LEARNING TO BE TE/

"What makes this book a necessity for teacher leaders is that it provides information that they can immediately implement into their personal instruction and the work they are doing with their colleagues."

Aimee Morewood, Associate Professor, College of Education and Human Services, Curriculum and Instruction, Literacy Studies, West Virginia University, USA

"For aspiring and novice teachers, this text provides an excellent foundation in the critical elements of the field. For experienced teachers and those mentoring other teachers, it provides a tool for providing leadership and coaching for colleagues. The tone is friendly and inviting and demonstrates the expertise of the authors in the 'real world' of teaching practice."

K. Victoria Dimock, Chief Program Officer, SEDL, USA

Learning to Be Teacher Leaders examines three integrated components of strong pedagogy— assessment, planning, and instruction—within a framework emphasizing the knowledge, skills, and dispositions that can empower teachers to become teacher leaders within their schools. Woven throughout are a student-centered stance toward assessment, planning, and instruction and a teacher-centered stance toward leadership. At the same time, the text recognizes the outside factors that can challenge this approach and provides strategies for coping with them.

Combining the what, why, and how of teaching, the research-based concepts are presented in a pragmatic format, relevant across grade levels, classrooms, and content areas. Designed to be specifically helpful in supporting success on national licensure assessments, this comprehensive text brings together in one place the important features of learning to be an effective teacher and becoming a teacher leader who continues to grow and develop within the profession. Using this book as a guide and resource, preservice and beginning teachers will focus on the most important factors in teaching, resulting in strengthening their pedagogy and developing a language that helps them move forward in terms of agency and advocacy. A Companion Website provides additional resources for instructors and students.

> **Visit the Companion Website at www.routledge.com/cw/broemmel for video links, websites, and a glossary of terms that readers will find helpful and additional readings, digital presentations, and potential in-class activities for use by instructors.**

Amy D. Broemmel is Associate Professor, Department of Theory and Practice in Teacher Education, University of Tennessee, Knoxville, USA.

Jennifer Jordan is Clinical Assistant Professor, Department of Theory and Practice in Teacher Education, University of Tennessee, Knoxville, USA.

Beau Michael Whitsett is Graduate Teaching Associate, Department of Theory and Practice in Teacher Education, University of Tennessee, Knoxville, USA.

LEARNING TO BE TEACHER LEADERS

A Framework for Assessment, Planning, and Instruction

Amy D. Broemmel, Jennifer Jordan, and Beau Michael Whitsett

Routledge
Taylor & Francis Group

NEW YORK AND LONDON

First published 2016
by Routledge
711 Third Avenue, New York, NY 10017

and by Routledge
2 Park Square, Milton Park, Abingdon, Oxon OX14 4RN

Routledge is an imprint of the Taylor & Francis Group, an informa business

Library of Congress Cataloging-in-Publication Data
Broemmel, Amy.
   Learning to be teacher leaders : a framework for assessment, planning, and
instruction / by Amy Broemmel, Jennifer Jordan, and Beau Whitsett.
      pages cm
   Includes bibliographical references and index.
   1. Teaching.   I. Jordan, Jennifer, 1976–   II. Whitsett, Beau.   III. Title.
   LB1025.3.B755 2015
   371.102—dc23
   2015008607

ISBN: 978-1-138-80385-5 (hbk)
ISBN: 978-1-138-80386-2 (pbk)
ISBN: 978-1-315-75344-7 (ebk)

Typeset in Bembo
by Apex CoVantage, LLC

This book is dedicated to all the current and former mentors and interns who have allowed us into their classrooms and their lives. We are grateful for the opportunity to learn alongside them as they have transformed into teacher leaders who positively affect their classrooms, schools, and communities.

BRIEF CONTENTS

CONTENTS

FOREWORD

We found Amy, Jennifer, and Beau's new book, *Learning to Be Teacher Leaders: A Framework for Assessment, Planning, and Instruction*, a pleasure to read. A pleasure because their goal is developing novice teachers into autonomous and effective teachers and into teacher leaders. Essential topics such as the potentially powerful role of formative assessment in understanding students as learners and for planning useful and powerful instruction are presented in a practical but evidence-based manner.

They argue for a unique analogy for understanding instruction, noting in Chapter 6 that theirs is "an agricultural, organic analogy as opposed to an industrial, constrained one." Their analogy works to help teachers understand why instructional differentiation is absolutely central to teaching effectively. They also argue for a balanced model for effective teaching, a model that incorporates the best of what we have learned from both the direct instruction and the inquiry-based models of teaching. Effective teachers need to be able to provide the specific and explicit routines some learners will need to become good readers and writers. At the same time, direct instruction plays a small but critical role when delivering literacy lessons that foster student independence and self-regulation, two central outcomes of effective inquiry-based literacy lessons.

Chapter 7 focuses on developing students' academic vocabulary and academic language, both of which are critical if students are to read well. We know much about developing the academic language proficiencies of children, all children, but too often fail to see much of what we know practiced in the instruction commonly offered in American classrooms. Too often, as the authors note, children from low-income homes, as well as children who are English language learners, arrive at school with English vocabulary knowledge well below that of the native

English-speaking, middle-class children who are often their classmates. The authors point out that the very purpose of academic language differs significantly from the social purposes of language used outside of schools.

Because the goal of all reading is understanding what has been read, the authors ask in Chapter 8 the very pertinent question: Why do we only see outstanding uses of questions in effective teachers' classrooms? Along the same lines, the authors ask why do we see so little literate conversation in American classrooms? Developing reading lessons where children respond to higher-order questions after reading and talk with each other about what has been read is a proven method for enhancing children's understanding and improving their comprehension when they read independently (Taylor, Peterson, Pearson, & Rodriguez, 2002; Nystrand, 2006). Unfortunately, as the authors point out, few classrooms offer students either the opportunity to respond to higher-order questions or to engage peers in literate conversations.

In the end, this book argues that effective teachers must make themselves heard: They must ask questions when mandates concerning daily practice run counter to effective practice. Learning to be that sort of teacher is the ultimate goal of this book. The content and the advice presented here will help new teachers develop into effective teachers and into teacher leaders. We couldn't ask a book to do much more.

Richard L. Allington and Anne McGill-Franzen
University of Tennessee

References

Nystrand, M. (2006). Research on the role of classroom discourse as it affects reading comprehension. *Research in the Teaching of English, 40,* 392–412.

Taylor, B. M., Peterson, D. S., Pearson, P. D., & Rodriguez, M.C. (2002). Looking inside classrooms: Reflecting on the "how" as well as the "what" in effective reading instruction. *The Reading Teacher, 56,* 270–279.

PREFACE

Far too often, novice teachers are viewed through extreme lenses. Either they are assumed to be proficient teachers upon entering the classroom for the first time, ready to face the challenges of teaching and the associated accountability measures that are increasingly part of teacher evaluations, or they are thought to know so little about effective teaching that they are required to follow a script or other program, with fidelity to the program rather than to their students. This book is our attempt to find a middle ground by respecting the knowledge and experiences that novice teachers bring with them and using straightforward, professional language to pull the important features of learning to be an effective teacher together in one place. We examine three integrated components of strong pedagogy: assessment, planning, and instruction, as well as a fourth component of leadership. We believe that addressing both effective teaching and leadership without situating them within a specific content area makes this a unique contribution to the available literature.

We are dedicated to preparing teachers who emerge with the knowledge, skills, and dispositions that champion not only effective teaching, but also leadership within elementary schools. We believe that the most effective teaching involves leading at many different levels. This book, then, is written with the intent of supporting novice teaching professionals who are looking for ways to tap the potential of all students and continue to grow professionally. We believe that in using our work as a guide and resource, beginning teachers will be able to focus on the most important factors of teaching, resulting in strengthening their pedagogy and developing a language that will allow them to move forward in terms of both agency and advocacy. Overall, our writing is devoted to addressing the pragmatic needs of the reader by presenting research-based concepts of effective teaching in practical language, accessible to novice teachers—even those in the earliest stages of learning and leadership.

After a short introductory chapter, the book is divided into four sections: Assessment, Planning, Instruction, Teacher Leadership. Each chapter builds on and draws upon the concepts discussed in the previous ones. The arrangement of topics mirrors how we believe effective instruction works: It starts with assessing students, uses that assessment data to plan for instruction, and carries out instruction while continuing to observe and assess. This instructional cycle is mediated by the depth of knowledge and growing body of experience that teachers bring with them into the classroom. How teachers see themselves affects their efficacy and, as a result, their students' learning, so developing the kinds of thinking and actions associated with leaders can be empowering and can serve to sustain beginning teachers through their challenging first years in the classroom. Throughout the book, we take a student-centered stance toward assessment, planning, and instruction, and a teacher-centered stance toward leadership. A final chapter sums up our hopes for our own students and readers: that they consistently take responsibility for making the instructional decisions that have the potential to affect their students in the most positive ways possible.

The book is filled with examples and anecdotes drawn from our own educational experiences. These examples come from all content areas and span the elementary school years. Each chapter concludes with a list of sources where readers can go to find more information on major topics, and the content chapters (those that fall under each of the four main components) also include activities that serve to link the ideas presented to opportunities to think about them and put them into practice. We have also attempted to integrate teachers' voices, particularly in the sections on leadership, so that readers know that the kinds of things we are advocating can and do really happen in classrooms across the country. We hope the voices within both inform and inspire novice teachers.

In addition, a Companion Website developed specifically for use with this book (www.routledge.com/cw/broemmel) contains additional readings, digital presentations, and potential in-class activities for use by instructors, as well as video links, websites, and a glossary of terms that readers will find helpful. Most importantly, we have included arrows at various points throughout each chapter in order to indicate the presence of a corresponding video on the Companion Website. We encourage readers to stop reading and take a moment to visit the site at these points along the way in order to watch examples of teachers carrying out the kinds of assessment, planning, and instruction described in the text.

We wish to thank all of the teachers who allowed us to come into their classrooms and capture a bit of what they do on a daily basis on video, as well as the reviewers who so graciously gave of their time to provide us with feedback along the way. And we hope that all of the hard work and effort of all the contributors has resulted in a text that, if nothing else, makes the reader stop and think for a little while—think about what they have the power to affect in their classrooms and schools. It is often more than one might expect.

ACKNOWLEDGMENTS

As isolating an endeavor as writing can be, through the sometimes tedious and almost always long hours of working on this book, I never felt alone. It is likely that the words that often seemed to start in my brain really came from elsewhere. They came from my own teaching mentors, Steve, Sherri, Patti, Michele, and Jean, who humbly modeled what effective teachers do and gently smoothed my rough edges during my own first years of teaching, and from amazing teachers like Nancy, Alisa, Matthew, and Seth whom I got to watch through the eyes of a parent as my own children journeyed through their classrooms. The words came from students like Reggie, Karen, and Julie, who taught me so much about working with future teachers during my very first semester of being a professor and from mentoring teachers like Ellie, Kristi, and Shannon, who gave me time to figure out how to (mostly) balance my continued idealism with the realities of classroom teaching as I supervised the graduate teaching interns placed in their classrooms. And they came from former students and current classroom teacher leaders like Bill, Lori, Dave, and Ashley, who have become my friends and mentors in their own right. This book would have never come into being without the influence of these incredible teachers who embody the definition of "teaching professionals."

Many thanks go out to my dear friends, Ines and Bob, whose innocent dinner invitation turned into a lesson on normative ethics and started me on the road to exploring the field, snippets of which found their way into this book. Thanks, too, go to Lauren Hopson, who was willing to talk to me for an hour on the night before school started and agreed to write about how she became an outspoken teacher leader in her school district on top of fielding calls from the media, parenting, and planning for and teaching her third graders during the first two weeks of the school year. And, thanks go out to my co-authors who made this challenging process a little easier because of their flexibility, trust, and sense of humor.

Truthfully, none of this would've come to pass without my colleague, co-author, and partner in crime, Jennifer, who agreed to embark on this crazy endeavor with me from day one.

Finally, I never would have made it through the writing process with a shred of sanity without the support of many of those I love. My kids endured many Mom-less nights, weekends, and even a family vacation, which I know wasn't easy for my daughter in particular. I'm not sure the boys really minded much, but they made me proud when they were called upon to take on extra duties in my absence and when, more often than not, they gave me an unsolicited hug just when I needed it most. Much appreciation goes to my spiritual, sarcastic, grammar-oriented friend, Jim, who always seems to appear just when I need him and upon whom I can always rely for words of wisdom, reality checks, and good laughs. I am grateful for my best friend, Chris, who could always be counted on to give me perspective—with just the right balance of praise and tough love. Without the distraction provided by our conversations and his endless suggestions for creative home improvement projects, I might have spent fewer late nights writing, but would've missed out on so much more. And, of course, I couldn't have focused enough to write even the first word of this project without my husband, who is always there to take care of everything and who, despite often being frustrated with the way I work, has always seen more potential in me than I have ever seen in myself. I will always be in your debt, Jeff.

—Amy D. Broemmel

Throughout the process of writing this book, I have come to realize that learning and leadership can take on many forms. I have always used the term "lifelong learner" to describe myself, but the last several years have solidified my understanding of that phrase. I have had the wonderful opportunity to work with some amazing students and mentors over the last fifteen years that have made more of an impact on me than they will ever realize. They helped me realize that effective teachers love their students first and teach their students second. Many of them have become leaders in their own ways, making sure that they constantly do what is best for their students rather than what is easy for the teacher.

Around the same time I embarked on the journey of teaching preservice teachers, I was blessed with my son, Henry, and my daughter, Scout. They think they look up to me to lead and teach them how the world works, but in reality, I am looking to them to teach me and make me a better person every day. See? That is what is so funny about being a leader; it is through others' eyes that you gain insight into what it truly means to lead. Leadership sometimes has an authoritative connotation, but my definition of leadership involves so much more. It means loving others and providing them the support they need to accomplish their goals. So, last but certainly not least, I would like to thank my husband, Ben, the "leader" of our family. He encourages me to not be afraid when I want to be and to stand up for what I believe in.

—Jennifer Jordan

Many thanks to Dr. Gregory Risner for introducing me to teaching and its many joys, Scott McKinnon for teaching me how to walk and talk like a teacher, and Dr. Jeffrey Davis for being a mirror to scholarly writing reflection and a window to the world of academia.

—Beau Michael Whitsett

1

OUR VISION OF EFFECTIVE TEACHING AND TEACHER LEADERSHIP

Let's be honest: Teaching looks pretty easy. Teachers are done working by 3 o'clock every day, they have summers off, and some even get snow days! They are in charge. They tell students what to do and then decide how well assignments are done. Teachers have power in the classroom, and they use it. Many of us believe these notions of teaching are true because of our experiences as students. As a result of compulsory education in the United States, we have all watched and listened to teachers for up to eight hours a day, five days a week, thirty-six weeks a year, for thirteen years. Lortie (1975) calls this our "apprenticeship of observation" (p. 67). These in-school experiences lead us to believe we know what teaching is all about—that the years we spend in classrooms make us experts on teaching. This informal apprenticeship can be likened to watching a chef prepare a meal. It looks so simple. All the ingredients are prepared, the appliances are ready, and the oven is preheated. We watch as the chef adds a dash of this and a little extra of that, creating a seemingly perfect plate, both in looks and in flavor. What we don't see are the complex decisions the chef makes beforehand based on the available fresh, local food. Nor do we understand exactly how the chef determines what subtle touch the dish needs to make it perfect. Even though the chef makes it look easy, when we try to replicate it in our own kitchen, it doesn't typically turn out with the same exact results. Like cooking, there is more to teaching than meets the eye, and, like the chef, a teacher must make complex decisions on a daily basis.

Still, it seems that when it comes to education, everyone has an opinion, idea, or reform that is intended to fix the reportedly broken system in the United States. The media often portrays teachers as lazy and ineffective or kindhearted but naïve. Certainly, we acknowledge that although there are some teachers who do fit these descriptions, most teachers we know are hardworking, intelligent, thoughtful people who care deeply about their students. Our view seems to be supported by years of national surveys conducted by PDK International/Gallup in which respondents answer a number of questions related to the state of public schools in the United States. One telling indicator involves the United States' trust in teachers. Nearly three quarters of those surveyed responded that they trusted the men and women who are teaching in public schools. They also rated their own neighborhood schools positively, with 53 percent of respondents giving an A or B rating to their community schools—the highest percentage ever recorded (Bushaw & Lopez, 2013).

In the current educational environment, where scripted curricula are common, students' standardized test performance is tied directly to teacher evaluation, and change seems the only constant, it is not surprising that many teachers are feeling overwhelmed. Far too often, these feelings are accompanied by claims of powerlessness, silenced voices, and resentment that lead to increasingly negative school and classroom environments. There is little doubt that teachers face challenging circumstances on a daily basis, but we believe that teachers do indeed hold power—power that can be used to influence the external voices of authority attempting to dictate what goes on in day-to-day classroom instruction.

Although out-of-school factors like student health, secure housing, and socioeconomic status, affect student achievement far more than in-school factors (Berliner, 2009), as classroom teachers, we have no control over them. However, when it comes to in-school factors, it is teachers that are most significant (Goldhaber, 2002). Although estimates posit that in-school factors account for approximately 20 percent of variation in student achievement, with teacher quality contributing less than 10 percent of that, one heavily relied upon study found that if a student has a good teacher three years in a row, that student's achievement scores could be as much as 50 percent higher than a student with ineffective teachers during the same time span (Sanders & Rivers, 1996). Despite the fact that out-of-school factors contribute more significantly to student achievement, we cannot overlook the impact of the teacher, both in the classroom and in the school, since those are factors over which educators can yield some level of influence. Thus, we believe it is important to consider the key characteristics of effective teachers.

What Does Effective Teaching Look Like?

We think everyone agrees that teachers should all possess a certain repertoire of knowledge, skills, and dispositions. Should a fifth-grade teacher understand the difference between a proper and improper fraction? Absolutely. Should a first-grade teacher understand how to teach phonemic awareness through shared writing activities? Most educators would agree that this is important. Take a look at the list of characteristics of effective teachers listed in Figure 1.1. Which knowledge, skills, and dispositions do you think are most important and contribute to effective

Responsive	Caring	Dedicated	Honest
Enthusiastic	Responsible	Principled	Curious
Committed	Fair	Perceptive	Decisive
Empathetic	Knowledgeable	Resourceful	Intelligent
Accepting	Accessible	Organized	Reflective
Professional	Reliable	Flexible	Communicative

FIGURE 1.1 Characteristics of effective teachers (based on: Gabriel, 2005; Stronge, 2007)

teaching? Do you already possess many of these? Which might be challenging for you?

Not only are what you teach and how you teach imperative; it is crucial to look at who you are as a teacher as well. We believe "[g]ood teaching cannot be reduced to technique; good teaching comes from the identity and integrity of the teacher" (Palmer, 1998, p. 10); teaching techniques are only as powerful as the teacher presenting them. As we begin our journey to become effective facilitators of student learning, we must first look inside ourselves and examine our own beliefs related to what education means. Teacher enthusiast Parker Palmer theorizes "we teach who we are," and

> . . . teaching holds a mirror to the soul. If I am willing to look in that mirror and not run from what I see, I have a chance to gain self-knowledge—and knowing myself is as crucial to good teaching as knowing my students and my subject.
>
> *(p. 2)*

It is just about impossible to disconnect who we are from how we teach. We are shaped by our prior experiences, for better or worse, and these experiences leave an indelible mark on our decision-making processes. By examining experiences and beliefs, we can begin to identify possible biases, assess our own dispositions, and explore how these dispositions can influence student learning. We suggest considering how you apply your knowledge, skills, and dispositions within three broad categories:

- Who are my students?
- What should I teach?
- How should I teach?

Once you begin looking within yourself, you can examine what is occurring around you.

Who Are My Students?

Effective teachers understand where their individual students are coming from, where they are going, and how to get them there. The individual life stories that students enter your classroom with can serve as powerful entry points for instruction. Effective teachers consider students' prior knowledge and experiences, the language they possess, their interests, and what motivates them as they set instructional goals and carry them out.

The community in which your school is located will likely have a strong impact on how your students perceive themselves. Some students are surrounded by the big city, ride the subway to school each day, and have never seen a live cow or cornstalk. Others may live on a farm, can drive a tractor, and have never seen a building over ten stories tall. When examining your own beliefs, you may realize that you feel students from certain geographic locations are better suited for school or might be more likely to be successful in school. Perhaps you believe a student whose background is most similar to yours will be most successful, or maybe you think just the opposite. It is imperative that you unpack all of your preconceived notions. Instead of focusing on what some students might be 'lacking' in their own background, you need to begin to focus on the unique funds of knowledge (Moll, Amanti, Neff, & Gonzáles, 1992): the language (Chapter 7), their interests, and their motivations (Chapter 9) that each child brings to school each day.

The term "funds of knowledge" developed out of the research conducted by Moll and González (1994) to examine the literacy practices of working-class Latina/o children. They define funds of knowledge as:

> These historically accumulated and culturally developed bodies of knowledge and skills essential for household or individual functioning and well-being. As households interact within circles of kinship and friendship, children are 'participant-observers' of the exchange of goods, services, and symbolic capital which are part of each household's functioning.
>
> *(p. 443)*

As children enter school, they bring with them their understandings of the dominant culture of the community and the expected behavioral norms. These forms of capital are sometimes overlooked or undervalued by the dominant school culture when a deficit view is taken. The goal of any effective teacher should be to instruct students in a way that mediates "the schools' class-based norms and the students' values, knowledge, and instead of" (Tozer, 2000, p. 158). Instead of viewing students as an empty vessel to be filled (deficit view), teachers should respect the unique 'capital' that each child brings to school, thus, building a reciprocal relationship in which the teacher and student learn from one another without the assumption that one's prior knowledge and social norms are more important or useful than the other's. Building this common ground of respect for each child's background will provide a more equitable learning environment for all students.

What Should I Teach?

Effective teachers also understand how to perform the balancing act between teaching the breadth and depth of the curriculum (Chapter 4) and adapting their teaching based on what their students need (Chapter 5). Think back to when you were a student in elementary school. Do you remember all the textbooks, workbooks, and supplementary materials you and your teacher had at your disposal? If you had effective teachers, they not only understood the goals of the district's curriculum, but also took into account the needs of their individual students—you! Their instructional goals most likely went beyond the curricular materials located inside your desk or on a bookshelf. Effective teachers constantly engage in a decision-making process to determine what material should be taught, the extent to which it should be taught, and how it can be best conveyed to a variety of learners.

How Should I Teach?

The National Academy of Education (2005) purports that "a teacher has not taught if no one learns" (p. 6). Merely covering all of the standards presented in your curriculum is not effective if your students fail to grasp and retain the material you present. Effective teachers employ instructional frameworks that empower student learning (Chapter 6). These instructional frameworks are even more robust when paired with the differentiation and a variety of instructional groupings and materials (Chapter 5) and teacher responsiveness to individual students' needs (Chapters 2, 3, and 8).

Some teachers simply think that teaching is all about instruction. This is obviously an important component of effective teaching, but it is not enough. Less effective teachers tend to focus almost exclusively on instruction, whereas more effective teachers realize it's important to invest in planning and assessment as well. Effective teachers first think about their individual students, what is most important to teach those particular students, and how to provide responsive instruction to the unique group of individuals.

What Makes an Effective Teacher Leader?

We've established that although teaching may appear to be a simple task to the observer, it certainly is not. We believe that, at a minimum, teachers must be classroom leaders. Interestingly, although we've all had years of experience watching leaders, most people don't view leadership as an easy task. This belief may explain why the word leadership can be defined in so many ways. The Oxford Dictionary (2014) defines it as, "The action of leading a group of people or an organization," but a simple Internet search for "definition of leadership" returns literally millions of results. Northouse (2010) defines leadership as, ". . . a process whereby an individual influences a group of individuals to achieve a common goal" (p. 3), whereas Bennis and Nanus (2003), scholars and pioneers in the contemporary field of leadership studies, define it in a more complex manner, indicating that leadership is a function of knowing yourself, having a vision that is well communicated, building trust among colleagues, and taking effective action to realize your own leadership potential. Even though definitions of leadership like those presented here tend to be associated with politics, sales, and other business-related endeavors, these definitions can quite easily apply to educational leadership. However, educational leadership itself typically refers to leadership by those in administration—curriculum directors, principals, and superintendents—rather than teachers. Despite the fact that few people typically view teachers as leaders, teachers do indeed have a history of leadership.

York-Barr and Duke (2004) indicate that the concept of teacher leadership recognizes that ". . . teachers rightly and importantly hold a central position in the ways schools operate and in the core functions of teaching and learning" (p. 255). Although it is not a new concept, recognition of the term 'teacher leadership' has really only come about within the past thirty years. In the industrial age of the early 1900s, efficiency was the goal of education, and as such, teachers were seen in a manner similar to that of a factory leader managing production of packaged goods. However, the educational reforms of the 1980s resulted in a shift from student learning efficiency to student learning agency; a focus on high-quality teachers and professionalization of teaching came into being alongside the term teacher leadership. The 'teacher as leader' should be viewed as a key maker, unlocking potential for students and stakeholders (Arends, 2011), although even now this view is not as commonplace as you might expect.

Silva, Gimbert, and Nolan (2000) have described the evolution of teacher leadership in three waves. The first wave is the narrowest sense of the term, in which teachers are formally appointed to managerial roles and simply serve as extensions of school administrators, helping to focus on running the school efficiently. The second wave focused on the instructional expertise of teachers and valued this instructional leadership by assigning teachers to roles that include staff development, curriculum building, and mentoring new teachers. Finally, the third wave looks to teachers as critical to the process of educational change. Definitions of teacher leadership under this umbrella still vary widely, but Childs-Bowen, Moller, and Scrivner's (2000) explanation aligns closely with this third wave of teacher leadership, stating, "We believe teachers are leaders when they function in professional learning communities to affect student learning; contribute to school improvement; inspire excellence in practice; and empower stakeholders to participate in educational improvement" (p. 28). York-Barr and Duke (2004) conclude that ". . . teacher leadership involves leading among colleagues with a focus on instructional practice, as well as working at the organizational level to align personnel, fiscal, and material resources to improve teaching and learning" (p. 261).

We agree with George, McLean, and Craig (2008), who note that not only is leadership a choice, but that you are never too young or too old to step up. Our beliefs are situated on the ideas that teacher leaders use thinking (Chapter 10) to set goals and take action (Chapter 11) in order to lead students, themselves, and others toward the future, whereas managers deal with immediate problems as they arise in the present, one after the other. This distinction is a broad encompassment of the many responsibilities and activities capable of influencing positive outcomes and combating negative consequences for students and stakeholders (Danielson, 2006; Lieberman & Miller, 2004).

Our Goals for Our Readers

We are writing this book because we want inspired teachers full of cutting-edge knowledge and new ideas to find success in their twenty-first century classrooms. Although teaching has always been a challenging profession, since the passing of the No Child Left Behind Act in 2001 (No Child Left Behind [NCLB], 2002), teachers have found themselves, at best, under the microscope and, at worst, under attack.

The teaching profession is dominated by women; 84 percent of all public schoolteachers are women according to the National Center for Education Information (Feistritzer, 2011). It is likely that this influences both how the profession is viewed from the outside and how it functions internally. In their book *How Great Women Lead*, St. John and Deane (2012) suggest that despite the scientific controversy surrounding the idea that women's brains are more adept at linking disparate ideas, in the real world, women do seem to make so many connections that they often have a hard time filtering out the minutiae. In classrooms and schools, where so many decisions are made daily, where these decisions have real and lasting consequences, and where kids' and sometimes families' lives are affected by these decisions, it is not surprising that often *everything* feels utterly important and overwhelming. We have experienced those feelings as classroom teachers and often continue to feel that way as teachers in the field of higher education.

Interestingly, as part of our writing journey, we have found Covey (1989) provides a clear lens for our work and that of future teacher leaders. He writes about two circles that contain our lives: the circle of concern and the circle of influence, pictured in Figure 1.2. Although his work focuses on life in general, we have approximated it to apply to our professional work. We have many concerns regarding education and many concerns for educators. However, many of those (e.g., low teacher pay, students living in poverty, overreliance on standardized test scores) are outside the focus of this book and, therefore, outside of our circle of influence. We have thus focused our work on those aspects of teaching that should be inside teachers' circles of influence; the aspects of teaching we write about are aspects of teaching in which individual teachers have a say.

We also appreciate that Covey takes the idea of influence one step further, noting that when people focus on what is in their realm of influence, they become proactive, whereas those who are more reactive don't, causing their circle of

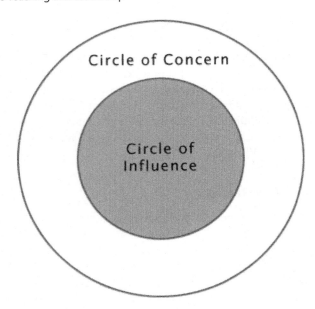

FIGURE 1.2 Covey's (1989) circle of concern and circle of influence

influence to shrink, as shown in Figure 1.3. We believe Covey's model can also help teachers filter out the minutiae, providing a means of helping them focus their work. In short, Covey's model provides a relatively simple lens that can have a lasting and positive influence on your professional teaching life.

Forty to fifty percent of teachers don't make it past the five-year mark in the profession. In one sense then, surviving the first years—making it to year six—is certainly laudable no matter how it happens. Yet, there is something about that approach that reminds us of Tom Hanks' character in *Cast Away*; it's great that he survived, but wouldn't it have been better if he had never been shipwrecked in the first place? We have endeavored to write this book because we want teachers to do more than survive their first years (or any years!) in the classroom, and we believe that part of moving beyond 'survival mode' comes from empowerment. We believe that understanding what you can and can't influence and then taking a proactive stance toward changing what you can will set the stage for a long and successful teaching career. As John Dewey said over a century ago,

> It is . . . advisable that the teacher should understand, and even be able to criticize, the general principles upon which the whole educational system is formed and administered. He is not like a private soldier in an army, expected merely to obey, or like a cog in a wheel, expected merely to respond to and transmit external energy; he must be an intelligent medium of action.
>
> *(Goldstein, 2014, p. 1)*

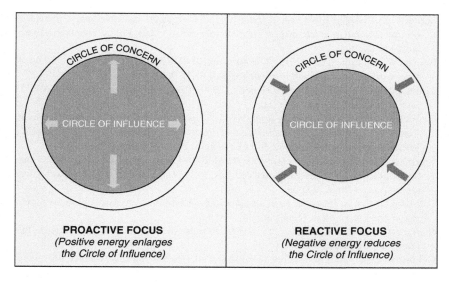

FIGURE 1.3 The effect of proactive and reactive foci on the circle of influence (Covey, 1989)

We hope that the rest of this book serves to empower teachers to become such intelligent mediums of action by providing them with the knowledge and understanding of what our experiences and research lead us to believe are the keys to successful teaching. We want to set our readers on the course to becoming teacher leaders, helping transform their classrooms, schools, and the profession from the inside out.

IF YOU WANT TO KNOW MORE ABOUT POLITICS AND EDUCATIONAL REFORM, CHECK OUT THESE RESOURCES:

Berliner, D. C. & Biddle, B. J. (1996). *The manufactured crisis: Myths, fraud and the attack on America's public schools.* New York, NY: Basic Books.
Ravitch, D. (2013). *Reign of error: The hoax of the privatization movement and the danger to America's public schools.* New York, NY: Alfred A. Knopf.
The Commission on Excellence in Education. (1983). *A nation at risk: The imperative for educational reform.* Washington, DC: The Commission on Excellence in Education.

References

Arends, R.I. (2011). *Learning to teach.* Boston, MA: McGraw-Hill.
Bennis, W. & Nanus, B. (2003). *Leaders: The strategies for taking charge.* New York, NY: Harper & Row.

Berliner, D. C. (2009). *Poverty and potential: Out-of-school factors and school success.* Retrieved August 20, 2014, from http://greatlakescenter.org/docs/Policy_Briefs/Berliner_NonSchool.pdf.

Bushaw, W.J., & Lopez, S.L. (2013). The 45th annual PDK/Gallup poll of the public's attitudes toward the public schools. *The Kappan, 95*(1), 9–25.

Childs-Bowen, D., Moller, G., & Scrivner, J. (2000). Principals: Leaders of leaders. *NASSP Bulletin, 84*(616), 27–34.

Covey, S.R. (1989). *The 7 habits of highly effective people.* New York, NY: Simon & Schuster.

Danielson, C. (2006). *Teacher leadership that strengthens professional practice.* Alexandria, VA: Association for Supervision and Curriculum Development.

Feistritzer, C.E. (2011). *Profile of teachers in the U.S. 2011.* Washington, DC: National Center for Education Information. Retrieved July 9, 2014, from http://www.edweek.org/media/pot2011final-blog.pdf.

Gabriel, J.G. (2005). *How to thrive as a teacher leader.* Alexandria, VA: Association for Supervision and Curriculum Development.

George, B., McLean, A., & Craig, N. (2008). *Finding your true north: A personal guide.* San Francisco, CA: Jossey-Bass.

Goldhaber, D. (2002). The mystery of good teaching: Surveying the evidence on student achievement and teachers' characteristics. *Education Next, 2*(1), 50–55.

Goldstein, D. (2014). *The teacher wars: A history of America's most embattled profession.* New York, NY: Doubleday.

Lieberman, A., & Miller, L. (2004). *Teacher leadership.* San Francisco, CA: John Wiley & Sons.

Lortie, D. (1975). *Schoolteacher: A sociological study.* Chicago, IL: University of Chicago Press.

Moll, L. C., Amanti, C., Neff, D., & Gonzales, N. (1992). Funds of knowledge for teaching: Using a qualitative approach to connect homes and classrooms. *Theory into Practice, 31,* 132–141.

Moll, L. C., & González, N. (1994). Lessons from research with language minority children. *Journal of Reading Behavior, 25,* 439–56.

National Academy of Education. (2005). *A good teacher in every classroom: Preparing the highly qualified teachers our children deserve.* San Francisco, CA: Jossey-Bass.

No Child Left Behind Act of 2001, P.L. 107–110, 20 U.S.C. § 6319 (2002).

Northouse, P.G. (2010). *Leadership: Theory and practice* (5th ed.). Thousand Oaks, CA: Sage.

Oxford Dictionary (2014, July 12). Re: leadership. Retrieved July 12, 2014, from http://www.oxforddictionaries.com/us/definition/american_english/leadership

Palmer, P.J. (1998). *The courage to teach: Exploring the inner landscape of a teacher's life.* San Francisco, CA: Jossey-Bass.

Sanders, W.L., & Rivers, J.C. (1996). *Cumulative and residual effects of teachers on future student academic achievement.* Knoxville, TN: University of Tennessee Value-Added Research and Assessment Center. Retrieved August 19, 2014, from http://www.cgp.upenn.edu/pdf/Sanders_Rivers-TVASS_teacher%20effects.pdf.

Silva, D.Y., Gimbert, B., & Nolan, J. (2000). Sliding the doors: Locking and unlocking possibilities for teacher leadership. *Teachers College Record, 102,* 779–804.

St. John, B. and Deane, D. (2012). *How great women lead: A mother-daughter adventure into the lives of women shaping the world.* New York, NY: Center Street.

Stronge, J.H. (2007). *Qualities of effective teachers* (2nd ed.). Alexandria, VA: Association for Supervision and Curriculum Development.

Tozer, S. (2000). Class. In D.A. Gabbard (Ed.), *Knowledge and power in the global economy: Politics and the rhetoric of school reform* (pp. 149–159). Mahwah, NJ: Lawrence Erlbaum Associates.

York-Barr, J., & Duke, K. (2004). What do we know about teacher leadership: Findings from two decades of scholarship. *Review of Educational Research, 74,* 255–316. DOI: 10.3102/00346543074003255.

SECTION I

Assessment

Section 1: Assessment

The purpose of assessment is to prevent student failure and ensure student success. Period. In the current testing climate, this guiding principle seems to have been pushed aside in favor of a more self-serving agenda. Instead of conducting assessments to collect data to inform subsequent instruction, which will support students and prevent failure, testing has become an enormous part of the moneymaking industry from which children receive little, if any, benefit. On the contrary, in many cases, testing is actually harming students. The psychological stress it places on some children (not to mention their teachers) has likely led to an increase in school-aged children suffering from test anxiety and subsequently receiving psychological services (Segool et al., 2013). Pressure for children and teachers to succeed on these assessments has served as a catalyst for many experienced teachers, including some of the most influential, to leave the profession. Teachers who remain in the classroom are sometimes inclined to give in to the pressures to teach to the test rather than teaching the skills that their own students most desperately need.

High-stakes tests have become a measuring stick to determine which school systems, schools, and teachers are performing well. Unfortunately, several faulty assumptions regarding the potential application of data are being drawn. The first assumption is that these tests are valid and accurately measure a student's achievement. Many have argued that the tests do not consider the socioeconomic or cultural factors that influence student learning (Jencks & Phillips, 1998; Lacour & Tissington, 2011). The second assumption is that these tests were designed to illustrate causation and can be used to determine whether or not a teacher or school are adding one year's worth of "value" to each student each year (Chetty, Friedman, & Rockoff, 2011). Statistically, the tests were never developed to be used in such a way, and many have argued that using standardized test scores to evaluate teacher effectiveness is inappropriate (American Statistical Association, 2014).

> Educational Testing Service and other standardized test makers are the first to inform educators that their tests are never meant as the sole diagnostic tool for an individual student. They are meant to indicate trends and patterns for a school or district, and to be included as one of many sources of information about a student. Yes, they may provide an initial indicator of achievement or aptitude regarding a student, but they should always be used in conjunction with other assessment tools in order to make decisions regarding an individual child. This applies to evaluating teachers of that individual as well.
>
> *(Wormeli, 2006, pp. 30–31)*

Another concern with our obsession with standardized tests focuses on reform. U.S. students are the most tested in the world (Darling-Hammond, 2013). We have enough test data to illustrate how our students are achieving relative to other same-aged peers, but national standardized tests (National Assessment of Educational Progress [NAEP], Partnership for Assessment of Readiness for College and Careers [PARCC]) continue to be used to illustrate the strengths and deficiencies of students and schools in each participating state. We also know how our students perform in relation to other countries (Programme for International Student Assessment [PISA]). Some argue that standardized testing will lead to higher achievement, but that is likely not the case. Historically, standardized testing has not successfully driven educational reform because the data provided are not robust enough to base instructional decisions upon. On the contrary, the results of standardized testing have been punitive at best.

It would be ludicrous to practice the doctor's physical exam as a way of becoming fit and well. The reality is the opposite: If we are physically fit and do healthy things, we will pass the physical. The separate items on the physical are not meant to be taught and crammed for; rather, they serve as indirect measures of our normal healthful living. Multiple-choice answers correlate with more genuine abilities and performance; yet mastery of those test items doesn't cause achievement (McTighe & Wiggins, 2001).

An understanding of the disparity between what assessments should be used for and what they are being used for is paramount for teachers. With this understanding, effective teachers can begin to muddle through the plethora of assessments they are instructed to conduct with their students each school year and determine which, if any, will be of benefit to their students. Assessment should not be viewed as a chore for teachers and for students, but a natural part of instruction that is not considered separate or intrusive. Having a grasp of the intended purposes for each assessment, what data will be provided, and the ways in which the data can inform instruction will empower the effective teacher to make deliberate choices whenever possible to transform assessment from a disheartening hoop-jumping activity to a more meaningful process used to prevent student failure and promote student success.

References

American Statistical Association. (2014). *ASA statement on using value-added models for educational assessment.* Alexandria, VA: American Statistical Association.

Chetty, R., Friedman, J. N., & Rockoff, J. E. (2011). *The long-term impacts of teachers: Teacher value-added and student outcomes in adulthood.* Cambridge, MA: National Bureau of Economic Research (NBER), Working Paper No. 17699.

Darling-Hammond, L. (2013, April 10). 'Test-and-punish' sabotages quality of children's education. Retrieved June 1, 2014, from http://www.msnbc.com/melissa-harris-perry/test-andpunish-sabotages-quality-childr.

Jencks, C., & Phillips, M. (1998). *The black-white test score gap.* Washington, DC: Brookings Institution Press.

Lacour, M., & Tissington, L. D. (2011). The effects of poverty on academic achievement. *Educational Research and Reviews, 6*(7), 522–527.

McTighe, J., & Wiggins, G. (2001). *Understanding by design.* Alexandria, VA: Association for Supervision and Curriculum Development.

Segool, N. K., Carlson, J. S., Goforth, A. N., von der Embse, N., & Barterian, J. A. (2013). Heightened test anxiety among young children: Elementary school students' anxious responses to high-stakes testing. *Psychology in the Schools, 50*(5), 489–499.

United States. National Commission on Excellence in Education. (1983). *A nation at risk: The imperative for educational reform: A report to the Nation and the Secretary of Education, United States Department of Education.* Washington, DC.: The Commission.

Wormeli, R. (2006). *Fair isn't always equal: Assessing and grading in the differentiated classroom.* Portland, ME: Stenhouse Publishers.

2

WHAT IS ASSESSMENT?

Assessment in our schools is not a new phenomenon. Children have been sub-jected to paper-and-pencil tasks for over a century. What has changed recently is the emphasis on achievement testing and standards-based education. This swing-ing of the pendulum was precipitated by the publication of *A Nation at Risk*, a document commissioned by President Ronald Reagan to examine the state of our schools (National Commission on Excellence in Education, 1983). This study identified several areas of concern, including the fact that the illiteracy rates of minorities was approaching 40 percent; high school graduates were producing declining SAT scores, therefore requiring college remediation courses; there was a dilution of material in the content areas; and there was a lack of consistency regarding expectations upon graduation. Most, if not all, of these concerns have remained at the forefront of educational reform efforts and at the heart of education-related conversations in the mainstream media. This fear that academic performance of students was not as strong as previous generations was again the impetus for the passage of both the No Child Left Behind Act (NCLB, 2001) signed into law by then-President George W. Bush, and the Race to the Top (U.S. Department of Education, 2009) funds offered by the Barack Obama administra-tion. Each of these iterations has led to added pressure for students, teachers, principals, and schools to perform with increasingly greater gains on yearly achievement tests.

Learning achievement can be assessed in many formats and at many times throughout the school year. The decision to allow students to participate or not in annual achievement tests is not within the teacher's control, but how students are prepared for the tests within the classroom is. Engaging in standardized test prep for an inordinate amount of time during the school day has been shown to be less effective than quality instruction (Evers & Walberg, 2004). This chapter and the next will focus on how effective teachers choose and employ assessments that are appropriate for students and provide information that guides instruction, therefore precluding failure.

How Do We Define Assessment?

If we were to ask ten people in the field of education for their definition of assessment, we might hear ten different versions. Some might discuss the use of standardized tests employed once a year, whereas others might mention how daily observations of students can be considered an assessment tool. So who is correct?

According to the Merriam-Webster online dictionary, assessment is defined as "the act of making a judgment about something." If we examine this definition a little further, we can begin to understand what is meant by the words "judgment" and "something." Educationally, the something is pretty straightforward, referring to a student's progress or understanding at a particular point in time. The term judgment, on the other hand, may be what leads to some disagreement in the field of education. The Merriam-Webster dictionary definition of judgment is "the act or process of forming an opinion or making a decision after careful thought: the ability to make good decisions about what should be done." Without the act of thoughtful consideration, teachers are not actually assessing their students. Instead, they are gathering percentage scores to place in the grade book or using these scores to rank their students for intervention services. Not only do effective teachers gather assessment data, but, more importantly, they know how to analyze the data to make informed decisions about their subsequent instruction. In the following sections of this chapter we will describe three categories of assessment tools (summative, diagnostic, and formative) and examine how they each fit into the definition of assessment discussed earlier.

Assessment Design

When determining which assessments are best suited for a particular situation with particular students, it is important to understand how the tests were designed and for what purposes they were designed. Many tests provide numeric data or descriptions that can be challenging to interpret or understand. Sometimes scores are simply a calculation of the number of correct items out of the total number of items. Other times, student scores are determined by complex statistical methods and derived from comparing individual scores to other similar students. By understanding terms such as reliability, validity, criterion-referenced, and norm-referenced, the effective teacher can better determine which assessments best fit the needs of students at a variety of points throughout the school year.

With any form of assessment, it is important to understand the reliability and validity of the assessment to make sure the tools you are administering are free of bias—or that you can at least identify the biases. Reliability refers to the consistency of results. A test with a high degree of reliability would yield the same results repeatedly independent of outside factors. For example, when you go to order a 20-ounce coffee at your favorite coffee shop, you expect to receive 20 ounces of coffee. It does not matter what time of day it is or what part of town you are traveling through; if you receive 20 ounces each time, then the coffee shop is producing reliable results. The same is true for a reliable assessment. The time of day, location of the school, or any other factors should not influence the results of the given assessment if it is deemed reliable.

Validity refers to the accuracy of the assessment. In other words, it examines if the assessment actually measures what it intends to measure. Imagine if you were perpetually late for any engagement you might set all your clocks ahead by fifteen minutes so that you had a better chance of being punctual. All of your clocks would still be considered reliable because they can still tell time accurately, but they would no longer be valid since the time reported is no longer aligned with Greenwich Mean Time (GMT).

Another consideration is content validity. Not only should the assessment be testing what it purports to test, but the format of the test should be similar to how students interacted with the material during instruction. This becomes difficult when developing a widespread achievement test. Multiple-choice questions are easy and inexpensive to score, but hopefully, students were not taught the material in this manner. Valid assessments provide results that express a student's true nature of learning. Tests can be considered reliable and valid if they are used appropriately, and assessments that are valid are almost always reliable.

In addition to confirming that the assessments being used in the classroom are valid and reliable, it is important to understand what the tests are intended to measure. All assessments can either be considered norm referenced or criterion referenced. Norm-referenced assessments purport to measure individual student achievement in relative comparison to a larger population of similar students. This similarity is usually defined by chronological age. Therefore, the achievement of a third grader who is nine years and seven months old would be compared to a large group of other children who are also nine years and seven months old to determine if the student is progressing at a similar rate.

Some examples of norm-referenced tests are achievement tests such as the Partnership for Assessment of Readiness for College and Careers (PARCC) and the Stanford Achievement Test, 10th Edition (SAT-10). Results are usually reported as percentiles, stanines, or grade equivalents and then used to compare individuals, classrooms, or schools to each other. Percentage scores are quite easy to understand and are calculated by dividing the total number of questions on an assessment by the total number of answers correct. A stanine score ranges from one to nine, with five being the mean and nine a high score. Therefore, if a student does well on an assessment, he or she will earn a stanine score of an eight or nine. This roughly correlates to a percentage score of 80 percent to 90 percent correct.

Grade-equivalent scores tend to be widely misunderstood. Let's say that a third grader completes a reading comprehension test and receives a grade-equivalent score of eighth grade. Some might think that this student should be reading texts on an eighth-grade level, but in actuality, the grade-equivalent score illustrates that the student is reading like an eighth grader would read on this third-grade test. If eighth-grade material is placed in front of this student, he or she will likely struggle to comprehend it. The results from a norm-referenced test will indicate that a particular student is doing as well as, better, or worse than his or her peers, which is something most teachers would already likely be cognizant of. The data provided by these tests are helpful in ranking students, but do not offer feedback on the particular areas of students' strengths and weaknesses, and more importantly, the data do not offer the teacher enough information to make informed decisions about subsequent instruction.

Criterion-referenced assessments, on the other hand, do not compare students against similar peers, but instead confirm whether or not students have met a predetermined or established criterion. Although some standardized tests fit this description, many criterion-referenced assessments are teacher made. For instance, a teacher might be interested in knowing whether or not a classroom full of first-grade students can accurately read sixty words from a passage in one minute. Sixty words per minute is the predetermined criterion upon which all the students will be judged. The teacher can time each student's reading and check off on a list whether or not the individual hit the mark, but this assessment does not inform the teacher whether a student could actually read 100 words in a minute or what the average number of words the entire class can read. Therefore, an effective teacher would take anecdotal notes regarding total words read and misread, mark which words were misread, and then analyze the miscues for trends. Then, the teacher would consider the needs of each individual student and determine the next steps for instruction. To prevent issues with validity of criterion-referenced assessments, there should be direct alignment between the test and the curriculum.

Summative Assessment

Summative assessments measure the level of proficiency that has been obtained at the end of an instructional unit. Usually, a summative assessment score is then compared against a predetermined standard or benchmark. If they are valid, summative assessments should illustrate how effectively students have learned the material presented. The most appropriate use of summative assessments is that they give a snapshot in time. Teachers must realize that one snapshot will not give a true understanding of what a student does and does not know. For example, think about the updates that you post on social media (Twitter, Facebook). What if an outside observer only looked at one of your tweets or posts? Do you think that this observer would be able to understand who you are, what you believe in, and what your aspirations are? Would that one exchange be indicative of your life? It probably depends on which post was analyzed. Giving students assessments every month or so creates a similar predicament. Depending on what students' preferred testing styles are and what other outside-of-school factors are weighing on their minds, the results of a summative test may not accurately portray students' academic growth.

Placing summative assessment first does not imply some sort of hierarchy of importance among assessment types, but rather emphasizes the importance of knowing where students should end up in order to know where to begin. Before any daily lesson plans are written, the effective teacher decides which essential understandings are the goals of instruction. The next step is to develop a summative assessment (portfolio, performance task, project, test) that is directly aligned with that goal. We have worked with teachers who wait until the night before the end-of-unit test to write the test. When this occurs, the test is generally based on a collection of facts and skills loosely related to the desired essential understandings and therefore becomes an invalid test of student knowledge.

At this point, it is also probably important to point out some of the inappropriate uses of summative assessments. Because these types of assessments only give a snapshot of a student's learning at one point in time, it is important to remember not to overgeneralize the data provided by these tests. Making decisions about remedial or advanced placements of students or the quality of instruction provided by teachers is not deemed an accurate or appropriate use of this information. Think back to when you were in school. Were you a good test taker? Did you get anxious or excited on testing days? What if you missed the bus? What if you were sick but had to go to school? There are many factors outside of whether or not a student has an understanding of the tested material that may influence his or her ability to perform up to his or her potential on a summative test. Examples of summative assessment are included in Figure 2.1.

Standardized Tests (PARCC, SAT-10)	Norm-referenced, commercially developed tests with high-stakes consequences (tracking decisions, grade retention). These assessments are generally given annually, and a numerical achievement score is assigned. These assessments are also used to gauge teachers' effectiveness by comparing students' test scores to their test scores at the end of the previous school year.
End-of-Chapter or Unit Tests	Criterion-referenced tests (commercially or teacher made) to determine if students have mastered the essential understandings and objectives of the chapter or unit. These are usually composed of multiple-choice, true/false, and short-answer questions.
End-of-Course Exams	High-stakes, criterion-referenced assessments to determine if students have mastered the content of the course and can therefore move into the subsequent course. Those who do not pass must retake the course.

FIGURE 2.1 Examples of summative assessments

Measureable Outcomes

Teachers need to be wary of the numeric scores provided by summative assessments. These scores can be a starting place to begin thinking about whether or not a particular student mastered the topic, but can rarely paint a vivid enough picture to truly understand what the child mastered and what he or she still needs support with. Some teachers transform summative data into formative data by developing a visual representation of which students missed particular questions and by charting the mistakes individually and by class to determine the next steps for instruction (see Figure 2.2).

Long O Spelling Pattern: *o_e, oa, ow,* and *o*

Student Name	Summative Score	Correct	Incorrect	Next Steps
Lindsey	10/10	home blow nose hold boat cold coat go show no		Move on to *long U* words
Kaitlin	6/10	home cold nose go hold no	bot blo cot sho	Review *oa* and *ow* spelling patterns
John	4/10	hold no cold go	hom cot nos sho bot blo	Review *short O* and *long O*
Madelyn	4/10	hold no cold go	hom cot nos sho bot blo	Review *short O* and *long O*
Curtis	10/10	home blow nose hold boat cold coat go show no		Move on to *long U* words
Henry	6/10	home cold nose go hold no	bowt blo cowt sho	Review *oa* and *ow* spelling patterns

Groups:
Lindsey and Curtis
Kaitlin and Henry
John and Madelyn

FIGURE 2.2 Visual representation of class assessment data

Pros and Cons

One benefit of summative assessment includes providing data to assess long-term patterns of achievement. The effective teacher can reflect on this data to inform her decisions about making instructional changes. Future curricular planning can be guided by the results to better meet the needs of all students. Additionally, professional development opportunities can be sought out to build capacity in weak areas. Summative assessment data can also be used to make placement decisions. As long as the information provided by these tests is valid, then these are all reasonable outcomes of summative assessment. Additionally, it is important to realize that effective teachers can use summative assessment data in a formative manner provided enough information is given by the assessment to allow subsequent decision making.

Formative Assessment

Formative assessment includes the subtle changes that teachers make on a moment-to-moment basis based on their evaluation of student understanding. It provides ongoing feedback to both the teacher and the student, which is then used to guide instruction and set goals for students. These tests are considered low stakes in that they do not typically affect a student's grades or place a teacher in jeopardy of losing her instructional position. When teachers and students are actively engaged in developing and implementing formative assessments, they can take some ownership in the process, which begins to authenticate the activities and experiences and reduces the negative aspects sometimes associated with testing.

Formative assessment can be used to determine students' content knowledge and related skills necessary to master the instructional material. This includes students' knowledge of facts and associated vocabulary terms, knowledge of the processes and procedures, and their ability to transfer this information and make connections to other material. Knowing this information will help the effective teacher pace instruction. Let's say that diagnostic testing showed that the majority of the students were ready to begin writing a simple story with a beginning (describing the characters and setting), a middle (the problem or conflict), and an end (the resolution). Therefore, instruction plans were developed to teach a unit on story writing. Day one would be an overall discussion of each part of the story, and each subsequent day would focus on a mini-lesson explaining each segment in detail followed by the authentic application of individual student writing. As the teacher circulates during independent writing time on day two (writing the beginning part of a story), he quickly realizes that the students are confused. These observations inform him that he needs to slow his pacing down and spend an additional day reteaching how to write the beginning of a story. Some examples of formative assessments are described in Figure 2.3.

Questioning and Observation	Questioning and observational techniques can offer significant insight into the depth of student understanding. By looking closely at the ways in which students speak and act (or don't speak and act), misconception and misunderstandings can be revealed. Observations can be followed up with probing questions, which should go beyond basic recall and challenge students to think about their own learning.
Admit/Exit Slips	Admit slips are employed at the beginning of class and exit slips at the end of class to determine student understanding of key concepts. Admit slips can cover the previous day's instruction and can serve as a refresher to engage students at the beginning of class. Exit slips provide feedback on the day's instruction and provide cues for reteaching and extension for the following class.
Whiteboards	Individual whiteboards hold all students accountable for participating in the lesson. The teacher (or student) asks a question of the group, and all students are responsible for holding up their board with their response. The teacher can immediately notice who is struggling with the material and adjust instruction. This may include calling a small group of students together to reteach the material.
Appointment Clock	The teacher directs students to make appointments with three other students at quarter past the hour, half past the hour, and quarter of the hour. Then, at predetermined points within the lesson, the teacher asks students to meet with their appointment and answer questions designed to engage students in higher-order thinking. The teacher circulates and collects anecdotal records to make instructional adjustments during the remainder of this lesson and for subsequent lessons.

FIGURE 2.3 Examples of formative assessments

Measurable Outcomes

The measureable outcomes of formative assessment will likely not be in the form of a percentage score or ranking. Rather, the intended outcomes will be purposeful, explicit feedback that guides both teacher instruction and student learning. The feedback will be helpful if it pinpoints the content, strategy, or transfer of knowledge that the student struggles with, but more importantly, the feedback should analyze the reasons why the student had difficulties and offer suggestions to support acquisition of the new knowledge. This is where knowledge of students becomes paramount. Effectively knowing where and why a student is making a mistake will generate an opportunity for academic growth.

Pros and Cons

Formative assessment can be a very powerful teaching tool if used wisely. It can provide information from minute to minute in real time to help determine whether or not your students are grasping the information you are teaching. Instead of waiting until the end of a chapter or unit to gauge understanding, these assessments provide immediate feedback so that you can tailor your instruction to the students' in-lesson needs. One negative aspect of formative assessments that teachers sometimes complain about is how much time they consume. When teachers are already overwhelmed by the amount of content they feel they must cover in a day, week, or school year, they question how they can add another thing to their already overflowing plate. The answer is surprisingly simple. By carefully planning your instructional activities (more about this in Chapter 4) you can design instructional activities that can also serve as your formative assessments; there is no need to write another multiple-choice test or hand out another work-sheet. You can just use the higher-order thinking activities that your students are already engaged in to determine their mastery of the topic. This might take the form of grading, but could also take the form of observations or conversation and questioning.

Diagnostic Assessment

Diagnostic and formative assessments are closely related and in many respects can be considered as the degree of intervention on a continuum. When teachers provide feedback and students still have a difficult time grasping the information is when diagnostic assessment comes into play. Diagnostic assessment can be considered a subcategory of formative assessment because it is an avenue to provide feedback to students who are struggling in a timely fashion. One difference is that commercially available diagnostic tests tend to be norm-referenced, whereas formative assessments are generally teacher created and criterion-referenced. Formative assessment differs from diagnostic assessment in that it is usually administered consistently throughout the school year rather than merely at the beginning of a unit or semester or when gross misunderstandings occur.

When you are not feeling well, you may decide to make an appointment with your physician. When you arrive at her office, you are generally expecting her to examine you, collect vitals, make an informed decision about your prognosis, and determine a course of action to help with a speedy recovery (perhaps physical therapy or medication). A diagnostic tool in education works in many of the same ways. When effective teachers begin their instruction, generally some form of diagnostic assessment is an early component of their lesson plan. Although this type of assessment is often undervalued or overlooked, it offers invaluable guidance for planning and pacing a lesson or unit. A diagnostic test, such as a pretest, should be developed after a summative assessment has already been decided upon.

The two assessments should correlate; that is, they should asses the same essential understandings and objectives that are most valued for student learning.

Diagnostic assessments generally serve three distinct purposes (Saubern, 2010): to understand the current situation, to garner knowledge about how to improve, and to determine required resources. The first purpose is to understand the current situation. These tests are sometimes referred to as a "screener." They determine a student's readiness regarding the essential understandings and objectives of instruction. Screeners are sometimes considered proactive rather than reactive because they are designed to discover weaknesses before they begin to impede learning. Some widely used screeners include Curriculum-Based Measurement (CBM), and the Dynamic Indicators of Basic Early Literacy Skills (DIBELS). These screeners sometimes are used multiple times throughout the school year to determine ongoing performance levels to gauge progress. It can be given early on (hopefully before any signs of struggle even occur) to determine a student's areas of strength and areas of weakness. This is where teacher judgment comes into play—the effective teacher looks for patterns of errors and determines a plan of action to intervene and support the student in mastering these areas. Unfortunately, some ineffective teachers rely on failure as a diagnostic tool. We believe that waiting for children to fail before providing support is a disservice and unnecessarily cruel.

Conducting diagnostic assessment before instruction begins offers a starting point for instruction. Obviously, not all students will be at the same point in instruction, so the results of this diagnosis may show several entry points for instruction. This is where grouping techniques can come into play. (Grouping strategies will be discussed more in Chapter 5.) By analyzing the data from the diagnostic tool's subcategories, the effective teacher can determine which areas students struggle with and then provide more instruction. For example, if a diagnostic pretest is given on two-digit subtraction, the teacher could form two groups with the data provided: those who mastered the concept and those who did not. This can serve as a starting point for remediation, but when taking a closer look, it may become clear that three remediation groups should be formed. One group might need to focus on mastering single-digit subtraction with accuracy, one group might need to practice regrouping, and the final group may need a tutorial on place value. This highlights the need for diagnostic assessments to provide an adequate amount of information on which to base planning decisions. Simply knowing whether a student "knows" or "doesn't know" the information is not sufficient. For the group that has already mastered two-digit subtraction, instructional time does not need to be wasted on this concept. This group is ready to move on to more complex activities.

The next purpose of employing diagnostic assessments is to garner knowledge about how to improve. This includes how the student can improve and how the teacher can improve her instruction. Simply collecting scores from a diagnostic assessment would be a waste of valuable time if there was no plan to analyze the results to determine the next steps in teaching and learning. This application of diagnostic assessment tools is used to pinpoint specific issues when general struggles are evident. Knowing that a student is having difficulty comprehending text or calculating multidigit subtraction problems is important, but might not be sufficient enough to provide student support. Diagnostic tools can drill down within a topic more deeply to determine the specific strategy or skill that a student is struggling with. By administering a battery of tests and then charting the results in relation to a large sample of same-aged peers, a visual representation of student needs becomes apparent. Next, determinations about instruction can occur. Should remediation include alternative teaching strategies or alternative curricula? In the two-digit subtraction example, a change in curricula would be appropriate for the students who have not mastered an understanding of basic subtraction. These students may not be developmentally ready to perform complex subtraction tasks and should take a step back to create a strong foundation upon which to build upon. Similarly, the students who mastered the diagnostic assessment should be provided more challenging curricula that requires critical thinking and problem solving. On the other hand, those students who struggle with place value and regrouping likely need the concepts illustrated again in a different manner. Perhaps visual representations or acting out the problem would be beneficial.

The final purpose of diagnostic assessments is to determine the required resources needed to implement subsequent instruction. Obviously, when an instructional plan is determined, the required materials for instruction are important to consider. Depending on the school and community, there may be more or fewer resources on hand. The effective teacher uses available resources, writes mini-grants, and asks stakeholders to donate supplies. Figure 2.4 describes some widely used diagnostic assessments.

Measureable Outcomes

Many diagnostic assessments provide a numeric score, which may be helpful in guiding your instruction. More than likely, you will need to look more closely at the information provided to make informed decisions about subsequent instruction. What does 42/44 words correct on the Dolch sight word list or 128 words correct per minute tell you about a student's reading ability? Can he or she decode unknown words with blends? Can he or she comprehend what was read and make inferences? We have no idea. It is important to examine the mistakes (as well as the correct answers) that a student provides on a diagnostic assessment. By looking at trends—for example, Julie usually forgets to regroup when adding large numbers—you can focus more precisely on what students can do well and what they still struggle with. Then you can plan your instruction to target those gaps in student understanding. Noticing these trends tends to be a difficult task for ineffective teachers, but over time, effective teachers begin to uncover common mistakes that students tend to make year after year.

Pretest	Commercially developed or teacher-developed assessments conducted before instruction on a particular topic begins. These assessments should inform the teacher of general gaps in achievement, as well as mastery of skills. Data collected should be used to plan instruction and for group formation.
DIBELS/ CBM	DIBELS were developed based on measurement procedures for CBM. These assessments are composed of short fluency measures (one minute) designed to regularly monitor reading and math development. These assessments were designed to identify children having difficulty so support could be offered.
DRA-2+	The Developmental Reading Assessment is administered at the start of the school year and at the midpoint of the school year to determine an individual student's reading level. The test examines nine categories of literacy subsumed within accuracy, fluency, and comprehension. The data provided by this assessment is then used to determine instruction.
Yopp-Singer	This assessment determines a student's ability to separately articulate all of the sounds present in a given word in the correct order. For example, the word *man* has three distinct sounds: /m/-/a/-/n/ and *keep* also has three sounds: /k/-/ē/-/p/. For students who are struggling with decoding unknown words, this assessment can be administered to determine their understanding of how phonemes are combined to make up words.
Woodcock Johnson III	Norm-referenced assessment, which includes twenty subtests related to reading, math, and writing achievement. These subtests include auditory processing, long-term retrieval, visual-spatial thinking, and fluid reasoning.

FIGURE 2.4 Examples of diagnostic assessments

Pros and Cons

The biggest benefit of employing diagnostic assessments is the ability to determine where to go next. Teaching skills and strategies in which your students may already be proficient or which may be developmentally inappropriate based on students' current understandings is a waste of valuable instruction time. The only downside to regularly using these types of assessments is the amount of time they consume. If you imagine giving a pretest over every skill and strategy you plan to cover in a school year, you may use an entire week of instructional time. Some teachers may consider this "wasted time," but in actuality we contend that you will be gaining much more instructional time because you will not be spending time on material that is too easy or too hard, but rather, right in your students' zones of proximal development (Vygotsky, 1978).

Diagnostic assessments can be conducted by school personnel, classroom teachers, or even by the students themselves! Allowing students to think aloud and formulate their feelings about their own strengths and weaknesses can be empowering to students. Our experience has shown that even the youngest children can verbalize what they are struggling with when given the tools and support needed (see Chapter 8). According to Brigance and Hargis (1993), "self-assessment as an integral part of instruction should be common policy. Students should be engaged in monitoring their own progress, seeking corrective feedback, and in deciding what to engage in next" (p. 92).

Final Thoughts on Assessment

> Tests have the wrong focus. They rank and label. Most tests don't provide real help. They produce only letters or numbers. We seem willing to measure only to compare, either to others or to the scale of items on a test.
>
> *(Brigance & Hargis, 1993, p. 24)*

The standardization movement in education is fatally flawed because it does not take into consideration all of the unique characteristics children inherently bring to school. Examining and comparing two children of the same age is like racing a bicycle and a motorcycle to see which is faster. The motorcycle will always win, but that doesn't mean it is somehow more superior. The view from the bicycle might be better because you can see more detail when you aren't speeding by. The bicycle can explore nature trails and greenways that do not permit motorcycles.

Effective teachers know that assessment tools must be sensitive enough to uncover the different gifts and needs of students, and these teachers are knowledgeable enough to recognize the nuances of the data to support student success. They employ assessment in a fluid manner based on the learning needs of each student, rather than in a prescribed, lock-step format, and use the data to inform their planning and instruction. We believe that if robust formative assessments are given all along, there might not actually be a need for a summative assessment. Teachers who give formative assessments on a daily basis already understand what their students know.

WANT TO LEARN MORE ABOUT IMPLEMENTING FORMATIVE AND DIAGNOSTIC ASSESSMENTS IN YOUR CLASSROOM? CHECK IT OUT!

Diagnostic

DRA 2+: Developmental Reading Assessment, 2nd Ed. PLUS.

McGill-Franzen, A. (2006). *Kindergarten literacy: Matching assessment and instruction in kindergarten.* New York, NY: Scholastic.

Measures of Academic Progress (MAP). (2014). Northwest Evaluation Association. Portland, OR.

Formative

Chapman, C. (2011). *Differentiated assessment strategies: One tool doesn't fit all* (2nd Ed.). Thousand Oaks, CA: Corwin.

Earl, L. M. (2013). *Assessment as learning.* Thousand Oaks, CA: Corwin.

Frey, N., & Fisher, D. (2007). *Checking for understanding: Formative assessment techniques for your classroom.* Alexandria, VA: Association for Supervision & Curriculum Development.

Frey, N., & Fisher, D. (2011). *The formative assessment action plan: Practical steps to more successful teaching and learning.* Alexandria, VA: Association for Supervision & Curriculum Development.

Marzano, R. J. (2009). *Formative assessment and standards-based grading: Classroom strategies that work.* Bloomington, IN: Solution Tree.

Connecting Pedagogy to Practice

1. Locate assessments that are used by your local school system. Determine if they are designed to be used as a diagnostic, formative, or summative assessment.
2. How could you adapt these assessments so that they could be administered in more than one of the proposed ways?

Putting Leadership into Action

Effective teachers understand the purposes of each type of assessment and know how to use the results to inform their teaching. Teacher leaders, however, understand the bigger context and the role that assessment plays in characterizing the status of education in the United States. We suggest that in order to gain insight into this very politicized area of education, you set aside some time to read. Our suggestions include:

- *The Formative Assessment Action Plan: Practical Steps to More Successful Teaching and Learning.* (2011) by N. Frey and D. Fisher
- *The Death and Life of the Great American School System: How Testing and Choice Are Undermining Education* (2010) by Diane Ravitch
- *Smartest Kids in the World and How They Got that Way* (2013) by Amanda Ripley

References

Brigance, A. H., & Hargis, C. H. (1993). *Educational assessment: Insuring that all students succeed in school.* Springfield, IL: Charles C. Thomas Publisher.

Evers, W. F., & Walberg, H. J. (2004). *Testing student learning, evaluating teaching effectiveness.* Stanford, CA: Hoover Institution Press.

Merriam Webster Dictionary (2014, July 12). Re: judgement. Retrieved July 12, 2014, from http://www.merriam-webster.com/dictionary/judgement

No Child Left Behind (NCLB) Act of 2001, Pub. L. No. 107–110, § 115, Stat. 1425 (2002).

Saubern, R. (2010). Ping: The Web 2.0 future of education? *Teacher, 209,* 10–15.

U.S. Department of Education. (2009). *Race to the top program executive summary.* Washington, DC: Department of Education.

United States National Commission on Excellence in Education. (1983). *A nation at risk: The imperative for educational reform: A report to the nation and the Secretary of Education, United States Department of Education.* Washington, DC: The Commission.

Vygotsky, L. S. (1978). *Mind in society: The development of higher psychological processes.* Cambridge, MA: Harvard University Press.

3

PURPOSES OF CLASSROOM ASSESSMENT

Grading comprises the foundation material as well as the structural fabric of the educational system in the United Sates. In most of our educational system students are graded far more than most agricultural and manufactured products. Like eggs, students are sorted and grouped, labeled and ranked, compared and rejected.

(Brigance & Hargis, 1993, p. 131)

According to Durham (2006), "the primary function of schools is the education of students. Any activity not leading to that end should be eliminated" (p. 1). Some educators and parents use the terms "assessments" and "grades" interchangeably, but this is not the case. Assessment is the key to student progress through feedback, and grades are merely a way to boil this progress down into a number that can be reported to parents and other stakeholders. As we discuss the merits of grading and assessment, the needs of students should be considered first and foremost. Parents have come to expect that grades will be given as a way to communicate student learning. That may be considered one purpose of grading, but should not be considered the only purpose. It is difficult to define grades and grading without thinking about the purposes for taking grades. The working definition of grades that will be employed in this chapter states that:

A grade represents a clear and accurate indicator of what a student knows and is able to do—mastery. With grades, we document the progress of students and teaching, we provide feedback to students and their parents, and we make instructional decisions regarding the students.

(Wormeli, 2006, p. 103)

According to McTighe and Wiggins (2001), grading should support learning (rather than merely communicate it) and be accurate, meaningful, and consistent if the expectation is learner growth. Although grading will again be discussed at the end of this chapter, we frame the first sections of the chapter around the two main purposes for classroom assessment: knowing who your students are and knowing where your students are in relation to curricular expectations.

Knowing Who Your Students Are

When working with teachers who are new to the field, they often comment about how much time seems to be wasted at the beginning of the school year. Ample time is spent getting to know students through icebreakers and collecting student assessment data. Some teachers complain that they just want to start "teaching" and wish the first few weeks of school included more instructional time. We respectfully disagree with their observations. Although this time may seem "wasted" to the untrained eye, the effective teacher understands that this process of getting to know your students at the beginning of the year (and throughout the year as necessary) is vital to effective planning and student learning. Recall our discussion of diagnostic assessment and the fact that conducting pretests is time consuming, but actually serves as a timesaver when you consider the valuable information it provides. It alerts the effective teacher to areas of mastery and areas of weakness for individual students. Taking time to understand learners through informal data-gathering techniques such as observations and interview can correspondingly be considered instructional timesavers.

Observation

To observe in everyday life generally means to look at things going on around us. In the field of education, it means more than just simply watching students. It refers to the process of looking, but also includes the active processing of the observations to determine the needs of the students. Through these observations, learning preferences, academic strengths and weaknesses, and what motivates a student can be determined. For example, Julie may seem more engaged during math lessons than during writing lessons. Upon further examination, it becomes evident that Julie is engaged during math lessons because of the hands-on component of using manipulatives for support. The effective teacher realizes this learning preference and connects this information to her writing lessons. Beginning the following week, she provides a chest full of props (glasses, clothing and hats, stuffed animals, etc.) available for students to peruse and select at the beginning of the writing block. With this added stimuli, Julie, who was so successfully engaged in math, now is becoming more engaged and successful in composing written texts. In this way, observations can be used as an informal formative assessment because the information gathered from watching students can inform subsequent instruction.

Interest Inventory and Interview

Another informal data-gathering technique employed to learn about students includes interest inventories and interview protocols. Interest inventories are usually paper-and-pencil assessments in which students report their feelings toward certain academic subjects. The *Elementary Reading Attitude Survey* published by Kear, Coffman, McKenna, and Ambrosio (2000) is a widely used assessment for younger readers. Students read (or listen to the teacher read) statements about reading, such as: "How do you feel about spending free time reading?" and "How do you feel when the teacher asks you questions about what you read?" Then students circle the picture of Garfield the cat that most closely matches their feelings (a Garfield that is happy, slightly smiling, mildly upset, or very upset). One benefit of conducting interest inventories like this is the ease of administration. An entire class can complete the assessment at the same time and, once complete, the teacher can analyze the results to inform instruction. One cautionary note about interest inventories (and, really, any data collection techniques that rely on students to self-report their feelings or attitudes) is that sometimes students will report their feelings in the ways in which they believe the teacher wants to hear. So, for instance, when asked, "How do you feel when you read out loud in class?" some students will be inclined to please the teacher and report by circling the happy Garfield face. Another concern with assessments that ask students to self-report is that the very youngest children and students with language difficulties may struggle to articulate their actual feelings toward academics and school. When this occurs they may be inclined to answer in a positive manner because that is what they believe the teacher wants to hear. All of these concerns can produce invalid assessment results, so it is important to, first, be aware of this possibility and, second, conduct additional assessments to collect more information to ensure that the information collected is accurate. This can be accomplished through student interviews.

Student interviews can provide a wealth of information related to a student's likes and dislikes and strengths and weaknesses when conducted correctly. The first step is to determine what information you want to collect before beginning the interview. Of course, the questions asked during the interview can be flexible and considered as follow-up based on the responses that students provide to garner a deeper understanding, but a protocol should be decided upon in advance. First, the effective teacher determines what information she would like to gather, such as favorite subject in school, favorite hobbies outside of school, and preferred learning tasks. Questions such as current age, whether or not the student has an Individualized Education Plan (IEP) and receives special education services during the school day, or guided reading level should not be broached during the oral interview. This information is important, but any information that the teacher can collect via other means, such as through the student's cumulative file, should be collected outside of the instructional school day. Once interviews begin, it will become obvious how time consuming the process is, and therefore, additional time should not be wasted on extraneous data collection that can be provided through other avenues.

Once a list of questions is created, then the effective teacher can determine how to conduct interviews and record the data. Student responses can be written down as they are provided, but it may be more helpful to digitally audio record responses. The reasons for this are twofold. First of all, students may speak quickly and offer rich descriptions that cannot be fully captured when jotting down notes. Additionally, students may become anxious due to the furious note taking occurring. Previous school experiences may have conditioned students to think that teachers only take notes when incorrect answers are provided. Students may come to believe they are not furnishing the information you want and will either change their answers to try to please you or, more likely, begin to shut down and refuse to provide informative responses.

After the entire class has been interviewed, it is helpful to organize the data collected into a chart such as the one illustrated in Figure 3.1. This visual representation of the data allows the effective teacher to identify trends in the data, which can then be used when making grouping decisions. For instance, when considering students' hobbies, the chart may expose four out-of-school interests that can be used to motivate reluctant readers. Perhaps one reading group will read about the history of rifles, one about how to care for horses, one about football legends, and a final group about famous dress designers. It is critical to realize that interest inventories and individual student interviews can ask any questions that the effective teacher deems important, but without acting on the data collected, getting to know students becomes a wasted exercise in data collection. It is what the effective teacher *does* with the information that is essential to affecting student learning.

Classroom Profile Chart									
Student Name	Home Life & Culture	Preferred Learning Style	Learning Needs	Favorite & Least Favorite Subject?	Social? In what ways?	Musical? How?	Artistic? How?	Athletic? How?	Outside Interests, Activities & Hobbies

FIGURE 3.1 Classroom profile chart

Knowing Where Your Students Are in Relation to Curricular Expectations

> When we buy replacement parts for our cars we expect them to fit exactly ... Interchangeability is an important part of standardization in the manufacturing process. It has made mass production possible. Mass production has been of great benefit in the production of consumer goods, but it has a dark side, particularly when the technique is applied in mass education. The application of mass production techniques to mass education was and is an appealing notion. The industrialization of the country coincided with the institution of mass free public education. Millions of students needed to pass through the pedagogical manufacturing process. However, there is one problem in education that resists the solution used in industry. This is the problem of tolerance limits. Variation in shape and dimension need to be kept quite small in manufacturing. This is possible with machine-made parts.
>
> *(Brigance & Hargis, 1993, pp. 141–142)*

Variation among students is to be expected and is impossible to control for. The traditional notion of public education viewed students as cogs moving through an assembly line. All students received the same machining and if there was a problem with the part, it was simply discarded and removed from the factory. Thankfully, this is no longer the prevailing notion of how schools should operate. As educators have garnered knowledge on how students learn and how to support learners with differing needs, the classroom landscape has evolved (Tomlinson, 1999). In effective teachers' classrooms, students are no longer subjected to assessments that are much too easy or much too difficult, but rather they follow the Goldilocks principle and are "just right" (Ohlhausen & Jepsen, 1992). Additionally, because students work at differing paces, these "just right" assessments are given at variable intervals and to students at differing points in the school year.

Differentiation of instruction and of student work (which can then be used as formative assessments) will be discussed at length in Chapter 5. Here we will discuss how to differentiate assessments to determine where students are in relation to curricular expectations. Leveling the difficulty of the content students are required to master is one way to differentiate. When choosing an assessment to determine where your students are in relation to curricular expectations, performance tasks are always a strong choice.

> In contrast to indirect evaluations methods in which the student is asked to respond to questions *about* a subject, performance exams ask students to *do* whatever it is he is supposed to have learned—exactly, one notes, as does life.
>
> *(Durham, 2006, p. 65)*

Just as the experiences in life are differentiated, so should be the assessments chosen in school. Performance tasks require students to apply their knowledge to a real-world application, such as practicing fractions, by assuming the role of a chef following a recipe to make cookies or a meteorologist reporting the weather on the nightly news.

> Imagine a garage mechanic charged with fixing the timing in a car's engine, but it's a car he's never serviced or studied before. In such a circumstance, he consults the manufacturer's manual or even with the manufacturer directly. He can ask for guidance from a senior mechanic, and he can even extend the deadline by telling the customer that, though he promised it would be ready by 5:00 P.M., the car won't be ready until the next day at 10:00 A.M. In the real world, we gravitate toward careers with tasks for which we have some proclivity. We don't spend an entire day working in our weak areas.
>
> *(Wormeli, 2006, p. 7)*

Another facet of knowing where your students are in relation to curriculum expectations deals with student progress (Allington, 2002). Some might argue that assessing students based on their progress may give them a false sense of how the "real world" works and may actually be setting students up for future failure. Say, for instance, that a student graduates and enters the working world of business. If he is not performing his job duties, his boss will most likely let him go in favor of a stronger candidate rather than monitor his progress and offer support for his growth. We argue that gauging a child's progress in relation to himself (not being compared to the rest of the class) can be a powerful motivator for continued growth. When a student can see his growth charted on a regular basis, the notion that all the hard work and effort are paying off becomes a motivating factor. It should be noted that this charting of progress should be shared with the individual student in private. Publicly posting progress charts may lead to students comparing themselves to one another rather than to themselves. For these students who have struggled in the past, grades traditionally may not have served to motivate future learning (Guskey & Bailey, 2001). When compared to other students in the class, they always seem to be falling behind. In contrast, by allowing them the opportunity to be compared against themselves, they will notice progress and likely become more engaged and motivated to learn.

> Are we afraid, however, that adjusting grades based on student information is somehow weakening the curriculum and thereby, the student's mastery of course content? Sure, but we're in it for the big picture—students' learning of the material, not just having it tossed in their laps and told to make sense of it on their own.
>
> *(Wormeli, 2006, p. 92)*

If assessments are not differentiated to meet the needs of all students, then a portion of the class will be completely lost and nonmastery of the content will be just about guaranteed. Slowing the pace of instruction down or modifying the expectations is the most reasonable course of action.

Once we are convinced that assessment should illustrate individual progress toward curricular expectations, then the question of grading effort and participation emerges. Let's revisit the definition/purpose of grades, which states that:

> A grade represents a clear and accurate indicator of what a student knows and is able to do—mastery. With grades, we document the progress of students and teaching, we provide feedback to students and their parents, and we make instructional decisions regarding the students.
>
> *(Wormeli, 2006, p. 103)*

Just because a student has put forth effort and participated in the lesson that does not necessarily indicate that he or she has mastered the material. Of course we want to encourage effort and participation, but these actions can be considered a means to a desired end, not the end within itself. Another issue to consider is how to objectively measure effort. How do educators know if a student really is putting forth an appreciable amount of effort or if he or she is merely skating by? The effective teacher focuses on mastery of content as a sole indicator of grades.

Taking grades and providing report cards are institutional proclivities that are here to stay, but many educators would argue that our society places too much emphasis on making the best grades. These grades are not always predictive of students' subsequent success in college or in the workplace. The emphasis should rather be focused on using assessment data to inform instruction. That means that assessments need to be within a student's zone of proximal development (Vygotsky, 1978) to provide valid assessment data. Differentiation of assessments so that students can illustrate their actual understanding of material instead of designing difficult tests that students memorize the answers to one day but forget the next should be the goal.

Keeping Track of Grades

Once all the assessment data is gathered, it must be organized and kept track of. Some teachers claim that they do not need to record formative assessments and document observations because it is "all up here" as they point to their head. Trying to memorize and remember the nuances of what motivates students and how and what mistakes were made is just about impossible when you are working with anywhere from eighteen to twenty-five students. Although keeping records can be time consuming, it does allow the teacher to see trends among the data and will also provide a means for communicating the data to other teachers and parents. Commercially developed record-keeping systems are available for purchase or for download off the Internet, but these were developed without keeping in mind the needs of your particular students. Record keeping should be developed based on your knowledge of which assessments will be conducted and which information you need to collect to best support the learning of your students. Each class is unique from year to year and so it is important to revisit previous record-keeping systems to determine if changes need to be made based on the needs of a new class of students.

It was emphasized in the previous chapter that all assessments should be directly tied to the standard being taught, so it makes sense to organize your gradebook around those standards that you are teaching. Many less effective teachers organize their gradebooks by subject and then enter grades chronologically based on the date they were administered. This method of recording grades does not provide adequate information on whether all the curriculum standards were mastered. Figure 3.2 illustrates how an effective teacher might consider organizing a gradebook.

In this particular example, the columns are labeled across the top with the Mathematical Common Core State Standards (National Governors Association Center for Best Practices & Council of Chief State School Officers, 2010) for the geometry strand in fourth grade. The students' names are listed by row, and a section for anecdotal notes is also available for each student. Organizing the gradebook in this manner ensures that all the standards will be covered. If a student masters the standard through a different type of activity or at a different point in the grading period based on the pacing and needs of the student, this gradebook

	Draw and identify lines and angles, and classify shapes by properties of their lines and angles.			
Student Name	CCSS.Math. Content.4.G.A.1 Draw points, lines, line segments, rays, angles (right, acute, obtuse), and perpendicular and parallel lines. Identify these in two-dimensional figures.	CCSS.Math. Content.4.G.A.2 Classify two-dimensional figures based on the presence or absence of parallel or perpendicular lines, or the presence or absence of angles of a specified size. Recognize right triangles as a category, and identify right triangles.	CCSS.Math. Content.4.G.A.3 Recognize a line of symmetry for a two-dimensional figure as a line across the figure such that the figure can be folded along the line into matching parts. Identify line-symmetric figures and draw lines of symmetry.	Anecdotal Notes
Julie				
Chris				
Sara				
Garrett				
Michele				

FIGURE 3.2 Standards-based gradebook

Does this format respond to the differentiated approaches I am using with my students? If so, how?

Does this gradebook format render an accurate statement of students' mastery—what they know and are able to do?

How does using this gradebook format make grading and assessing students more manageable for me?

Does this gradebook format support my teaching/learning beliefs?

Is this gradebook easily understood by others who may need to see and interpret its pages without me being present?

By using this gradebook format, will I be able to keep up with grading and record keeping so that I can provide feedback to students, document progress, and inform my instructional decisions in a timely manner?

FIGURE 3.3 Questions to consider when designing a responsive gradebook

scenario can support those decisions. The information that is vital to communicate is whether or not the standard was mastered—not the date and activity that provided this information. Within the area provided for anecdotal notes any additional information regarding differentiation and analysis of errors can be recorded. Wormeli (2006, p. 161) asserts that,

> As we enter data on our students, we reflect on their growth and how the lessons we provided helped or hindered that growth. Our gradebooks are records of our actions, in this sense. Since our teaching/learning beliefs are revealed via our actions, we better make sure our beliefs and actions are consistent with one another. If we embrace differentiation, then we need to use gradebook practices that support differentiation.

Wormeli (2006, pp. 161–162) also provides a valuable list of questions to ask yourself when considering how to set up your gradebook (Figure 3.3).

A Few Key Points to Keep in Mind

There are a few additional factors related to assessments and grading that the effective teacher keeps in mind. These include using homework as practice and not for a grade and how to grade collaborative group work. Additionally, who will be administering the assessment and where and when the assessments will be given must be considered.

Avoid Grading Homework

Homework should be viewed as an opportunity for students to practice what they are learning or to solidify mastery of a given topic. When a young child is learning to play the piano, he or she is encouraged to practice placing the fingers on the correct keys. Music teachers offer feedback and assistance during lessons and do not place any judgment on mastery at this point. The purpose of these lessons is to practice, not to perform (that will come at a later date). The effective teacher realizes that homework is a time for practice and feedback, not evaluation and grading. Also, homework may not be a valid indicator of student understanding. We have all had conversations with well-meaning parents who complete their child's homework as a way of "supporting" their learning. The child has learned nothing, and now the teacher has a skewed image of what the child actually understands. On the other end of the spectrum is the child whose parents are working two jobs and are not available in the evening to help with homework. This particular student may be the oldest sibling and is in charge of caring for his younger siblings. In this case, he may have mastered the material covered within the homework, but does not have the time to complete the assignment with accuracy. Because of this, the teacher holds the erroneous belief that he does not understand the material and she will likely assign him *more* homework on this topic!

What about Group Work?

When considering how to assess group work, things sometimes get a bit messy. Research has illustrated that collaborative learning is helpful for student growth, but that group grades should not be a part of collaborative working environments (Brookhart, 2013). Another pitfall of collaborative assignments is that when assessments are attempted to be given independently, they usually focus on the process of the assignment rather than on the acquisition of content during the activity. A few examples of process assessments include having students reflect on the group process, completing a participation rubric, or peer evaluations of the learning process. All of these assessment types have merit and can provide valuable feedback in regard to how well students participated in the activity, but they do not inform the teacher whether or not each individual student has mastered the objective and standard of the lesson.

Some ineffective teachers stop at this point and place the grades demonstrated by these process assessments into their gradebook, but the effective teacher takes group grading one step further and ensures that she understands how well each of her students grasps the material. Some of these assessments include verbal questioning/feedback while taking anecdotal notes during group work. Some teachers will assign a post-project test for students to illustrate their learning, but we feel that this extra step is a waste of time and effort. When group work activities are designed well, they engage students in higher-order thinking and provide ample data (in the form of observations or written work) for the effective teacher to place in the gradebook, analyze, and use to inform instruction.

The Who, When, and Where of Assessment

Testing should occur in situations that are familiar and comfortable to students. If the desired outcome of conducting assessments is to collect valid data, then it is imperative that students are tested in environments that closely mirror everyday classroom experiences. This means that students should not be herded into the gym or cafeteria where dozens of examiners are sitting at desks and students are processed through the testing stations in a fashion reminiscent of an assembly line. This may sound like an outrageous scenario, but we have observed testing conducted in this manner. Students should be tested within the classroom in a quiet setting and free of distractions whenever possible.

Additionally, students should be assessed by their own teacher. First of all, teachers have typically built rapport with their students, thus making students feel more comfortable responding to their classroom teacher. Especially younger children may get nervous when tested by a stranger and, therefore, the student may not provide data that accurately reflects his or her understanding of the material. Second, a wealth of information is available through observing students completing assessments. Keeping anecdotal records of a student's mistakes when completing the assessment can serve as a record of the internal thought processes occurring when mistakes are made. Over time, the effective teacher gains insights into why mistakes are occurring and what can be done to reteach the material. Finally, the classroom teacher understands the student, including their strengths and weaknesses, better than the school psychologist or other school staff. Which assessments are chosen and how the data provided inform instruction should be the concern. The effective teacher also should act on her knowledge of each individual student to adapt assessments based on the needs of each student. Only the classroom teacher will know if a student is having a "bad day" from lack of sleep the previous night or is anxious about missing the bus this afternoon. The effective teacher considers all of these factors to ensure that the test chosen and the testing conditions provided will result in valid results that express the student's true understanding.

Teacher Introspection

As you collect data on your students over the course of a week, month, or entire school year, you will be excited to see how much growth they are making. Concepts that were confusing at the beginning of the year, such as how the Earth orbits around the Sun or how to multiply fractions with unlike denominators, will now come to your students seemingly naturally. On the other hand, your students will continue to struggle with some concepts, and this can provide you with the opportunity to reflect on your own instruction.

Assessing students and collecting grades just to fill up columns in a gradebook to "prove" you are teaching and collecting data is not what effective teachers do. Instead, they purposefully plan assessments that are directly aligned with the objectives being taught, they plan performance tasks that help them learn about their students, and they use the data collected to make changes in instruction. The effective teacher looks inward when determining how to better help students succeed. Rather than placing the blame on the students (or their parents or the community), the onus is on the teacher to plan how instructional strategies (more on this topic in Chapters 4 and 5) can support student learning.

DO YOU WANT TO KNOW MORE ABOUT GRADING AND ASSESSMENTS? CHECK THESE OUT!

Brookhart, S. M., & Nitko, A. J. (2007). *Assessment and grading in classrooms*. New York: Pearson.

Marzano, R. J. (2007). *Classroom assessment & grading that work*. Alexandria, VA: Association for Supervision & Curriculum Development.

Marzano, R. J. (2010). *Formative assessments & standards-based grading: Classroom strategies that work*. Centennial, CO: Marzano Research Laboratory.

Connecting Pedagogy to Practice

1. Think about how you would create your own class profile sheet. What information is important to you? What categories would you create?
2. Search for gradebook formats online or ask your colleagues to look at their gradebooks. What do you notice? Are they standards based? Do they allow for differentiation based on individual student needs?

Putting Leadership into Action

Most of us who have spent our lives in schools understand how grading works. An A is best, a B is okay, and, after that, well, we would rather not think about it. Effective teachers have justifiable reasons for giving their students the grades that they do—some might even say that they don't give grades; students earn them. But not everyone shares the same opinion of the traditional system of grading, and it is worth considering another perspective. In his well-known book, *Punished by Rewards*, Alfie Kohn presents a challenging premise about the negative impact of grades specifically, and rewards in general, on student learning. Teacher leaders take the information presented in the book and reflect on where their own position lies on the continuum between traditional grading systems and the kind of system Kohn proposes. They might ask whether they have ever seen classroom grading practices that match what they believe in, but they would go one step further in considering how they could make their grading system more closely align with what they believe. We challenge you to do the same!

References

Allington, R. (2002). What I've learned about effective reading instruction from a decade of studying exemplary elementary classroom teachers. *Phi Delta Kappan, 83*(10), 740–747.

Brigance, A.H., & Hargis, C. H. (1993). *Educational assessment: Insuring that all students succeed in school.* Springfield, IL: Charles C. Thomas Publisher.

Brookhart, S.M. (2013). *Grading and group work: How do I assess individual learning when students work together?* Alexandria, VA: Association for Supervision & Curriculum Development.

Durham, Q. (2006). *The realities of classroom testing and grading: A guide to performance issues.* Lanham: MD: Rowman & Littlefield Education.

Guskey, T. R., & Bailey, J.M. (2001). *Developing grading and reporting systems for student learning.* Thousand Oaks, CA: Corwin Press.

Kear, D. J., Coffman, G.A., McKenna, M. C., & Ambrosio, A. L. (2000). Measuring attitude toward writing: A new tool for teachers. *The Reading Teacher, 54*(1), 10–23.

McTighe, J., & Wiggins, G. (2001). *Understanding by design.* Alexandria, VA: Association for Supervision and Curriculum Development.

National Governors Association Center for Best Practices & Council of Chief State School Officers. (2010). *Common Core State Standards for Mathematics.* Washington, DC: Authors.

Ohlhausen, M. M. & Jepsen, M. (1992). Lessons from Goldilocks: Somebody's been choosing my books but I can make my own choices now! *The New Advocate, 5*(1), 31–46.

Tomlinson, C.A. (1999). *The differentiated classroom responding to the needs of all learners.* Alexandria, VA: Association for Supervision and Curriculum Development.

Vygotsky, L.S. (1978). *Mind in society: The development of higher psychological processes.* Cambridge, MA: Harvard University Press.

Wormeli, R. (2006). *Fair isn't always equal: Assessing and grading in the differentiated classroom.* Portland, ME: Stenhouse Publishers.

SECTION II

Planning

Section II Introduction: Planning

The National Academy of Education (2005) says, "Much of teaching relies upon anticipating and preparing for student understanding ahead of time" (p. 17). That means effective teaching doesn't just happen because you step into a classroom armed with lots of knowledge about teaching and learning. It doesn't even just happen because you've spent time getting to know your students' academic strengths and interests. It does mean that effective teaching, if it is going to have a chance of resulting in real learning, takes time to plan on the front end—even before your students step foot in your classroom. Planning of this nature presents opportunities for the kinds of critical decision making characteristic of strong teachers.

Planning is, in a sense, akin to creating a map—or a series of maps—for your teaching. Sure, it might be easier to have a sort of teaching global positioning system (GPS) guiding you through your day, giving you directions like, "Slow down a little, you're losing Patrick and Andrea," or, "You're going to need to continue this lesson tomorrow; there's not really enough time to finish it in a meaningful way before we head to lunch," or even, "Don't forget to connect today's work to the science unit you'll be starting in a couple weeks," but it might also be annoying. Anyway, since we don't—thankfully—have this technology, the task of planning the year-long journey is left to the classroom teacher. It isn't as though you have to start from scratch; the state or school district typically provides standards, pacing guides, and textbooks. Simply having access to these, however, is not enough. O'Shea (2005) says, "Externally prepared guides and curriculum resources can be helpful, but only teachers can make the planning decisions that will result in improved student learning" (p. 26). It is clear that simply following a script or staying on the same page as everyone else is not likely to garner strong academic growth. In fact, we believe a willingness to enter the classroom without well-developed plans designed with the specific group of students in mind foreshadows ineffective teaching and limited learning.

We recognize the fact that many experienced classroom teachers manage to effectively fit their lesson plans neatly in the 2" × 2" squares that seem to be present in every standard lesson plan book, but also know that those teachers have internalized the lesson planning process and have the details of each lesson they teach clearly articulated in their heads. It is the rare novice who has developed the ability to articulate an effective lesson plan in four square inches, and even rarer to find one who has the vision to effectively teach the content associated with grade-level standards by looking at only one week at a time. The next two chapters are designed to help combat this piecemeal approach to "covering" the curriculum. In them, we lay out guidelines for both long- and short-term planning, discuss the importance of considering both student needs and curriculum expectations, and highlight ways in which teachers can actually use the assessment data they collect to inform their instruction.

References

National Academy of Education. (2005). *A good teacher in every classroom: Preparing the highly qualified teachers our children deserve.* San Francisco, CA: Jossey-Bass.

O'Shea, M.R. (2005). *From standards to success.* Alexandria, VA: Association for Supervision and Curriculum Development.

4

LEVELS OF PLANNING

Teachers "need to have a sense of where they are going, why they want students to go there, and how they and their students are going to get there" (National Academy of Education, 2005, p. 16). That kind of clarity doesn't happen unless you sit down and consider your long- and short-term plans for your students. We realize that in one sense, this is asking a lot. Teachers face enormous pressures on a daily basis: Class sizes are going up, while available space is typically not; required standardized assessments are eating away at instructional time; there is precious little money allocated by the school to buy supplies for classrooms; your planning time is filled with answering emails and phone calls or filling out paperwork that was due yesterday; and, things keep changing (the Common Core standards are in . . . no, they're out . . . no they're in . . .). The truth is that teachers continue to have more and more items added to their job descriptions, but nothing—nothing— is ever taken away. It's no wonder that planning often takes a back seat to the issues that demand immediate attention. However, we believe that careful planning with a clear focus on what it is you want your students to be able to do actually saves time and increases learning in the long run. You have to plan with the end in mind: the end of the year, the end of the unit, the end of the week, the end of the lesson.

Long-Term Planning

Long-term planning provides a mechanism for thinking about how the big pieces fit together, and we believe there are two parts to effective long-term planning. The first component involves planning classroom procedures that will help your classroom run smoothly and support students' independence. The second involves planning how best to allocate the time necessary to teach each of the associated grade-level standards. Both are challenging and critical for a successful school year.

Procedures

A procedure is defined as "a series of actions that are done in a certain way or order; an established or accepted way of doing something" (Merriam-Webster Online Dictionary, 2014). Dedicating time early in the year to establishing these accepted ways of doing things in the classroom helps alleviate disorder and over-reliance on the teacher so that time can be spent in more constructive ways. It is true that you can (and should) develop procedures as you see they are needed in your classroom throughout the year; however, there are many things that we know students will need to know how to do before they ever walk through the class-room door. It is your responsibility to decide exactly how those things will happen before they ever enter your classroom. We know that students need to know expectations for noise levels, how to sharpen their pencils, and how to line up at the door, among many other things. See Figure 4.1 for a list of procedures that have potential benefits in the classroom (Wong & Wong, 2004). Intentionally establishing these kinds of procedures provides students with clear expectations, allowing them to work toward functioning with autonomy rather than constantly relying on the teacher for guidance.

Denton and Kriete (2000) suggest that establishing these kinds of procedures in the classroom should be one of the primary goals of the first six weeks of school. We agree that they need to be firmly in place as quickly as possible, but generally, the more experience children have in school, the faster they are able to take ownership of these procedural expectations. That is not to say that, in addition to teaching content, kindergarten teachers should plan to spend six weeks teach-ing and practicing procedures, whereas fifth-grade teachers should only allocate a few days; generally, we have found it takes anywhere from two to six weeks for students to get the hang of a new classroom. We do believe, though, that regardless of the grade you teach, it is imperative that you plan exactly how you want these procedures to flow in your classroom and that you dedicate time to model them, provide students with opportunities to practice them, and, once established, remind students to follow them and reteach them as necessary.

Planning for procedures is one place where creative teachers tend to sneak in a lot of fun. Consider the wide range of options for getting students to line up on

Procedures to Rehearse With Students

Entering the classroom	Moving about the room
Getting to work immediately	Going to the library or tech center
Listening to and responding to questions	Structuring headings on papers
Participating in class discussions	Returning to a task after an interruption
Keeping your desk orderly	Asking a question
Checking out classroom materials	Walking in the hall during class time
Indicating whether or not you understand	Responding to a fire drill
Coming to attention	Responding to an earthquake
Working cooperatively	Responding to a severe weather alert
Changing groups	Saying "thank you"
Keeping your notebook	When you are tardy
Going to the office	End-of-period class dismissal
Knowing the schedule for the day or class	When you need a pencil or paper
Keeping a progress report	When you are absent
Finding directions for each assignment	When you need help or conferencing
Passing in papers	When you finish early
Exchanging papers	When a schoolwide announcement is made
Returning student work	When visitors are in the classroom
Getting materials without disturbing others	If the teacher is out of the classroom
Handing out playground materials	If you are suddenly ill

FIGURE 4.1 Possible classroom procedures (Wong & Wong, 2004, p. 193)

the playground after recess. There is certainly nothing wrong with a traditional means of calling students to attention through blowing a whistle or calling the teacher's name aloud, at which point they know to stop what they are doing and proceed to the spot designated for lining up. However, we observed one teacher who chose instead to bellow, "Whoop-de-doo!" when he wanted his kindergarteners to line up. In response, the five- and six-year-olds would chime, "Caribou!" from wherever they were on the playground, put their hands to the side of their heads in the form of mock antlers, and dash to wherever the teacher was waiting. Although the same approach would not likely be embraced by fourth graders, older kids are just as likely to embrace procedures that actively engage them in some way. Whereas some teachers make creative use of hand signals, singing, and clapping routines, others find that more standard procedures fit their style. As long as you have procedures that serve the dual purposes of saving time and making the students less reliant on teacher direction, then what those procedures look like is generally left up to the discretion of the teacher.

Curriculum

Just as having procedures in place from the first day of school serves to reduce wasted classroom time, developing a year-long plan for addressing grade-level standards can help streamline instruction. In 1999, it was estimated that on average it would take a teacher 15,000 hours to teach all of the expected standards. It is likely that everyone would agree that is a lot of hours, but since there are typically only 9,000 hours available in a given school year, it's not tough to see why teachers often give in to the pressure of 'covering' standards rather than 'teaching' students (Marzano, Kendall, & Gaddy, 1999). In keeping with the idea that the most effective teaching and learning begins with keeping the end in mind, we urge you to consider two different levels of long-term planning: year long and unit.

Year-long planning is sometimes also called curriculum mapping. It can be especially challenging for teachers in self-contained elementary classrooms because it should be completed for each subject. The good news is that many schools have completed a process like this at some point and will likely make it available to beginning teachers. Generally, these school- or district-wide documents are based purely on curricular standards, which may come from national organizations, the state, or in some cases, the school district itself. Such documents may be called by different names as well. We have worked in districts where they were called curriculum maps, pacing guides, standards frameworks, and grade-level benchmarks. Regardless of what the document is called, it has a purpose and is worth asking for if it is not offered outright.

If your school does not have such a document, then it is well worth the initial time investment to dig in yourself (or with a group of colleagues who are equally convinced of its value!) and plan your year. Curriculum maps typically organize all of the standards in a given content area into a developmental sequence that serves as a guide for what to teach when. In essence, it becomes what is often labeled the "scope and sequence" when it is included as part of any textbook series. In comparison, curriculum maps based on standards have benefits over programmatically derived scope and sequences because standards are not tied specifically to purchased materials, but are rather established as a general set of expectations for students at any given grade level in any content area. Thus, they remain relatively stable from year to year, unless a state chooses to overhaul its standards in response to national movements. Interestingly, two such movements are currently going on as the Common Core State Standards (CCSS) (2010) for math and literacy and the Next Generation Science Standards (2013) are being implemented in many districts across the United States, so depending on how proactive your district is about curriculum mapping, you may get an opportunity to participate in the process early in your career.

Units of Instruction

Once you understand what you have to tackle across the school year, it becomes a bit easier to think about how to break the standards into manageable chunks of related material, which can be addressed in a series of lessons we call units. These units of instruction typically last anywhere from two to nine weeks, depending on the topic and grade level. In our experience, this is the level of planning most often missing from classrooms.

There is, of course, not one single way to approach planning a unit. Guillaume (2008) cites three approaches:

- Backwards design (Wiggins & McTighe, 2005)
- Big idea approach
- Thematic instruction

Both the big idea approach and thematic instruction follow similar processes in that they identify related themes or generalizations in the standards, select appropriate associated resources, and plan instructional activities to support the content to be learned. Typically, the big idea approach remains within a single content area (e.g., social studies or science), whereas the thematic approach crosses content-area boundaries as they apply to the broad theme (e.g., community, adaptation, leadership). Although these are certainly legitimate and appropriate ways in which units can be planned, we gravitate toward the backwards design approach advocated by Wiggins and McTighe. They suggest that this kind of thoughtful planning diminishes what they call the "twin sins of traditional design" (p.16), which they suggest contribute little to actual learning. The first sin, they say, is activity-focused teaching. This approach to planning tends to equate learning with participation in fun and engaging activities, but fails to consider where, if anywhere, the activities intellectually lead students. Imagine talking to a second-grade teacher who says, "We're doing a unit on pumpkins!" and goes on to explain how for the next two weeks students will be writing about pumpkins, estimating the weight and number of seeds that pumpkins contain, reading pumpkin stories, tasting pumpkin products, and even taking a field trip to the pumpkin patch. Although these activities are undoubtedly fun and engaging, you might leave the conversation wondering whether the students are actually making progress toward achieving any long-term instructional goals. The second design sin is the coverage approach, in which teachers lead the students through the textbook or series of lectures step by step, ensuring that all necessary information is addressed within the semester or school year. Users of this approach may say things like, "I don't have time to spend three days on the Constitution. We have to get all the way through the Civil War before the test in April." A perfect example of a coverage approach to teaching involved a teacher who once told us, "I have to cover a year's worth of content by March so I can review everything prior to spring standardized assessments." Although some may think that the activity-based approach is more prevalent at the elementary levels and the coverage approach in secondary settings, there seems to be a fair amount of both across the spectrum. In fact, it seems as though the increasing emphasis on standardized test performance may actually be contributing to more coverage-oriented teaching, even in the primary grades.

As opposed to activity and coverage-focused approaches, the backwards design approach outlined by Wiggins and McTighe highlights a three-stage process that clearly values learner outcomes and assessment, and plans "with the end in mind"

(Routman, 2008, p. 55). They suggest that there is often too much emphasis on teaching and not enough on learning, and so their model first focuses on the learning that should take place, how learning will be monitored, and finally, what the teaching will look like. The three stages are:

- Stage 1: Identify Desired Results
- Stage 2: Determine Acceptable Evidence
- Stage 3: Plan Learning Experiences

Identifying Desired Results

Wiggins and McTighe advocate a focus on developing and deepening understanding of important ideas. Thus, in the first stage of this model, the primary tasks are finding a central focus and identifying outcomes. Routman (2008) advocates selecting topics that are not only based in the standards, but also:

- Have enduring value beyond the classroom
- Reside at the heart of the discipline and be encountered in context
- Need to be uncovered
- Engage students (p. 65)

Wiggins and McTighe (2005) would use different language to describe this process, but advocate that teachers use a similar thinking process to determine how standards might be pulled together to establish the central focus or big idea: "a conceptual tool for sharpening thinking, connecting discrepant pieces of knowledge, and equipping learning for transferable applications" (p.70) of the unit. One example of a central focus is included in Figure 4.2.

Once the central focus is clear, it is important to consider what key knowledge, skills, and/or procedures students should acquire as a result of the unit of study. In addition, we suggest identifying any common misconceptions or potentially confusing information within the unit. For example, in a unit of study on forces and motion, teachers might anticipate student misconceptions about gravity, as many adults struggle with the idea that a bowling ball and golf ball dropped from the same height at the same time would hit the ground simultaneously. By clearly articulating what we want students to do, we can more easily design both lessons that support their growth toward these expectations and assessments that let us know how that process is going.

The central focus of this unit is to create a basic understanding in students about the relationship between groups of people and the land they inhabit, through study of regions and landforms from local, regional, and global perspectives.

FIGURE 4.2 The central focus of a third-grade social studies unit

Determining Acceptable Evidence

The second stage of the backwards design model focuses on planning for assessment. There should be clear links between the knowledge and skills identified in the first stage and the informal and formal assessments developed in this stage. Wiggins and McTighe advocate using performance tasks as at least one form of summative assessment, but also stress the importance of other acceptable evidence, including more formal tests and quizzes and less formal observations, checklists, and self-assessments.

Planning Learning Experiences

Only after the central focus, big ideas, and assessments have been planned should the focus shift to actual resources and activities. Guillaume (2008) lists five types of resources that should be explored in planning for a unit of instruction: text materials (books, primary sources, textbooks, etc.), visual images, disciplinary tools (what 'experts' use in the real world), people (community members, local organizations), and technology. Specific activities, grouping structures, and modifications and adaptations for students with varied needs would be taken into consideration at this point, and will be discussed in greater detail in Chapter 5, though we include a possible template for planning a unit here, in Figure 4.3.

UNIT PLAN

Subject Area:
Standards to be addressed:
Central focus of the unit:
Common errors and/or misunderstandings to be addressed:
Knowledge, Skills, and Procedures needed:
Academic language demands:

- Language functions
- Language forms
- Essential vocabulary, symbols, and/or phrases

Resources and materials needed:
Evaluation: How will you know if each student understands the central focus of your unit?

    Informal assessments:
    Formal assessments:

FIGURE 4.3 Unit plan template

Short-Term Planning

Short-term planning is where teachers tend to spend most of their time. Although some schools require plans be turned in to the principal ahead of time, most teachers are simply expected to have plans available for review upon request or observation. Most use some sort of plan book provided by the school; however, many teachers make thoughtful adaptations to the straightforward squares that typify these books, and some even create their own templates that more closely mirror the time allocations of their schedules. What is rarely seen are the kinds of lesson plans that preservice teachers are regularly asked to do. There is good reason for this! Most experienced teachers have internalized the parts of a strong lesson and automatically plan their lessons to address the key components. In this section, we hope to spur you to think about weekly planning in terms of maximizing instructional time through a thoughtfully planned schedule and carefully selected routines. Then, we discuss the important considerations that must accompany daily lesson planning.

Weekly Planning

Teachers do not have complete control over their weekly schedule. In fact, middle and secondary teachers who teach different sections of the same class may have no control at all. In elementary schools, though, special classes (physical education, art, music, computer lab, etc.), lunchtimes, and recess times are typically set at the building level and provided to teachers prior to the first day of school. In addition, teachers at any level have very little control over when students with additional needs are pulled out for speech services, occupational therapy work, or special education classes. And, to top it off, individual schools may have other school-wide initiatives or customs that can interrupt potential instructional time. Once those things are set, however, teachers need to thoughtfully consider how to use the remaining blocks of time. Most elementary teachers look for at least two large blocks of time, ideally at least ninety minutes long, to teach literacy and math. Science and social studies instruction are generally fit into the smaller spaces and are sometimes taught on alternate days or in alternating units, or even meaningfully integrated into literacy instruction. Deciding on a weekly schedule that works can take a few weeks, so keep an open mind and don't be afraid to try something different if your original plan isn't working out as you hoped it would.

Instructional routines are another means of making things run smoothly in the classroom. They are similar in nature to procedures, discussed earlier, though they typically relate directly to a content area. In essence, they are recurring events within a schedule that are designed specifically to decrease complexity of the classroom, minimize confusion, and prevent loss of instructional time (Ryan & Cooper, 2012). For example, the weekly literacy routine in one classroom may involve mostly whole-group instruction on Mondays, followed by four days of literacy station work while the teacher pulls small groups for guided reading. In another classroom, the literacy routine may take the form of a workshop, with a daily mini-lesson followed by individual reading and responding, and concluding with a short sharing session. The important thing is that routines are established so that the students know what to expect, which enables them to take responsibility for themselves, and ultimately saves time.

We want to conclude the section on weekly planning with a cautionary note. We believe teachers become very dependent on fitting instruction into a five-day cycle, likely in part because of the way textbook materials are structured and also simply because most teachers we know are organized beings who like things neatly and tidily wrapped up at the end of the week. Planning almost exclusively on a five-day cycle, however, presents two specific challenges to meaningful instruction. First, there is nothing magical about a series of five days of instruction on learning. Just because five days were spent on a topic doesn't mean students will 'get' it. Maybe they will, but maybe it should've only taken two, or maybe it needed seven. Instruction should not be driven by what can be accomplished in a week; it should be driven by the students' needs and their progress toward the instructional outcomes. Second, there are an amazing number of three- and four-day weeks in a school year! If your primary mode of planning is completed in five-day chunks, when a three- or four-day week appears, one of two things typically happens. In the case of a three-day week, the five-day cycle and all of its associated routines are often thrown out the window and something completely different (usually labeled "fun") happens instead. We are in favor of fun and engaging instruction, but at a time when the expectations for student learning are high and there is never enough instructional time, we simply cannot advocate activity-focused instruction. In the case of a four-day week, teachers often find themselves scrambling to fit five days of instruction into four. Overloading students in this manner contributes to the problem of simply covering material with little regard for actual learning. We believe teachers who can step away—even just a little—from seeing weekly planning as their primary focus and move instead toward more thoughtful daily planning will soon recognize the benefits.

Daily Planning

We firmly believe that no teacher should ever enter the classroom wondering, "What should I do today?" though we have heard reports that such things do happen. We do our best to prevent that. In fact, our novice teachers are often frustrated by the fact that they are expected to write full-fledged lesson plans for any lessons they plan to teach their students. They, sometimes with the support of their mentoring teachers, sometimes argue that writing detailed lesson plans for every lesson isn't realistic. In truth, we agree that it is quite a lot to expect a teacher—especially an elementary teacher who is responsible for four to six (or more!) separate lessons a day—to formally write out full-fledged daily lesson plans for each and every lesson. (Such plans can come in handy when you need a sub-stitute at the last minute, but that chance rarely compels teachers to write them on a regular basis!) However, we believe novice teachers need detailed daily lesson plans in order to help compensate for their understandable lack of automaticity. What is automaticity you ask? It is the ability to do something without paying attention to the lower-level details. Think back to the first time you sat behind the steering wheel of a car. It is likely that you had to actually exert effort to think through the process of starting the car: turning the key, putting your right foot on the brake, taking your hand off the wheel and shifting the car into gear, putting your hand back on the wheel, moving your foot from the brake to the gas pedal, and then gently pressing down. It seemed like a challenge to turn on the turn signal or the headlights or the windshield wipers, let alone mess with the stereo. Now, as an experienced driver, you simply jump in and go without giving any of those things a second thought, and sometimes even arrive at your destination with no memory of how you got there. Those procedures that once seemed daunting and took a lot of thought have become automatic, allowing you to focus mental energy on other things—maybe following the directions your global positioning system (GPS) is giving you, eating your breakfast, or chatting on the phone (where that kind of thing is legal!). We view lesson planning as the key to helping you develop teaching automaticity. If you have put thoughtful effort into your daily lesson planning ahead of time, it actually frees you to pay attention to aspects of effective teaching that might otherwise go unnoticed.

Generally speaking, daily lesson plans can last anywhere from five to ten min-utes (which might be called a mini-lesson) to an hour or more; some lessons can actually last a few days! They are structured around a specific objective or two, require particular resources and materials, include a means of assessing student progress toward the objective(s), and typically follow a gradual release of respon-sibility model (Pearson & Gallagher, 1983).

Objectives

We can feel you rolling your eyes as you begin reading this section. In the past, many teachers have simply used the associated state standard as a learning objective since many of these standards were narrow and specific. However, with so many states now relying on the very broad CCSS as a guide, that practice is no longer feasible. Effective teachers have a clear focus regarding what they want to accomplish—their intended lesson outcomes—thus, although writing specific lesson objectives often feels time consuming, it is a critical step in the lesson planning process. Objectives are typically written in a clear and consistent format that includes an observable behavior. A simple Internet search will reveal a plethora of verbs specifying observable behaviors, usually associated with Bloom's taxonomy, recently revised by Anderson and Krathwohl (2001). The more specificity you have in your objectives, the better, although the most important part of an objective is being able to describe exactly what it is that you want students to be able to do by the end of the lesson. Consider the following two examples:

After reading *Memoirs of a Goldfish*, students will be able to independently identify the setting, main character, and problem of the story in writing.

Students will understand the parts of a story after reading *Memoirs of a Goldfish*.

They both could lead to similar lessons, but the second one is far too open to interpretation. What does "understand" mean in this context? What parts of the story will be identified? How will they show that they understand? The clarity of the first objective makes designing an associated assessment relatively easy.

Assessments

Assessment has been discussed in depth in previous chapters. Our emphasis here is twofold. First, group assessment is not enough. Asking questions does give you a sense of where those students who are called upon to give answers are in terms of understanding, but it is not a sufficient gauge of all students in the class. Each lesson should incorporate some means of collecting evidence related to individual performance. Second, all assessments are not created equally. It is critical that what students are asked to do is actually a valid assessment of the objective. In relation to the previously stated objective, if the students were given a multiple-choice worksheet from which they selected the setting, main character, and problem of the story, would they be fulfilling the objective? Is "selecting" the same as "independently identifying?" We would say no. Effective teachers make sure that their assessments are both directly linked to the objective and formatted in the same way the students learned the material. If students learned to identify the parts of a story in writing, they should be assessed by identifying the parts of a story in writing.

Resources and Materials

Not all resources have equivalent instructional value, nor does one size necessarily fit all. Mindless worksheets that are found online are no better than mindless worksheets that come from the textbook. The good news is that if you have clearly articulated your objective and developed associated assessments, finding the resources and materials to accompany the lesson is a lot easier. We realize that we are suggesting that planning is a time-consuming task, and it is. The good news is that we don't advocate reinventing the wheel! We are not suggesting that you should sit in front of your blank plan book attempting to generate creative and engaging lessons from scratch. There are so many great ideas at your fingertips—as long as you have access to colleagues, teaching resources, and the Internet. However, it is important that you realize those lessons were designed for someone else's students (or in some cases, someone's vision of what "typical" students might be!). It is your responsibility to adapt those lessons to meet the needs of your students, find texts that fit your students' needs, and make certain that you are not wasting time on extraneous 'stuff' that doesn't really contribute to helping students move toward accomplishing the lesson objective.

Lesson Structure

Whether a lesson lasts twenty minutes or two days, the most effective ones follow a model that engages students, gradually releases responsibility for learning to the students, and brings the lesson full circle by reviewing the learning and establishing next steps. Teachers have a responsibility to share the lesson's purpose with students. (It's hard to do if you haven't taken time to think about why you're teaching what you're teaching!) Although there are instances in which teachers intentionally structure lessons where students are expected to discover big ideas on their own (see Chapter 6 for more on instructional frameworks), in many lessons, it seems like teachers are actually trying to keep the purpose secret. In general, we say share it! Build enthusiasm for it! Hook the kids and make them want to learn what you are trying to teach. (See more on engagement in Chapter 9). The heart of the lesson involves modeling, guided practice, and independent practice. However, we prefer to organize it as Routman (2008) discusses in her book *Teaching Essentials as the Optimal Learning Model*: "I do it, We do it, We do it, We do it, You do it" (p. 91). We frame ours only slightly differently, preferring to expand on the "You do" part rather than the "We do," as Routman does. We suggest:

- I do—Teacher modeling, demonstration, and think-aloud
- We do—Whole-group-involved guided practice with teacher feedback
- Ya'll do—Small-group guided practice with teacher feedback
- You two do—Partner-based guided practice with teacher feedback
- You do—Independent practice and application

Not all lessons will require all five steps, but at the very least we believe that every lesson should include modeling, guided practice, and independent practice. Sometimes teachers neglect the "I do" step, simply telling students what the topic is and sending them off to practice independently. If you have ever tried to sight-read music, you know how frustrating operating without a model can be! It's stressful, and though there are times when you want kids to struggle a little (inquiry approaches to science instruction come to mind), usually, showing students what we want them to do is good practice. Another common problem involves jumping straight from the "I do" to the "You do" section, causing students to miss out on valuable learning that comes from actually working and engaging in much-needed practice. A basketball coach who simply lectured athletes about how to play and then told them to show up to the game without any practice would likely not last long. Practice matters on the court, field, or anywhere else! It's no different in the classroom. If you are modeling and giving your students sufficient practice time, your lesson may last twice as long as you expect, but the likelihood that your students' learning will last will increase greatly.

Lesson plan formats are varied and diverse. Sometimes, teachers are expected to follow a common form developed or adopted by the school or district. Some are based on teacher evaluation rubrics, or in other cases, teachers are simply left to their own devices. Miller (2008) indicates that her lesson design plans take the form of answers to a series of questions, including, "What do I want students to learn?" "How do I use this skill or strategy myself?" and "What connections can I help students make?" (p. 80). However, she also includes a section she entitles, "Showing Students How" (p. 86), which more specifically details what both she and the students will do throughout the lesson. Pelletier (2000), on the other hand, includes space for key vocabulary, questions, materials, and homework, in addition to instructional procedures and means of assessment. In Figure 4.4, we have included a format that is built around the components we have addressed earlier, as well as a few others that will be discussed in upcoming chapters.

Planning never ends; it is simply one part of an ongoing effective instructional cycle that includes teaching and assessing. We believe that one of the most overlooked components of planning actually takes place during and after teaching: adjusting and tweaking future daily lessons based on observations and formative assessment. Planning forces teachers to think about what needs to be accomplished and how to most productively use class time toward that end (Stronge, 2007). Though there is never enough time in a classroom, we hope that teachers take a minute at the end of every lesson, or at least at the end of every day, to consult their observational notes and other assessments, reflect on the impact of their lessons, and consider how the results should affect their next instructional steps. Lesson plans should not be seen as final products; they are works in progress, scaffolds, so to speak, ready for adaptation and revision for both related lessons and future students.

LESSON PLAN

Standard:
Objective(s):
Teacher Knowledge of Students:

- Students' learning difficulties (academic, social, emotional)
- Students' interests in instruction
- Students' individual needs

Introduction:

- Background Knowledge: Connections to students' lives
- Motivation/Engagement

Resources and Materials:
Academic Language Requirements:
Forms of Assessment:
Instructional Procedures:

- "I Do" (Modeling, Showing, Demonstrating)
- "We Do" (Guided Practice)
- "You Do" (Independent Practice and Application)

Closure:

- Review in relation to objective
- Set the stage for next steps

FIGURE 4.4 A standard lesson plan template

Challenges to the Planning Process

There are a number of challenges associated with effective planning strategies. The National Academy of Education (2005) offers what they call four "age-old curriculum concerns" (p. 16) for teachers to consider as they plan:

- Balancing breadth and depth
- Incorporating both cognitive and affective goals for learning
- Avoiding fragmentation
- Striving for both relevance and rigor

These four items certainly warrant such consideration, though as a result of the movement toward a standards-based approach to instruction, teachers may have limited options for individually addressing these issues. We offer three additional challenges that we believe both affect effective planning and are within most teachers' control, at least to some extent: the use of instructional time, the role of textbooks, and the balance between collaboration and conformity.

Use of instructional time. It should be clear, based on earlier discussions of the estimates of time needed to effectively teach standards, that there is no room for wasted time in classrooms. Stronge (2007) indicates that only 70 percent of classroom time is focused on teaching and learning, and the remaining 30 percent is dedicated to administrative and behavioral concerns. It is clear, then, that teachers must make every effort to minimize interruptions and maximize engagement, since it is engagement coupled with understanding that will ultimately result in durable learning—that which lasts long beyond 'the test.' In some cases, the most effective teachers have reportedly found ways of securing an extra thirty minutes of academic engaged time per day. At that rate, they would gain a day's worth of instructional time in just over two weeks!

Research on the brain also indicates that time is necessary for learning to occur. Jensen (2009) reports that time is an essential ingredient for mastery of learning, and Jacobs, Schall, and Scheibel (1993) suggest a correlation between brain development and actual time spent engaged in complex learning. Allington (2002a) and Routman (2008) echo the importance of having students spending time actually engaged in the process of doing work rather than simply hearing about it, yet an estimated 90 percent of actual instructional time is teacher focused. Jensen indicates that teacher talk should never exceed 51 percent of class time and states that "[t]he brain needs enough processing time to make and strengthen connections that are the foundation . . . of learning" (p. 23). He makes practical suggestions, such as planning to introduce new content in ten-minute chunks, followed by ten to fifteen minutes of processing (work) time, and simply taking a brief pause every minute or so to allow students' brains more time to assimilate the new information. We also suggest that you make the tough decisions about how to match your daily instruction to your long-term goals and plans at the same time that you focus on teaching and learning rather than just 'covering' content.

Textbooks. Because textbooks are typically the primary resources provided for teachers by their schools, many teachers feel compelled to use them as the primary source of instruction. Although it is beyond the scope of our work to offer a specific critique of textbooks, there have been a number of criticisms offered in the literature. Often texts that claim to be "standards based" contain superficial treatment of content (O'Shea, 2005), contain inaccuracies and biases (Loewen, 2007), and are typically written above the grade level for which they are intended (Allington, 2002b). Yet, whether because they are written by so-called experts, because the district paid a lot of money to make them available to the teachers, or because they are purported to have premade plans that are designed specifically for students at the associated grade level, there remains pressure to use these one-size-fits-all books.

We suggest using them as a resource rather than as the source for instructional planning. Dunn (2000) agrees, suggesting, among other things, that teachers use texts as (1) a framework for identifying key ideas, (2) a source of possible questions and activities, and (3) a reference and background reading. We believe that planning to use primary sources and other content-area documents is much more effective than textbooks in terms of facilitating learning. Not only are these resources typically more interesting, they also serve to develop academic language, particularly that associated with the discourse of the discipline, and understanding of the contexts in which the content might appear in the real world.

Balancing Conformity with Collaboration

Teachers are generally congenial people who like to get along. Group planning seems to be a common way veteran teachers attempt to help alleviate the 'overwhelmed' feelings most beginning teachers face in the first months of school. In some cases, plans (and even associated worksheets!) are simply provided, seemingly accompanied by the expectation that they will be implemented. Too often, the pressure to conform leads to planning via textbook, neglecting the long-term vision for students and their associated learning needs in favor of doing what's next in the book. Despite the well-intentioned efforts of teachers and administrators alike, we agree with Guillaume (2008) that although there are benefits to collaboration, "every teacher . . . should be involved deeply in planning" (p. 77). Beginning teachers need to learn about the standards they are expected to teach, and they need to practice selecting appropriate materials and activities for their students. Collaborative planning can be invaluable if it generates a number of instructional ideas and meaningful activities from which teachers can select in order to best match their specific instructional purposes and student needs.

We have each been part of a team whose planning sessions were generative and invigorating and where each member's contributions were valued. Unfortunately, we have also observed team planning in which one or more members dismissed any ideas that didn't follow preconceived notions of what 'should be' happening instructionally. In more than one case, we have seen beginning teachers told things like, "Well, that might work, but we have to stick to the text." In cases like this, we would encourage you to find out if that is a real or perceived expectation by humbly asking a trusted colleague or your administrator. You might be surprised to find out that it is a misperception, but even if the answer you get is, "Yes," you have the option to ask for clarification regarding what "stick to the text" actually means. In one case, one of our former students asked that question in her first year and found out that in relation to the district-adopted reading text, it meant her students had to read the weekly story and take the associated test. As a result, she adjusted her instructional schedule to take care of those requirements on Monday and spent the rest of her week engaging her students in authentic reading and writing activities that she determined would better meet their needs.

Final Thoughts on Planning

Planning is not the same as finding stuff; fun does not equal worthwhile; cute does not mean meaningful. Being an effective teacher means that you will be spending lots of planning time outside of the required workday. Eventually, as you become intimately familiar with the standards and learning expectations associated with your grade level, internalize the structures associated with a coherent lesson plan, and gain the experiences that will help you make appropriate in-lesson modifications to meet the needs of your students, planning will become easier and less time consuming. But as long as states keep modifying their curriculum standards, districts keep purchasing new programs, and you keep getting new students, the need for adapting and updating your lesson plans remains. There are simply no shortcuts when it comes to meeting the learning needs of your students.

Connecting Pedagogy to Practice

1. Select two or three procedures (how to walk down the hallway, how to sharpen a pencil, how to ask to use the restroom, etc.) and plan exactly how you want them to happen in your classroom.
2. Find a teacher's guide from a reading or math series and select a lesson. Analyze it and answer the following questions:

   a. What Common Core State Standard(s) does the lesson support?
   b. Is there a central focus or big idea that connects it to surrounding lessons?
   c. Do the lesson objectives include observable behaviors?
   d. Do the assessments match the objectives?
   e. Does the instruction link the objectives to the assessment?
   f. What, if anything, would you change in order to make the lesson more effective?

3. Next time you are in a classroom, take a stopwatch and keep track of how much time is focused on teaching and learning. Make note of any interruptions (assemblies, announcements, bathroom breaks), and consider how you might adjust the schedule to maximize instructional time.
4. Interview a teacher. Ask:

   - How is long-term planning done?
   - How much time is spent planning each week?
   - Is there a particular form required for unit and/or lesson plans?
   - What elements are to be addressed in unit plans?
   - What elements are to be addressed in daily lesson plans?
   - What type of teacher plan book is used?

Putting Leadership into Action

It is relatively easy to plan for instruction if you put faith in the textbooks and materials provided by your district. You simply follow the instructions. In some schools and with some students, this might even be enough to facilitate student growth. And, "Do pages 45–50 in book" fits in the squares of the lesson plan book. Teacher leaders, however, rarely use those books—textbooks and lesson plan books—in their original form. One small step toward leadership might involve taking a look at your weekly schedule and designing a lesson plan book template that matches it. If you're ready to take a bigger step, you might consider trying to make a year-long plan, based on units of instruction, for one subject area.

References

Allington, R.L. (2002a). What I've learned about effective reading instruction from a decade of studying exemplary elementary classroom teachers. *Phi Delta Kappan, 83,* 740–747.

Allington, R.L. (2002b). You can't learn much from books you can't read. *Educational Leadership, 60*(3), 16–19.

Anderson, L.W. & Krathwohl, D.R. (2001). *A taxonomy for learning, teaching, and assessing: A revision of Bloom's taxonomy of educational objectives.* Boston, MA: Allyn & Bacon.

Denton, P., & Kriete, R. (2000). *The first six weeks of school.* Greenfield, MA: Northeast Foundation for Children.

Dunn, M.A. (2000). Closing the book on social studies: Four classroom teachers go beyond the text. *Social Studies, 91,* 132–136.

Guillaume, A. M. (2008). *K–12 classroom teaching: A primer for new professionals* (3rd Ed.). Upper Saddle River, NJ: Pearson.

Jacobs, B., Schall, M., & Scheibel, A. (1993). A quantitative dendritic analysis of Wernicke's area in humans. II. Gender, hemispheric, and environmental factors. *Journal of Comparative Neurology, 327,* 97–111.

Jensen, E. (2009). *Fierce teaching: Purpose, passion, and what matters most.* Thousand Oaks, CA: Corwin Press.

Loewen, J. (2007). *Lies my teacher told me: Everything your American history textbook got wrong.* New York, NY: Touchstone.

Marzano, R., Kendall, J., & Gaddy, B. (1999). *Essential knowledge: The debate over what American students should know.* Aurora, CO: Mid-Continent Research in Education and Learning.

Merriam-Webster Online Dictionary. (2014, August 16) Re: procedure. Retrieved August 16, 2014, from: http://www.merriam-webster.com/dictionary/procedure.

Miller, D. (2008). *Teaching with intention: Defining beliefs, aligning practice, taking action.* Portland, ME: Stenhouse.

National Academy of Education. (2005). *A good teacher in every classroom: Preparing the highly qualified teachers our children deserve.* San Francisco, CA: Jossey-Bass.

National Governors Association Center for Best Practices & Council of Chief State School Officers. (2010). *Common Core State Standards.* Washington, DC: National Governors Association Center for Best Practices, Council of Chief State School Officers.

NGSS Lead States. (2013). *Next generation science standards: For states, by states.* Washington, DC: The National Academies Press.

O'Shea, M.R. (2005). *From standards to success.* Alexandria, VA: Association for Supervision and Curriculum Development.

Pearson, P.D. & Gallagher, M.C. (1983). The instruction of reading comprehension. *Contemporary Educational Psychology, 8,* 317–344.

Pelletier, C.M. (2000). *Strategies for successful student teaching: A comprehensive guide.* Needham Heights, MA: Allyn & Bacon.

Routman, R. (2008). *Teaching essentials: Expecting the most and getting the best from every learner, K–8.* Portsmouth, NH: Heinemann.

Ryan, K., & Cooper, J.M. (2012). *Those who can, teach* (13th Ed.). Belmont, CA: Wadsworth, Cengage Learning.

Scillian, D. (2010). *Memoirs of a goldfish.* Ann Arbor, MI: Sleeping Bear Press.

Stronge, J.H. (2007). *Qualities of effective teachers* (2nd Ed.). Alexandria, VA: Association for Supervision and Curriculum Development.

Wiggins, G., & McTighe, J. (2005). *Understanding by design.* Upper Saddle River, NJ: Pearson.

Wong, H.K., & Wong, R.T. (2004). *How to be an effective teacher: The first days of school.* Mountain View, CA: Harry K. Wong Publications.

5

USING FORMATIVE ASSESSMENT IN PLANNING

Almost every time we talk with administrators about what's going on in classrooms at their schools, they mention data-driven instruction. They tell us about the data coordinator in charge of collecting and maintaining data, and talk about in-service days dedicated to having teachers look at their own classroom data. They talk about Response to Intervention (RTI) initiatives and Universal Design for Learning (UDL) principles and the need for even more data to inform both. Schools are now collecting so much data that it sometimes amazes us that we can't simply see it oozing out from around the windows and under the doors of each and every classroom. And yet, we find a startling number of teachers only seem to go through the motions of analyzing and using this data in their instruction. We once worked in a school that gave an extensive (twenty to thirty minutes, one-on-one) diagnostic reading assessment to each student in grades K–3. If the teachers were unable to find time to do it themselves, trained aides or, in some cases, the reading specialist gave the assessment, scored it, and gave the results to the teacher. Within the first few weeks of school, every K–3 teacher had detailed data about each student's decoding, fluency, and comprehension strengths and weaknesses. Unfortunately, far too often, those data were simply received and put on a shelf—as if the only reason the assessment existed was to be given and checked off the teacher's "to do" list. Maybe the teachers were overwhelmed by the information they were given, or maybe they were underwhelmed by it, viewing it simply as a hoop-jumping exercise. Our guess was that either way, they really didn't stop to think about the potential power of the data they were being handed. They didn't realize that they were being given information that could focus their instruction and maximize their reading instructional time.

We will agree that all data are not equally beneficial to instructional planning. However, as we mentioned in Chapter 2, even standardized test data may help us see patterns of strength and weakness in our own teaching over time if we take the time to look. We believe that for teachers, the primary purpose of assessment should be using it to inform their instruction—to make data-driven decisions about how to best meet the needs of students; there should be a cyclical and ongoing relationship between effective assessment and effective instruction. There is no doubt that all "teachers should be able to use data from different kinds of assessment to evaluate patterns of student strengths and target instruction where it is needed" (National Academy of Education, 2005, p. 24), but effective teachers are the ones who actually do it.

We recall a fifth-grade teacher who once told us that she spent one week teaching each part of speech every year so that she could be sure her students knew them by the time the big test rolled around. When we asked if her ten- and eleven-year-olds really needed a week-long review of nouns and verbs, she replied that it took a lot of time, but teaching it to them was the only way she could be sure they knew it. We would argue that in this case, when most students engage in some study of nouns and verbs every year of elementary school (and beyond!) that some sort of grammar-related preassessment would have been beneficial in this instance. Had this teacher collected this type of data, she may have found that most of her class had a solid understanding of these basic parts of speech, whereas only two or three struggled to remember that nouns named a person, place, or thing and verbs demonstrated action or a state of being. In essence, had she carried out some type of formative content assessment far enough in advance, she could've used the data to shape her instructional planning, potentially allowing her to use at least a portion of the eight weeks of language arts instruction dedicated to the parts of speech in a more meaningful and productive manner. She may have been able to strike a balance between not duplicating what her students already knew and not moving too quickly for their current levels of understanding (Gregory & Kuzmich, 2004).

If teachers make the choice to ignore all the assessment data at their fingertips, they are bound to waste valuable instructional time, no matter how long they spend planning for instruction. Furthermore, even if they spend time looking at the data but continue to either plan whole-group lessons or simply move through the teacher's edition from one lesson to the next, they are missing the big idea. The primary purpose of using assessment to inform instruction is to differentiate and group according to the needs of the students in relation to the content and skills they are expected to learn. Again, we reiterate the idea that putting time into assessment and planning on the front end actually maximizes instructional time and leads to more learning throughout the school year.

Differentiation

When differentiated instruction is mentioned, some teachers automatically think of Gardner's (1983) theory of multiple intelligences or learning style theories based on whether learners prefer auditory, visual, or kinesthetic approaches to instruction. Despite the fact that educators quickly embraced these visions of differentiating instruction, research has debunked at least some of it. The work of Kratzig and Arbuthnott (2006) suggests that focusing on sensory modalities may be a waste of time, as "most people are likely multimodal and multi-situational learners, changing learning strategies depending on the context of the to-be-learned material" (p. 245).

Differentiated instruction is not, then, about catering to a specific "intelligence" or mode of sensory learning. Rather, Tomlinson (1999) asserts that at its heart, differentiation ensures "that struggling and advanced learners, students with varied cultural heritages, and children with different background experiences all grow as much as they possibly can each day, each week, and throughout the year" (p. 2). Wormeli (2006) simplifies the definition even further in saying simply, "Differentiated instruction is doing what's fair for students" (p. 3). He goes on to caution that differentiation is not about making learning easier for students, but rather to provide "the appropriate challenge that enables students to thrive" (p. 4) and to give them "the tools to handle whatever comes their way" (p. 5). As schools have become more diverse, filled with students with more exceptionalities, languages, and struggles, we must become more "mindful of and responsive to diverse learning needs" (Tomlinson, Brimijoin, & Narvaez, 2008, p. 1).

In order to differentiate instruction, though, teachers do need to know their students. They need to have some sense of their interests and motivations, how ready they are for specific instruction, and the funds of knowledge they bring to the classroom. Stefanakis (2011) and Routman (2008) both emphasize the need to focus on students' strengths first; when we focus on the deficiencies, home life, etc., those things become 'can'ts,' immediately limiting our ability to affect students. The most effective teachers set high expectations for all of their students (Stronge, 2007) and then provide the scaffolds, modifications, and accommodations to help them meet those expectations. Thus, teachers must be both proactive and intentional in order to meaningfully differentiate instruction for all students as the need arises. As pictured in Figure 5.1, Tomlinson (1999) suggests that

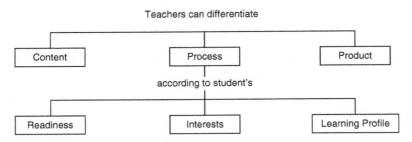

FIGURE 5.1 Tomlinson's (1999, p. 15) model of differentiation

teachers can differentiate content, process, or product based on students' readiness, interest, and learning profile. These considerations, then, lie at the core of effective instructional planning.

Student Considerations

Teachers are concerned with the success of all learners; however, effective teachers recognize that although there are certainly grade-level expectations, individual expectations are also important—especially to students at both ends of the spectrum. Knowing a student's level of readiness in relation to curricular expectations allows teachers to make the most of instructional time. Just because a high-achieving student comes into the classroom proficient at most all of the associated grade-level standards, it does not mean that the child should be left alone to work on his or her own. Similarly, struggling students should not be exposed to a barrage of grade-level expectations when they do not yet have the skills or knowledge to reach them. Teachers must understand the individual's readiness for content and skills in relation to the grade-level expectations and must adjust instruction to set goals that accelerate learning for that student. The goal of differentiation based on readiness, then, is what Tomlinson, Brimijoin, and Narvaez (2008) term "teaching up: supporting students in achieving at a level higher than they thought possible" (p. 4). Adjustments to content entry points, pacing of delivery, and activities may be necessary based on students' needs, though the instructional focus should always remain on moving all students forward in their learning.

Students' interests can and should affect instruction. Some teachers interpret this to mean students' choice is the ultimate goal and either turn too much over to the students too quickly or simply relieve themselves of the responsibility to differentiate because they think it means giving up too much control. Differentiation is not about either extreme; it is about balancing teacher choice with student choice depending on the instructional goals and potential for moving students (or a student) along. For example, it is a rare teacher who doesn't value wide and varied reading among students, and yet there are many children and adults who emerge from their public schooling thankful to never again read a book. How does this happen? Although there are many factors, one is certainly the skewed balance between teacher-required reading and student-selected options. Certainly, if a teacher is in the midst of a unit focusing on plot elements (exposition, rising action, climax, falling action, and resolution) he may require students to read a fiction book with strong narrative structure—maybe even the same fiction book so that he could model and think aloud in front of the entire group as he identified the plot structures. However, if the teacher's purpose for asking students to read a book is to practice applying comprehension strategies in order to understand the plot, there would not be a strong need to have all students reading from the same book—or even in the same genre. Students could be allowed to choose a book that appeals to them. This concept of choice doesn't just apply to materials, but also can come into play in regard to tasks (Do some students prefer to work alone, whereas others prefer partners or groups?) and topics (If a student has a passion for something—insects, fractions, construction vehicles—capitalize on it!). The extent to which a teacher considers students' interests and choice in planning for instruction should be directly related to the purpose of the lesson or unit. Within the parameters of purpose, paying attention to interests and maximizing opportunities for choice will serve not only to build on what students know, but also to engage them in the learning process.

Finally, students' learning profiles should be taken into account. This doesn't refer to first labeling students as certain kinds of learners and planning instruction to fit those specific modes of learning. Tomlinson (2014) suggests instead that the use of learner profiles should offer multiple ways of supporting learning in a given instance. In math, for example, students may be more successful in starting with the procedural pieces as they work toward understanding the bigger concepts. But, the same learners who, in math, are more successful when they start with the pieces and move toward the whole, may, in social studies, prefer to see the big picture first. Differences in culture, gender, and self-image may also warrant consideration in differentiating according to learner profiles. The key is to keep in mind that the ultimate goal is to help students determine what works best for them in relation to finding success within a given subject or task. They will only be able to figure that out if we provide them with opportunities to explore a variety of learning options.

Curricular Considerations

In the planning stages, content, process, and products can all be modified in order to design lessons that will help all students grow. Differentiating content is probably the easiest of these three to tackle; it involves the "what" of instruction. This includes not only specific content, but also the materials associated with learning the content. Stefanakis (2011) suggests organizing instruction according to three levels—what all students will learn, what most students will learn, and what some students will learn—based on the essential content understandings. Where instruction starts should be based directly on the diagnostic preassessment, and should only be differentiated if there is a need or other evidence suggests that a student or students will understand the ideas or use the skills more effectively as a result (Tomlinson, 1999). Once the content of instruction is set, consideration of the materials should follow. Texts are of particular concern at this stage, although media of all sorts should be considered. Teachers are much more apt to differentiate texts if they are teaching reading, making sure that students of varying levels are provided with appropriate instructional or independent levels of text—that which can be read with higher than 90 percent accuracy and with better than 70 percent comprehension. However, reading level is arguably of more concern in content areas like science and social studies; if the content is inaccessible, how can students be held accountable for learning it? We suggest the responsibility of finding a variety of other means of accessing the information sits firmly in the lap of the teacher. Easier texts that address the same ideas and content, primary sources (newspaper and magazine articles, letters, journals, etc.), videos, audio books, and other digital media can be perfectly acceptable alternatives to challenging texts if the purpose of a lesson is to understand content. Considering the use of student choice, and thus affecting motivation and engagement, may also be particularly helpful in regard to the selection of materials. Ultimately, teachers should ask, "What changes should I make to this lesson's content and materials so that all of my students can work on the same concepts in ways that are appropriate for their needs?"

Differentiating process has to do with the 'how' of instruction, as in how might students go about making sense of the ideas and information I want them to learn? Both the kinds of instruction (hands-on, lecture, etc.) and the audiences (whole group, small group, individual) come into play when considering differentiating the process. Consider the math concept of addition with regrouping. It is not unusual to find an entire classroom full of second graders who, even if they can carry out the procedures associated with regrouping, don't fully understand the concept. We will assume that the teacher in this case knew that all of her students needed to work on building conceptual knowledge around this topic. As such, she may have started with whole-group instruction in which all students were using manipulatives like base-10 blocks to physically carry out the regrouping process. After carefully observing her students, it seemed as though everyone understood what they were doing, so she removed the manipulatives as a scaffold and invited them to try a few problems. It quickly became apparent that about half of the class was successful in transferring their understanding to the more abstract pencil-and-paper process, but the other half struggled. She then planned to differentiate the next day's lesson by splitting the students into two groups, with those who demonstrated understanding working together in partners to solve increasingly challenging problems, while she pulled the manipulatives back out for the other group and spent more time modeling and thinking aloud as a means of supporting their learning. As she continues to observe and assess the students in her group, she may find that some appear to be ready to move on and others need a different means of practicing this math skill. Over the course of a unit of study, a number of different processes, including work stations and centers, may be going on at the same time, as shown in Figure 5.2. Specific grouping strategies will be explored in more detail later in this chapter.

Finally, Tomlinson (1999) advocated differentiating products, that is, the ways in which students demonstrate what they have learned. When considering this aspect of differentiation, teachers may find themselves asking questions such as, "Did any of my students have a hard time relating to the materials or the products they will need to use to express what they know?" or "What other products will demonstrate that they have mastered the material I have taught?" Modifications

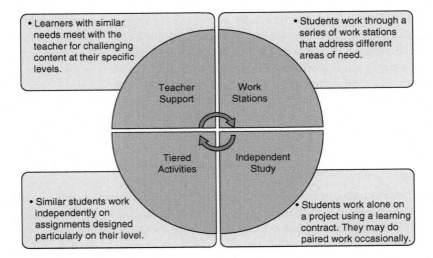

FIGURE 5.2 Multiple ways of differentiating processes in the classroom

in process might be as simple as letting a student who struggles with fine motor skills record his or her oral answers to essay questions rather than attempting to write them out by hand. Student choice can also once again come into play if the teacher provides multiple options for documenting understanding. For example, as part of a study on plant life, students may choose to create a model that includes accurate representation and labeling of plant parts, to write a report that includes a description of plant parts, or to videotape themselves giving a lecture on the parts of a plant. All three products, though different, would provide the teacher with similar insights regarding the students' understanding of parts of a plant. The key to differentiating products is making sure that each accurately reflects the objective of the lesson or unit of instruction.

Wehrmann (2000) cautions teachers to begin differentiation in small steps rather than leaping ahead at full speed. We believe that just as students have different needs, so do teachers. For some, it might be easier to jump in and go for it. Others might choose a subject they feel comfortable with to start differentiating. Still others might decide that they want to start differentiating products based on student interests. Like just about everything in teaching, there is not one correct way in which a teacher can differentiate. In fact, the only 'wrong' approach might be to avoid it altogether. Teachers can no longer simply "teach, test, and hope for the best" (Gregory & Kuzmich, 2004, p. 8).

Grouping

Grouping considerations for students are most often considered a component of the 'process' aspect of differentiation, but because whole-group instruction remains so prevalent in classrooms, we believe it warrants its own separate section of the chapter. Although there are appropriate times for whole-group instruction (when students have shared and similar background knowledge or the teacher is attempting to build such knowledge or the learning objective is appropriate for all students), using it as the primary means of delivering instructional content and guided practice is not the most effective use of time and energy, and actually tends to result in fewer engaged students and more off-task behavior. At the other end of the spectrum lies individual work or instruction. In most research, one-on-one instruction (like tutoring) comes out on top in terms of effectiveness. This is not surprising, as instruction provided in this manner is easy to attune to the specific needs and preferences of the individual student; however, the reality is that it is impossible to provide individual instruction for each of the twenty to thirty students in a classroom on a regular basis. Thus, this remains a preferred mode of reteaching a specific concept or skill, but is not employed as a regular instructional grouping strategy, except when working on completing individual assessment tasks.

Partnerships are another grouping structure that can play a significant role in the classroom, although these roles typically revolve around practice rather than instruction. Such partnerships can reduce risk and maximize student interaction, especially for those students who may feel intimidated to share ideas in a larger group. (It is important to note, though, that sometimes the social aspect of partnerships can decrease time on task!) We believe that, like most instructional decisions, partnerships should be made intentionally based on the task at hand. Sometimes there are benefits to working with like-ability partners (e.g., for tasks designed with specific student needs in mind), and sometimes matching more experienced students with less experienced partners can have benefits (e.g., providing a sort of peer tutoring). What often doesn't work is partnering students whose abilities are drastically different, like putting a struggling student with one who has mastered all the material, or one who likes to take charge and get things done with one who is willing to sit back and let that happen. When it comes to planning, it is important to avoid the temptation to write "Divide class into partners" in the lesson plans without thinking further about the purpose of the partnership and what specific partnerships might best support that purpose.

We believe that much classroom instruction and practice should take place in small groups. As such, it is important to understand the research behind such groupings. Lou et al. (1996) conducted a meta-analysis of research on within-class grouping. Their work suggested that students at all grade and ability levels who took part in small-group instruction performed moderately better than those who received whole-group instruction. Specifically, groups of three to four students were deemed most effective, suggesting that the common practice of dividing students into three (high, average, and low) reading groups advocated by most core reading materials is not 'research based,' as in a classroom of at least twenty students, that would mean each group would be composed of at least six students. According to the work by Lou and colleagues, the data on the impact of homogeneous (like-ability) and heterogeneous (mixed-ability) groups were more variable. Their work indicated that mixed-ability groups had a stronger positive impact on more struggling students, whereas like-ability groups were more beneficial for what they considered average students. In their work, high-achieving students were unaffected by these approaches to grouping, though an earlier study had conflicting results (Kulik, 1992). Other research suggests more dire consequences for ability grouping, especially for those students who struggle the most. In particular, low-ability readers tend to have fewer opportunities to read and write and receive more isolated skill as opposed to comprehension instruction (Allington, 1983; Collins, 1986; Stanovich, 1986). Furthermore, when working with low-ability reading groups, teachers tend to emphasize behavior more than academic learning (Oakes, 1994); rarely change group membership (Allington, 1983; Barr & Dreeben, 1991); and demonstrate lower levels of enthusiasm, preparation, and expectations (Gamoran, 1992). Furthermore, this approach often leads to generalizations about similarities among group members. In one study, researchers looked at students categorized as struggling readers and found that when assessment in the areas of word identification, meaning, and fluency was taken into consideration, the group of strugglers actually fell into six different categories of need (Valencia & Riddle-Buly, 2004). Students deserve instruction targeted to their needs.

As a result of the negative outcomes associated with fixed groupings based on ability and achievement, flexible grouping strategies are often promoted as a means of meeting the needs of all learners (Caldwell & Ford, 2002; Opitz, 1998). The idea behind flexible grouping is that the groups are chosen based on a specific purpose, they meet until the specific purpose is accomplished, and then new groups are formed. One grouping technique is not inherently better than another, and students can be part of multiple groups throughout the school day. Flexible groups also provide students opportunities to work with a variety of peers over time. Opitz (1998) offers eight different grouping techniques for teachers to consider, though there is some overlap among them. Figure 5.3 highlights the eight strategies, along with their purpose, selection process, and pros and cons associated with each.

As with planning for partner work, with rare exception, grouping students for instruction cannot be done on the fly. Planning for groups should be a deliberate process based on purpose, assessment, and evidence, and membership—even in flexible groups—should be continually monitored and adjusted based on

Grouping Technique	Purpose	Selection Process	Pros and Cons
Random	To form groups of equal size for informal tasks like getting to know each other	Most often, counting off, but can also be based on other characteristics: color of shirt, number of siblings, types of pet, etc.	Less stressful for students concerned with being left out; requires little planning; can lead to behavior issues
Achievement	To provide targeted instruction based on prior performance (most common in reading and math)	Typically these groups are made based on some sort of standardized measure of achievement or another form of assessment	Students are assumed to have similar strengths and needs; ability to differentiate materials; can lead to overgeneralization and assumptions about needs
Social/ Cooperative	To create mixed-ability groups where specific roles are assigned and cooperation is necessary to complete a given task	Consider leaders and followers, behavior, personality traits; the ultimate goal is working together	Balance between leaders and followers can be a challenge; not all students may feel equally valued
Interest	To generate motivation and engagement around a topic or idea	Students who are interested in studying the same thing within a given topic (grasshoppers, bees, beetles, ants, and flies as part of an insect study)	Interests may vary wildly (too many or not enough topics to form groups of three to four); students are generally excited by the opportunity to study something they are interested in
Task	To allow students who are good at/enjoy specific tasks to work together	Consider preferred modes of demonstrating learning (differentiating products), such as performing, writing, drawing, etc.	Allows students to demonstrate their knowledge without experiencing performance barriers (e.g., fine motor skills, shyness, etc.); provides practice in tasks students are already proficient in and does not provide opportunities to master other tasks
Knowledge of Subject	To differentiate content based on students' background knowledge	Groups are formed based on personal data collected via questionnaires, interest inventories, and observations	Allows for natural differentiated levels of support to extend student knowledge based on their schema; may have students of different ability levels included, making finding appropriate materials challenging
Skill/ Strategy	To provide focused instruction on a particular skill or strategy	Select only those who need extra support on the designated skill/strategy	May have students of different ability levels included, making finding appropriate materials challenging
Student Choice	To actively engage students and build interest/motivation around a topic or task	Students group themselves based on their preferences	Motivation is typically high among students who group themselves; some students may feel left out; off-task behavior is a risk

FIGURE 5.3 Grouping strategies and associated considerations

individual performance and growth. Small groups provide teachers with the ability to provide targeted instruction in a way that maximizes instructional time.

Final Thoughts on Planning for Differentiation

Tomlinson (2014) contends that effective differentiation is built on three pillars: philosophy, principles, and practices, as shown in Figure 5.4. Teachers must embrace the ideas that:

- All students can learn
- All students have strengths
- All students have areas to strengthen
- Students have funds of knowledge they bring with them to any context
- Students learn in different ways depending on the context and expectations
- Affective factors influence learning (Gregory & Chapman, 2013)

Teachers have to hold themselves accountable for understanding curricular expectations and establishing learning environments that allow students to capitalize on their strengths. They must use assessment as they plan instruction, and be both thoughtful and proactive as they plan and structure learning activities in ways that

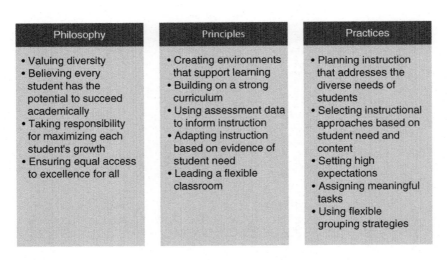

FIGURE 5.4 Supporting effective differentiation (adapted from Tomlinson, 2014)

provide scaffolding for all learners. They have to give all students a chance to show what they are capable of.

Tomlinson (2014) goes on to assert that differentiation is arguably a fundamental expectation in today's classrooms. We aren't sure that we completely agree, as the top–down agenda prevalent in our country today seems to include a message more akin to standardization and adherence to costly one-size-fits-all programs than to differentiation. However, if teachers are going to have a chance of finding success based on measurements of student growth and achievement, we believe that they must indeed be adapting their instruction to fit the needs of their students. They must pay active attention to the differences between and among students, making a "conscious effort . . . to analyze available data and make decisions about what is working and what needs to be adjusted" (Gregory & Chapman, 2013, p. 3). The responsibility to teach all students is simply "too important . . . to abdicate to others such as textbook publishers, software developers, or the teacher next door" (O'Shea, 2005, p. 78).

FOR MORE INFORMATION ON DIFFERENTIATION, CHECK OUT THESE RESOURCES:

Gregory, G. H. & Chapman, C. (2013). *Differentiated instructional strategies: One size doesn't fit all.* Thousand Oaks, CA: Corwin Press.

Tomlinson, C. A. (2014). *The differentiated classroom: Responding to the needs of all learners* (2nd Ed.). Alexandria, VA: ASCD.

Activities to Connect Pedagogy to Practice

1. Consider these three second-grade students. How might you differentiate for reading based on their readiness, interest, and learning profile?

   a. Liberty is an eight-year-old who loves school. She wears glasses and sometimes loses them when she takes them off to fidget with them. She is an 'average' student who occasionally gets in trouble for being out of her seat. She is energetic and chatty with everyone she meets, and always volunteers to help the teacher. Her first-grade teacher says she is a great speller and never misses a word on the weekly spelling test, but she does not transfer that ability to her writing samples. She recognized all the required sight words for first grade, but her reading often sounded disjointed and robotic as she read word for word. She reads on a Level J.

   b. Crosslan is a seven-year-old second grader with poor grades and perfect attendance. He loves math and science, and says he likes language arts and social studies, but he struggles to focus in those subjects. He rarely completes his work and is on grade level in reading.

He always checked out library books on the solar system until he lost one and was banned from checking out any others until he paid for the one he lost. He is the oldest of four children and lives with his single mother who works at two jobs. He is outgoing and has a good sense of humor, which he likes to show off. He reads at a Level J.

c. Gentry is the youngest of four girls. Her mother teaches at a nearby school and has expressed concern that her daughter doesn't seem to be reading on grade level. When Gentry reads, she does it fluently until she comes to a word she doesn't know—and then she looks to the teacher for an answer. She hates to read out loud in class and gets embarrassed if she makes a mistake. Her spelling is average, but the content of her writing is creative. She reads at a Level K.

2. Now take a look at the beginning of the year reading the following data for the members of a second-grade class. Consider how you would group them according to achievement and interest. What influenced your choices?

Name	Reading Level	Reading ZPD	Interests	Other
Alyssa	J	2.4–2.6	Reads a lot, hates bugs, and enjoys helping her mom cook	Is often the leader among groups of girls
Carter	I	1.4–1.6	Enjoys camping and playing baseball	Is the class clown and loves being the center of attention
Emmeline	H	1.8–2.2	Likes to read fairy tales and is an avid writer	New to school
Gentry	K	2.3–2.7	Loves to sing and play with dolls; lives on a farm	Doesn't read outside of school
Kaleb	G	3.0–3.4	Loves comic books and super heroes—especially Superman	Has been diagnosed with Asperger's syndrome and goes to speech therapy
Crosslan	J	2.0–2.3	Loves motorcycles and tanks and watching old Westerns	Often gets in trouble for being off task
Bo	K	2.3–2.7	Likes to talk about animals and insects—often brings them to school in jars	Quiet most of the time, but isn't afraid to speak up if asked

Name	Reading Level	Reading ZPD	Interests	Other
Liberty	J	1.9–2.3	Fashion—she always makes sure she has the right bows to match her outfits	Classmates say she's annoying because she talks too much
Zachariah	H	1.6–2.0	Adores his uncle who is in the army and stationed overseas	Is always doodling and draws in his free time
Brittany	D	1.0–1.4	Likes to listen to books, but not to read them; cheers for the pee-wee football team in the fall	Doesn't like school and often appears disengaged and grumpy
Nathaniel	E	1.4–1.8	Seems to know a lot about knights of the round table and medieval times	Doesn't seem comfortable around adults, though he is popular with the other boys
Nathan	F	1.6–2.0	Loves sports and plays them all	Rushes through everything school related
Scout	F	1.5–1.8	Athletic—plays softball and does gymnastics	Has to take care of her goats and donkeys after school
Henry	G	2.0–2.5	Loves construction vehicles and enjoys nonfiction books	Parents came to the United States from Central America when he was in kindergarten
Ryan	C	0.9–1.3	Loves puzzles and games and Dr. Seuss books	Doesn't know all his letters and sounds; has been in Tier 3 RTI since arriving at the school early last year
Meagan	D	1.2–1.6	Loves fishing with older brothers; has a pet snake	Placed in Tier 2 RTI
Shannon	N	3.5–3.8	Plays the piano and knows everything about pop music	Lives with her single dad, older sister, and younger brother

Putting Leadership into Action

Think about your own learning preferences. Do you like to work in groups or alone? Do you have a favorite subject? Would you rather act something out or design a poster to demonstrate your understanding? Then consider how your preferences play out in your instructional planning. Many teachers tend to lean on their own preferences rather than that of their students when they plan for instruction. Teacher leaders typically have a strong awareness of their own preferences and strive to put them aside in order to more effectively meet the needs of their students. Reflect on what personal preferences might be affecting your planning and consider how you might mitigate those preferences through integrating more student choice, using a wider range of materials, and providing more varied grouping structures.

References

Allington, R.L. (1983). The reading instruction provided readers of differing reading ability. *Elementary School Journal, 83,* 255–265.

Barr, R. & Dreeben, R. (1991). Grouping students for reading instruction. In R. Barr, M. Kamil, P. Mosenthal, & P. D. Pearson (Eds.), *Handbook of Reading Research* (pp. 885–910). White Plains, NY: Longman.

Caldwell, J. & Ford. M. P. (2002). *Where have all the bluebirds gone: How to soar with flexible grouping.* Portsmouth, NH: Heinemann.

Collins, J. (1986). Differential treatment in reading instruction. In J. Cook-Gumperz (Ed.), *The Social Construction of Literacy* (pp. 117–137). New York, NY: Cambridge University Press.

Gamoran, A. (1992). Is ability grouping equitable? *Educational Leadership, 50*(2), 11–21.

Gardner, H. (1983). *Frames of mind: How children think and how schools should teach.* New York, NY: Basic Books.

Gregory, G.H. & Chapman, C. (2013). *Differentiated instructional strategies: One size doesn't fit all.* Thousand Oaks, CA: Corwin Press.

Gregory, G.H., & Kuzmich, L. (2004). *Data driven differentiation in the standards-based classroom.* Thousand Oaks, CA: Corwin Press.

Kratzig, G.P., & Arbuthnott, K.D. (2006). Perceptual learning style and learning proficiency: A test of the hypothesis. *Journal of Educational Psychology, 98,* 238–246.

Kulik, J.A. (1992, February). *An analysis of the research on ability grouping: Historical and contemporary perspectives.* Retrieved August 22, 2014, from http://www.gifted.uconn.edu/nrcgt/reports/rbdm9204/rbdm9204.pdf.

Lou, Y., Abrami, P. C., Spence, J. C., Poulsen, C., Chambers, B., & d'Apollonia, S. (1996). Within-class grouping: A meta-analysis. *Review of Educational Research, 66,* 423–458.

National Academy of Education. (2005). *A good teacher in every classroom: Preparing the highly qualified teachers our children deserve.* San Francisco, CA: Jossey-Bass.

Oakes, J. (1994). Tracking: Why schools need to take another route. In B. Bigelow, L. Christensen, S. Karp, B. Miner, & B. Peterson (Eds.) *Rethinking our classrooms: Teaching for equity and justice.* Montgomery, AL: Rethinking Schools, Ltd.

Opitz, M.F. (1998). *Flexible grouping in reading: Practical ways to help all students become better readers*. New York, NY: Scholastic.

O'Shea, M.R. (2005). *From standards to success*. Alexandria, VA: Association for Supervision and Curriculum Development.

Routman, R. (2008). *Teaching essentials: Expecting the most and getting the best from every learner, K-8*. Portsmouth, NH: Heinemann.

Stanovich, K. (1986). Matthew effects in reading: Some consequences of individual differences in the acquisition of literacy. *Reading Research Quarterly, 21*, 360–407.

Stefanakis, E.H. (2011). *Differentiated assessment: How to assess the learning potential of every student*. San Francisco, CA: Jossey-Bass.

Stronge, J.H. (2007). *Qualities of effective teachers* (2nd Ed.). Alexandria, VA: Association for Supervision and Curriculum Development.

Tomlinson, C.A. (1999). *The differentiated classroom: Responding to the needs of all learners*. Upper Saddle River, NJ: Pearson.

Tomlinson, C.A. (2014). *The differentiated classroom: Responding to the needs of all learners* (2nd Ed.). Alexandria, VA: ASCD.

Tomlinson, C.A., Brimijoin, K., & Narvaez, L. (2008). *The differentiated school: Making revolutionary changes in teaching and learning*. Alexandria, VA: Association for Supervision and Curriculum Development.

Valencia, S.W., & Riddle-Buly, M. (2004). Behind test scores: What struggling readers really need. *The Reading Teacher, 57*, 520–531.

Wehrmann, K. S. (2000). Baby steps: A beginner's guide. *Educational Leadership, 58*(1), 20–23.

Wormeli, R. (2006). *Fair isn't always equal: Assessing and grading in the differentiated classroom*. Portland, ME: Stenhouse.

SECTION III

Instruction

Introduction

We know assessment drives instruction. We also know the word assessment does not have to be synonymous with the term standardized test. A healthy diet of assessments not only drives instruction, but also keeps a constant check on the operating systems. When assessments are used for the sole purpose of assigning grades or for punishment, students begin to feel like they have run out of gas and are stranded on the side of the road with no assistance in sight.

The effective teacher understands that after assessment is firmly seated then her attention can turn to planning the other components of the lesson. "If you fail to plan, you plan to fail," is a phrase often linked to planning. We know we need to plan, but even the planning stages sometimes leave more question than answers, such as: "How much is enough planning?" or "When will I know I'm ready to instruct?" You must keep in mind that planning is like establishing the road map for the lesson with multiple means to an end, and it should not be synonymous with drafting a battle plan to be ordered and followed regardless of casualties.

So once we know how to assess and plan, we can consider instruction. During instruction the teacher's goal should include modeling the strategies or skills being presented, but should also include ample time for students to practice and explore with the new material that is presented. These opportunities should be planned with your particular students' needs in mind, which may not match the plethora of teaching ideas that can be found at online sites such as Pinterest and Teachers Pay Teachers. Remember that mastery is the driver of instruction and should influence all decisions related to planning. Additionally, mastery does not have to be synonymous with the conceivably negative connotation of task mastery. We dare say instructing is the f-word—fun!

Although we know that instruction is the next logical step, some teachers experience the problem of enactment (Kennedy, 1999). Lesson plans may look engaging and promising on paper, but actually putting all the pieces of a successful lesson in motion can be daunting. Those who have attempted to stand in front of a classroom of children (or adults) and taught—not just presented—new material understand the numerous barriers to successful implementation. There are many 'moving parts' to a lesson that need to sequenced, synchronized, and balanced for learning to occur. This requires more than simply knowledge of one's subject matter, but rather, entails somewhat of a sixth sense for teaching. Although much of this can be learned through experience, it is important to point out that effective teachers purposefully consider how they will balance and connect the following 'moving parts' of their instruction: instructional frameworks, academic language, questioning and feedback, and engagement.

Reference

Kennedy, M. (1999). The role of preservice teacher education. In L. Darling-Hammond & G. Sykes (Eds.), *Teaching as the learning profession: Handbook of policy and practice* (pp. 54–85). San Francisco, CA: Jossey-Bass.

6

ESTABLISHING THE INSTRUCTIONAL ENVIRONMENT

It should be evident by now that we firmly believe teachers teach students, not curriculum. Of course, as explained in the last section on planning, curriculum is important—if we are not clear about *what* we are trying to teach kids, it is not likely that they will learn. It is important to note that it is really students' learning, not teachers' teaching, that is the measure of success. So how exactly do we facilitate that learning? Let's start by taking a look at Page's (2010, pp. 54–56) *12 Things Teachers Must Know About Learning* as a means for setting the stage for instruction.

1. Learning is personal.
2. Classes do not learn. Only individuals learn.
3. Learning is constructed.
4. Learning is meaningful.
5. Learning is interactive.
6. Learning is emotional.
7. Learning occurs in the brain.
8. Learning is a social activity.
9. Learning is predictable.
10. Memory is largely an associative process.
11. Conceptual learning is spontaneous learning that we do naturally, effortlessly, and unconsciously.
12. Learning that utilizes higher-level thinking effortlessly goes into our long-term memory.

If you didn't previously consider teaching a complex social interaction, we suspect that you surely do now after viewing this list. Although there are many different instructional models that teachers can employ in order to facilitate student learning, we believe that in the long run, there needs to be some sort of balance between a teacher-centered approach and a student-centered approach to instruction. Finding the right balance depends on the context, the content, and the purpose of the lesson. Still, understanding where basic instructional structures place their emphasis can help teachers, especially novices, be more intentional about facilitating learning from day to day and week to week.

An Existing Framework Analogy

Construction analogies are threaded through educational research and common language surrounding instruction (think 'building' prior knowledge, 'scaffolding,' and 'bridging' concepts). This idea of starting to build learning from the ground up works to explain how to instruct, though, much like the experience of building your own house, it often appears to be easier than it really is. You might anticipate that painting, laying tile, and installing new countertops and a backsplash in your kitchen will take you five days, but you soon realize that you underestimated the porous nature of the walls and find yourself spending more time than you anticipated in the paint stage. Later, just when you think you're back on target, you realize your measurements were off by a slight margin and you need to find more tile. Soon, you come to accept that it might take you seven or eight days to complete the project for which you had allocated only five, but if you want your kitchen to look good, you know you have to demonstrate flexibility. Although teaching is similar in many ways (e.g., not everyone learns in the same time frame, instruction you think is going to make sense finds you standing in front of twenty-five pairs of eyes blankly staring back at you, etc.), we think that, in most cases, the kinds of construction implied by the analogy are those that can be replicated again and again. Gawande (2009) defines these as complicated problems. A complex problem, on the other hand, is not such an easy process to repeat with the same results. Typically, anything that involves human development might be considered a complex problem, and we are certain that facilitating student learning falls under this category; it is rarely as neat and tidy as the steps associated with construction.

A New Framework Analogy

We offer a different analogy, then, for understanding instruction. Ours is an agricultural, organic analogy as opposed to an industrial, constrained one. Humans are organic beings that grow in many different ways; they are not simply cut or molded like blocks of wood or steel beams. Our analogy compares instruction to the growing of plants or crops. Everything starts with the soil; its richness (or lack thereof) influences what can grow, how fast it will grow, and what else it will need to grow. Even heavy doses of rain and sunshine will not produce desired results if the soil does not have the proper nutrients. In this case, the soil refers to the background experiences and funds of knowledge brought to the classroom by the student; we have to assess them in order to know what they have and what they need. Once we know what is necessary, we can plan for how much of everything (fertilizer, water, and sunshine) we think we will need. Plants and crops also need to be safe in order to flourish; thus, they need protection from many things: extreme weather, animals, and weeds. Like the farmer nurturing his crops, teachers must nurture their students' learning. Once the assessment and planning are complete, the teacher must focus on establishing an appropriate instructional environment in order to facilitate student growth. Like cornstalks, our students don't grow in standard increments across time. But if we establish the appropriate conditions, we anticipate that like corn that reaches "knee-high by the Fourth of July," our students, too, will demonstrate marked growth across the school year.

Instructional Models: The Components

In our analogy, we suggest that these models are like the water necessary for growth. Scaffolding is like the sunshine, which can be used to transform energy into growth. Finally, nurturing is presented as a means of guarding against numerous distractors. Let's start with the two models.

The Water: Instructional Models

A number of instructional models can be implemented to facilitate student growth. Although instructional models can be categorized in a number of ways, for our purposes here, we have simply used the labels "teacher centered" and "student centered," as pictured in Figure 6.1. Although many models could fall under each category, we are going to use our agricultural analogy to explore two that are

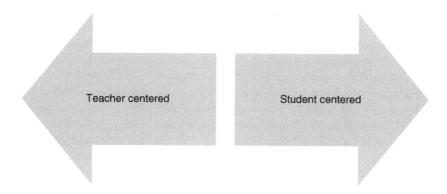

FIGURE 6.1 Instructional model continuum

typically considered to be on opposite ends of the instructional spectrum: direct instruction and inquiry learning. These models operate much like the watering of plants and crops. In direct instruction, teachers play a role in virtually pouring knowledge and skills into the brains of students. On the inquiry learning end, the teachers provide the water, but guide students to figure out how much water they need on their own. In general, neither of these extremes is desirable in and of themselves, since both drought and oversaturation can inhibit growth. Teachers are tasked with finding the balance that works for the topic, task, and student.

Direct Instruction

Direct instruction generally refers to the approach in which knowledge and skills are delivered in a step-by-step fashion. Other terms associated with direct instruction are active teaching, mastery teaching, and explicit instruction (Arends, 2001). Direct instruction aims at memory and the storage of knowledge. This model is often perceived as teacher centered with knowledge and skill holders (teachers) imparting that knowledge and skill to others (students), like the proverbial blank slate being filled with information or the vision of a teacher lifting the top of students' heads and pouring in information. There are many advantages and disadvantages to this instructional model as described by a variety of researchers. We'll start with the advantages. Administrators and other stakeholders often prefer models of direct instruction because it is thought to be able to be assessed with validity as a result of its structured nature (Mason, 1963). Students taught using this model may also receive more guidance, as teachers are typically expected to make sure that students have mastered one step before moving on to the next (Skinner, 1968). Direct instruction is also seen as one of the most organized ways of teaching (Qablan et al., 2009), and as such, many teachers consider it an easier method for teaching new content and skills (Robertson, 2007). It is also rooted in historical significance, and is accepted and promoted in many cultures (Lee, 2002).

Finally, in general, when most people think of teaching, this is the model they envision, and so it often 'feels' like we are embodying the spirit of teaching when we implement this kind of approach, though it is not without significant disadvantages. Typically, this model requires a strong understanding of the content and skills being taught, and teachers who are not as competent with the information may find it difficult to effectively transfer the necessary understanding to students (Chiappetta & Collette, 1973). Teachers who use this approach also tend to pose problems and then solve them without giving children opportunities to practice with guidance (Ray, 1961). And because this approach relies heavily on memorization, students may forget facts more easily (Vandervoort, 1983) and struggle to draw from their foundational knowledge (Wang & Wen, 2010; Vandervoort, 1983). Finally, students taught primarily with a direct instruction approach tend to fail to develop process skills and the abilities to make judgments (Wang & Wen, 2010; Vandervoort, 1983). These disadvantages indicate that students' learning may not be fully realized through direction instruction alone because it often fails to expect students to engage in higher-level thinking processes.

Still, there are times when students need to be provided with basic information, and this is the appropriate time to employ direct instruction. However, that doesn't mean that planning should be aimed at an hour-long lesson; time is key when planning for direct instruction. Jensen (2005) takes into consideration brain research as he offers guidelines for direct instruction of new content. Elementary guidelines suggest five to eight minutes for kindergarten to second-grade students, eight to twelve minutes for third through fifth graders, and twelve to fifteen minutes for sixth through eighth graders. Thus, it is evident that keeping direct instruction lessons short and focused is key to student success.

Inquiry Learning

Inquiry learning generally refers to the approach in which knowledge and skills are discovered. Concept learning is also associated with this model (Arends, 2001). This type of inquiry aims to promote thinking and its associated processes, and is typically perceived as both hands on and student centered. Although commonly linked to science education, it is certainly applicable across the curriculum. In this model, students take an active role in practicing what they have learned (Smart & Csapo, 2007), and the ensuing interactions build mental structures necessary for continued intellectual development (Lawson & Renner, 1975). This approach is often engaging, as teachers capitalize on students' natural activity and curiosity when learning about a new concept (Vandervoort, 1983; Dewey, 2009). Finally, teachers who use the inquiry method effectively are required to consider the needs of the child (Eshach, 1997; Henderson & David, 2007). The advantages of the inquiry learning model indicate that students' learning needs are more likely to be met due to the level of personalization, and their active role helps utilize their curiosity as a means of internalizing learning. However, teachers can experience difficulties in channeling and maintaining the interest of students (Bencze, 2009) and may be unprepared for the social demands of this type of strategy (Oliveria, 2009). It is, without a doubt, more challenging and time consuming to plan for this type of instruction (Robertson, 2007), and it still requires the teaching of some specific content. Thus, it cannot stand alone as the only means of providing instruction (Skinner, 1968).

The Best of Both Instructional Worlds

We believe that both instructional models, and many others that fall in between, offer opportunities to teach students. Teachers who use inquiry activities as a supplement to a curriculum based on a traditional, direct instruction or lecture method provide enhanced opportunities for student achievement (Marshall & Dorward, 2000), as they can deliver content knowledge through direct instruction and help students apply their knowledge and develop their process skills through inquiry activities (Wang & Wen, 2010). Similarly, teachers can use the inquiry method to provide students with a hands-on experience and follow up by giving students additional content information through direct instruction (Robertson, 2007). Teachers can provide opportunities to learn, but should also guide how the activities should be carried out and reinforce the content to be learned (Glassman, 2001).

Theoretical History of Both Models

If well-balanced doses of the two instructional models offer the best opportunities for students to learn, then why are both models commonly viewed as such an extreme dichotomy? The theoretical influences on direct instruction shaped its teacher centered structure. Behaviorism contends that learners' environmental factors can be manipulated by others to produce knowledge, whereas social cognitive theory contends that environmental factors are observed by the learner to produce knowledge. Both of these imply that the givers of information, like teachers, produce learning for the receivers, such as students.

The theoretical influences on inquiry learning shaped its student centered structure. Sociocultural and constructivist theories contend that learning is socially constructed through interactions between and among individuals, whereas cognitive and information processing theories contend that learning occurs through mental processes by individuals. Both of these suggest that individuals are responsible for their own learning through thinking processes and interaction. Figure 6.2 provides an overview of the theoretical basis of these two models.

Both of these models can be implemented in order to facilitate learning if teachers intentionally plan to transfer that responsibility from teachers to students through scaffolding.

The Sunshine: Scaffolding

Scaffolding for both instructional framework models can follow the model of the gradual release of responsibility (GRR), as discussed in Chapter 4. The concept is as easy to understand as the name implies: Teachers transfer responsibility to students through a process that uses an "I Do, We Do, You Do" approach (Fisher & Frey, 2008). If you recall, we added the stages of "Ya'll Do" and "You Two Do" as a means of further scaffolding between the "We Do" and "You Do" stages. In general, though, teachers instruct during the "I Do" stage, teachers and students

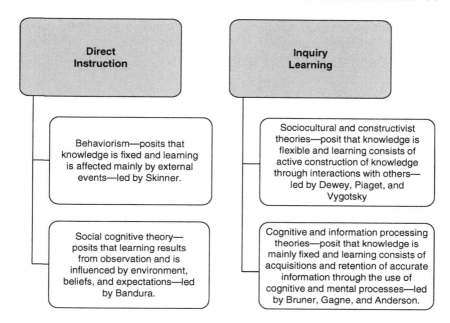

FIGURE 6.2 Theoretical model history (adapted from Arends, 2001, p. 261)

practice together during the "We Do" stage, and students practice alone during the "You Do" stage. Parents often seem to naturally employ this process as they teach their children to ride a bike. First, they often model how to ride by simply demonstrating it, followed by explaining and asking questions about the process. Then, parents may hold the handlebars while assisting the child as the bike slowly rolls. Finally, parents may let go of the bike to give the child the opportunity to succeed (or fail!) on his or her own.

We believe the GRR model is most appropriately used within the framework models in order for students to think and learn on their own while participating collaboratively as members of the class. If too much responsibility is released, then students can become overwhelmed and start to shut down, like the scorching and withering effect of too much sunshine. Teachers' assessment and planning skills should be utilized to release just the right amount of responsibility at just the right time. Just as the frameworks themselves offer the water of our agricultural analogy, the gradual release of responsibility provides sunshine in the form of scaffolding, transforming energy into learning growth.

Protection: Nurturing Growth

Like the crops in our farming analogy, students need nurturing and protection from the numerous factors that inhibit growth. Maslow's hierarchy of needs, in its expanded form (McLeod, 2007), supports a balanced, holistic approach to teaching, as seen in Figure 6.3. We believe knowing and applying Maslow's concepts in the classroom are an obvious must. Maslow's work suggests that the first four stages must be in place before cognitive needs can be met. Each of these four is heavily influenced by the instructional environment created by the teacher. Hunger, clothing, and shelter needs must be met, and classroom routines must be established to support physical and emotional needs and help students feel safe and secure. The love and belongingness stage indicates that students must feel liked and a part of the group, and the esteem stage implies that they also need regular opportunities to feel both respected and competent. Structuring a classroom environment that meets students' needs offers them the protection needed to grow to the next stages.

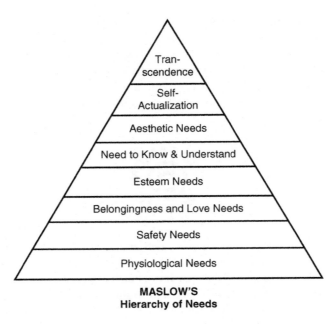

MASLOW'S
Hierarchy of Needs

FIGURE 6.3 Maslow's expanded hierarchy of needs (adapted from Huitt, 2007)

Putting the Picture Together

Students are fantastically complex organic beings. In order for learning to grow, they need a healthy blend of inquiry and instruction, scaffolding, and nurturing. Like the farmer who carefully plans for and observes his crops, continually making adjustments to (hopefully) increase his harvest, teachers must intentionally address each aspect of an effective instructional environment if the students are going to be able to reach their potential in the classroom.

The Frameworks in Action

Here we provide two instructional unit examples to demonstrate the major components of instructional frameworks. Examples of both instructional framework models with scaffolding through gradual release of responsibility are provided. The first, Figure 6.4, is an example of direct instruction with supplementary inquiry activities, and the second, Figure 6.5, is an example of inquiry learning supplemented with content information instruction.

The unit samples include ideas for a central focus, big ideas, and assessments, as described in Chapter 4. Effective activity planning follows these items during the construction of units of instruction. The emphasis of both of these unit samples is solely on instructional activities in order to demonstrate a blend of the models with socially interactive release of responsibility.

Direct Instruction with Inquiry Activities: Upper Elementary Unit Sample

The direct instruction model with added inquiry blends both models' aspects to promote learning. The gradual release of responsibility flows from teacher to students while allowing many forms of social interaction. The utilization of the "Ya'll Do" and "You Two Do" stages aids this flow. Embedding inquiry-based activities helps move it away from being solely teacher centered and drives it toward student centered to avoid the typical direct instructional model's disadvantages. Writing the same stories from two viewpoints reviews the components of narrative writing in a manner that allows multiple opportunities for mastery because mastery requires review. The many groupings allow the teacher to view and work with individual students to ensure personal teaching and learning.

Inquiry Learning with Direct Content Instruction: Lower Elementary Unit Sample

This sample unit follows the 5-E lesson phases intended to deliver inquiry-based learning. Many researchers, including those at Biological Sciences and Curriculum Study (BSCS), have developed the 5-E lesson phases (Bybee, et al., 2006).

Instruction

Upper Elementary Unit Sample

Central focus:

Narrative writing

Big ideas:

Community involvement

Pet care

Assessments:

Informal: Observation with checklists for students' knowledge of pets,
paragraph writing skills, and group interaction

Formal: Teacher-made narrative writing rubric

Learning experiences:

Supplemented inquiry-style activity one

The teacher may ask students what they are passionate about and have a class discussion.
After discovering that a class is highly interested in caring for pets, the teacher may
provide a shared experience of an animal shelter representative visiting and sharing
narrative pet stories orally and providing animal care information.

"I do" narrative writing: Teacher instructs with some help from students

The teacher may retell the first of the two animal shelter visitor's narrative stories aloud
with help from the students. The teacher may write the retold story for students to
see, explaining that the oral story told was a form of narrative. The teacher may do a
think-aloud to analyze the written story to identify the events and details that formed
the narrative.

"We do" narrative writing: Teacher instructs with much help from students

The teacher may repeat the process with the visitor's second narrative story with more
class guidance, especially in the identification and analysis of narrative events and details.

"Ya'll do" narrative writing: Student groups practice with much help from teacher

The teacher may provide a personal narrative about a pet story to groups of students. The
groups may read the story and then analyze to identify narrative components through
group discussion.

"You two do" narrative writing: Student pairs practice with some help from teacher

Pairs of students may share personal pet stories aloud to gather ideas for writing
narratives. Sharing may occur as one-on-one discussion of narrative events and details.

"You do" narrative writing: Students practice individually with some help from teacher

Students may write personal pet story narratives with teacher guidance.

Supplemented inquiry-style activity two

The teacher may bring the animal from the story personally shared with students to
school. The teacher may invite students to think about how the story would be different
if it was written from the pet's point of view.

Supplemented inquiry-style activity three

The art teacher may have students create self-portraits and pet portraits to illustrate the stories.

"I do" point of view: Teacher instructs with some help from students

FIGURE 6.4 Sample unit #1: Direct instruction with inquiry activities

The teacher may share the same narrative story through the point of view of the pet aloud and in written form. The teacher may do a think-aloud to analyze and reveal the differences in points of view for the two versions of the same story.

"We do" point of view: Teacher instructs with much help from students

The class may have a discussion about how the animal shelter visitor's stories would be different if told through the point of view of the pet.

"Ya'll do" point of view: Student groups practice with much help from teacher

Groups may share their ideas for crafting another version of their stories through the point of view of the pet and begin to write.

"You two do" point of view: Student pairs practice with some help from teacher

Pairs of students may work together to read each other's stories to analyze and reveal the author's purpose.

"You do" point of view: Students practice individually with some help from teacher

Students may publish and present both narrative stories.

Supplemented inquiry-style activity one continued

Students' stories may be shared with the local animal shelter. Students may also have follow-up discussion about seeing animal issues through the point of view of the pets in hopes of discovering ways to help in the community.

FIGURE 6.4 Continued

Adding direct instruction to explain and support students' experiences may help students grasp abstract concepts like categorical data. The gradual release of responsibility in the inquiry learning sample unit flows back and forth from students to teacher while allowing many forms of social interaction. Embedding direct instruction and guiding the activities helps move it away from being solely student centered and drives it toward teacher centered for the purposes of avoiding the typical inquiry learning model's disadvantages. Experiencing favorite fruit and vegetable selection in a variety of ways aids in mastery. The many groupings allow the teacher to view and work with individual students to ensure personal teaching and learning.

The Importance of Reflection

Teachers often forget to employ the final aspect of carrying out effective instruction: reflection! Reflection should be an ongoing part of instruction that focuses on gathering evidence demonstrating that learning is occurring. Routman (2008, p. 118) offers a list of questions that can support reflection after both individual lessons and units and aid in evaluating the effectiveness of the instruction.

- Is the teaching "responsive teaching" or "telling teaching?"
- Who is doing most of the work?
- What opportunities do students have to talk and interact?

Lower Elementary Unit Sample

Central focus:

Data collection and explanation

Big ideas:

School involvement

Nutrition

Assessments:

Informal: Observation with checklists for students' knowledge of fruits and vegetables, categorical data collection and explanation skills, and group interaction

Formal: Teacher-created performance assessment checklist for explaining categorical data

Learning experiences:

"We do" engagement: Students' prior knowledge accessed and interest engaged in the phenomenon

The teacher may access prior knowledge of fruits and vegetables by taking students on a tour of the cafeteria to view how these items are ordered, prepared, and served. Having a class discussion about favorite fruits and vegetables may activate students' interests.

"Ya'll do" exploration: Students participate in an activity that facilitates conceptual change

The teacher may have groups of students participate in an activity of interviewing other classmates to discover fruit and vegetable likes and dislikes.

"We do" explanation: Students generate an explanation of the phenomenon

Students, as a whole class, may be invited to share how they would communicate the answers and information from the interviews to others.

"I do" direct content instruction: Teacher instructs by providing examples

Teacher shares examples of collecting data with a three-category smiley face survey system: smile, not sure, and frown. Teacher explains how each example can be communicated to others.

"You two do" elaboration: Students' understanding of the phenomenon challenged and deepened through new experiences

In pairs, students use a three-category smiley face system to interview other classes about fruits and vegetables.

"You do" evaluation: Students assess their understanding of the phenomenon

Students individually explain their survey findings to the class. Then, students may be invited to share their findings with the cafeteria and school in an attempt to increase desired fruit and vegetable selection.

FIGURE 6.5 Sample unit #2: Inquiry learning with direct content instruction

- How does the pacing of your lesson affect student engagement?
- How is assessment embedded in the lesson?
- How is instruction adjusted to students' responses?
- How are you providing time for guided and independent practice?

- How are students' efforts and achievements celebrated?
- What went well?
- Is there anything you might have done differently?
- How independent are the students in problem solving, finding and using resources, self-monitoring, and self-evaluation?
- What have students learned? What is your evidence?
- How can you provide additional support for students who need it most?
- How are students evaluating their own learning and setting new goals?
- What are your next steps and why?

Final Thoughts on Establishing the Instructional Environment

In conclusion, what we know about learning and its many nuances should drive teachers' balance of instruction on the continuum between direct instruction and inquiry learning. Supporting learning by releasing responsibility can be a robust social exchange between many combinations of teachers and students, and taking students' personal needs into consideration when establishing the instructional environment is key in facilitating effective learning. Just as water, sunshine, and protection from harm are necessary components of effective farming, selecting effective means of instruction, scaffolding student learning, and making students feel safe and accepted are critical aspects of instruction that must be met if learning is going to happen. Learning is characterized in many ways throughout the literature, but we believe that, above all, it is personal.

DO YOU WANT TO FIND OUT MORE ABOUT INSTRUCTIONAL FRAMEWORKS?

Check These Out!

Framework models:

Arends, R. I. (2001). *Learning to teach.* Boston, MA: McGraw-Hill.

Scaffolding:

Fisher, D., & Frey, N. (2008). *Better learning through structured teaching: A framework for the gradual release of responsibility.* Alexandria, VA: Association for Supervision and Curriculum Development.

Direct instruction vs. inquiry learning:

Robertson, B. (2007). Getting past "inquiry versus content." *Educational Leadership, 64*(4), 67–70.

Connecting Pedagogy to Practice

1. Think back to your elementary school experiences as a student. Where would the instruction be categorized on the direct instruction or inquiry learning continuum? Is your instruction reflecting your experiences as a student for better or worse?

2. Highlight lesson plans with direct instruction one color and inquiry learning another to help recollection of balance.

Putting Leadership into Action

All teachers tend to get in instructional ruts now and then. Teacher leaders recognize when that happens and find ways to pull themselves out of them. Think about your teaching habits. What is your 'go-to' kind of lesson? If you're feeling ready to spread your wings and consider pushing yourself to the next level of teaching, you should consider reading *Teaching Essentials: Expecting the Most and Getting the Best from Every Learner, K-8*, by Regie Routman or *Teaching with Intention: Defining Beliefs, Aligning Practice, Taking Action*, by Debbie Miller. Their insights should serve to build your understanding of effective teaching and give you some new ideas to thoughtfully try out in your own instruction.

References

Arends, R.I. (2001). *Learning to teach*. Boston, MA: McGraw-Hill.

Bencze, J. (2009). "Polite directiveness" in science inquiry: A contradiction in terms? *Cultural Studies of Science Education, 4*, 855–864.

Bybee, R., Taylor, J.A., Gardner, A., Van Scotter, P., Carlson, J., Westbrook, A., & Landes, N. (2006). *The BSCS 5E Instructional Model: Origins and Effectiveness*. Colorado Springs, CO: BSCS.

Chiappetta, E.L. & Collette, A.T. (1973). *Process versus content in elementary science teaching*. Syracuse University, NY: The Department of Science Teaching.

Dewey, J. (2009). *Democracy and education*. Radford, VA: Wilder Publications.

Eshach, H. (1997). Inquiry events as a tool for changing science teaching efficacy belief of kindergarten and elementary school teachers. *Journal of Science Education and Technology, 12*, 495–501.

Fisher, D., & Frey, N. (2008). *Better learning through structured teaching: A framework for the gradual release of responsibility*. Alexandria, VA: Association for Supervision and Curriculum Development.

Gawande, A. (2010). *The checklist manifesto: How to get things right*. New York, NY: Metropolitan Books.

Glassman, M. (2001). Dewey and Vygotsky: Society, experience, and inquiry in educational practice. *Educational Researcher, 30*(4), 3–14.

Henderson, T., & David, A. (2007). Integration of play, learning, and experience: What museums afford young visitors. *Early Childhood Education Journal, 35*(3), 245–251.

Huitt, W. (2007). Maslow's hierarchy of needs. *Educational Psychology Interactive.* Valdosta, GA: Valdosta State University. Retrieved June 1, 2014, from http://www.edpsycinteractive.org/topics/regsys/maslow.html.

Lawson, A., & Renner, J. (1975). Piagetian theory and biology teaching. *The American Biology Teacher, 37*(6), 336–343.

Lee, O. (2002). Promoting scientific inquiry with elementary students from diverse cultures and languages. *Review of Research in Education, 26,* 23–69.

Marshall, J.A., & Dorward, J.T. (2000). Inquiry experiences as a lecture supplement for preservice elementary teachers and general education students. *American Association of Physics Teachers, 68* (7 Suppl 1).

Mason, J. (1963). The direct teaching of critical thinking in grades four through six. *Journal of Research in Science Teaching, 1(4)* 319–328.

McLeod, S.A. (2007). *Maslow's hierarchy of needs.* Retrieved June 1, 2014, from http://www.simplypsychology.org/maslow.html.

Oliveria, A.W. (2009). "Kindergarten, can I have your eyes and ears?" politeness and teacher directive choices in inquiry-based science classrooms. *Cultural Study of Science Education, 4,* 803–846.

Page, B. (2010). 12 things teachers must know about learning. *Education Digest: Essential Readings Condensed for Quick Review, 75*(8), 54–56.

Qablan, A., Al-Ruz, J., Theodora, D., & Al-Momani, I. (2009). "I know it's so good, but I prefer not to use it." An interpretive investigation of Jordanian preservice elementary teachers' perspectives about learning biology through inquiry. *International Journal of Teaching and Learning in Higher Education, 20*(3), 394–404.

Ray, W. (1961). Pupil discovery vs. direct instruction. *The Journal of Experimental Education, 29*(3), 271–280.

Robertson, B. (2007). Getting past "inquiry versus content." *Educational Leadership, 64*(4), 67–70.

Routman, R. (2008). *Teaching essentials: Expecting the most and getting the best from every learner, K-8.* Portsmouth, NH: Heinemann.

Skinner, B. F. (1968). Teaching science in high school: What is wrong? *Science, 159,* 704–710.

Smart, K., & Csapo, N. (Dec. 2007). Learning by doing: Engaging students through learner-centered activities. *Business Communication Quarterly, 70*(4), 451–457.

Vandervoort, F.S. (1983). What would John Dewey say about science teaching today? *The American Biology Teacher, 45*(1), 38–41.

Wang, J., & Wen, S. (2010). Examining reflective thinking: A study of changes in methods students' conceptions and understandings of inquiry teaching. *International Journal of Science and Mathematics Education, 6*(3), 1–21.

7

ACADEMIC LANGUAGE

Sara and Chris are both excited about entering kindergarten this fall. Sara comes from a home in which her mother is a high school music teacher and her father manages a small printing company. The family values education and reads together every night as part of their nighttime ritual. Whenever possible, the family takes weekend trips to local museums and other attractions. The family doesn't have to worry about whether or not there will be enough money to put food on the table or who will watch the kids while Mom and Dad are at work since both parents have secure jobs that also allow them to be home when school is not in session. Sara's dad reads the newspaper every night, and Sara enjoys sitting next to him in his big recliner and pretending to read over his shoulder. One of Sara's favorite activities to engage in with her mother is baking cookies by following a recipe that her grandmother has passed down.

Chris's home life looks a little different. Chris lives with his mom who works full time at the local convenience store. After school each day, Chris and his older siblings are left home alone until the early evening when his mother gets off work. By the time the family eats dinner and takes baths, there is little time left before bedtime to read books or have conversations about what the kids learned at school that day. The family struggles to keep food on the table and is worried that the utilities might be shut off since they are behind in their payments. When time allows, the family likes to spend time with the entire extended family sharing stories of "yesteryear" and of fond memories and experiences.

Which of these two students would be considered more likely to be academically successful? When Sara and Chris walk through the doors of their elementary school, they will already be placed on an uneven playing field before instruction even begins. It may not seem surprising that children come to school with varying levels of academic experiences, but what may be a surprise is that their experiences with language, both oral and written, are tantamount to success in school.

Early Experiences with Language

Most children first develop their receptive language and then their expressive language. Somewhere between the ages of one and two, most young children begin to speak their first words, then phrases, and eventually complete sentences. They mimic the language they hear around them, which is generally produced by family members or caregivers. The vocabulary they produce, the purposes for speaking, and the frequency of talk are all determined by the social factors of the community in which they are developing. Hart and Risley (1995) in their seminal work *Meaningful Differences in the Everyday Lives of Young American Children* followed families with preschool-aged children and noted how often both the parent(s) and the child spoke during one hour a week (Figure 7.1). The researchers then extrapolated the data to determine how much language would be spoken in a week, a year, and in a four-year period. They determined that by the time these children entered school, children from a welfare family would have heard 13 million words and a child from a professional home would have heard 45 million words. That is a difference of 32 million words heard!

When we again think of Sara and Chris and imagine them entering school, it doesn't seem surprising that the disparity between their language experiences entering kindergarten are staggering. What is equally disturbing is that this trend will likely continue as Sara and Chris progress through their school years. Some scholars have dubbed this phenomenon "the Matthew Effect" after a verse in the Gospel of Matthew, which translates, in essence, into the rich get richer and the poor get poorer (Stanovich, 1986).

	Words Heard per Hour	Words Heard in a 100-Hour Week	Words Heard in a 5,200-Hour Year	Words Heard Over a 4-Year Period
Welfare	616	62,000	3 million	13 million
Working class	1,251	125,000	6 million	26 million
Professional	2,153	215,000	11 million	45 million

FIGURE 7.1 The impact of socioeconomic background on language acquisition (adapted from Hart & Risley, 1995)

In fact, schools often operate in ways that advantage certain children and disadvantage others, causing distinct outcomes that align with social and political forces in the larger context. Institutional support for the primary language and students who speak it is a prime factor in school success for these students.

(Diaz-Rico & Weed, 2006, p. 24)

Students who have interacted with fewer novel vocabulary words struggle with acquiring a broader vocabulary set. This is likely due to their lack of relevant schema, or background knowledge. For example, when I recently came across the word fissiparous in a book I was reading, I was not sure of the word's meaning. Fortunately, the new word sounded similar to fissure, which is a word I am familiar with. By connecting the new word to my previous knowledge and using my skill of analyzing context clues, I was able to make a pretty accurate guess of the meaning. (By the way, it means tending to break up into parts, or creating disunity or dissension, similar to the definition of fissure, which means a narrow opening or break.) Children who have a narrow set of vocabulary to draw from are less likely to make these connections, and therefore, do not acquire new words as quickly as their peers who already possess a large vocabulary.

It is not only the amount of talk that occurs within the home before school even begins, but also the type of conversation and literacy practices that are occurring that need to be considered. Heath (1983) spent nine years studying three working-class communities, two of which exemplify the impact of home language on in-school success. One was predominately Caucasian and one predominately African American to document the ways in which language was acquired and expressed. In Roadville, the predominately white community, children were surrounded by parents reading and the children were encouraged to learn the alphabet and nursery rhymes. In Trackton, spontaneous verbal word play and competitive storytelling in which family members vied for the speaking floor were valued. When thinking about which culturally based literacy practices would be most conducive to learning in the traditional school environment, it is obvious that the children from Roadville would have a slight advantage when entering school over their peers in nearby Trackton, not because their language was better, so to speak, but because it more closely matched the language used and expected in schools.

Some working-class families view education as the teacher's role and do not want to impede on their child's learning by intervening in their academic development (Lareau, 1989). Parents who may seem aloof and not interested in their child's academic success may have had negative experiences when they were in school or view the teacher as the more knowledgeable and capable adult. Chris's mom wants her child to succeed just as much as Sara's parents do. It is the effective teacher's role to close the language gap to ensure equity among all students. Therefore, academic language becomes all about equity and access for all children. When children cross the threshold of the school doors, they are inevitably entering with a wide range of experiences with language. The ineffective teacher might assume that these children (and their families) are lazy or not smart enough to succeed. The effective teacher, on the other hand, realizes that these children are bright and do indeed have valuable language experiences, though they are different from those more commonly associated with school. They just need to be exposed to vivid vocabulary and language instruction.

Social vs. Academic Language

It is important to determine what exactly academic language is, and one way to do that is by comparing it to social language. Linguists refer to these as two examples of possible language registers that a person can possess. A register is language used in a particular setting for a particular purpose; it is highly influenced and built upon a community's culture, knowledge, and norms. Most adults adapt their register depending on their audience and context. Consider the manner in which you would speak to friends as opposed to an employer, a police officer, or a member of the clergy. Think about how the experiences of attending a fancy cocktail party or visiting a dairy farm can highlight the nuances of one's register. That feeling of being out of place, not knowing exactly what to say, and worrying that something might be said that would offend someone else are all related to language registers. Not fully grasping the culture, knowledge, and norms of a group can place someone at a disadvantage and may not be conducive to interacting with others from within the group.

Social language is used around family and friends as a way to communicate what is happening in our lives, to discuss needs, to make jokes, or to indicate agreement or disagreement. Depending on the circle of friends, one's social language may not fit the norms of the group. For example, Comic-Con is an annual event in which comic book fans meet (and even dress up as) their favorite characters. Attendees catch up with what is happening in each other's lives, joke around with each other, and discuss the pros and cons of their favorite characters. A plethora of social language occurs at these meetings, but someone who is not familiar with comic books would have a difficult time participating in the conversation taking place since they do not understand the knowledge and norms of the group.

Social language communication can take place face to face via e-mail, text, phone, or video conferencing. Some examples of social language include:

- Asking "What's up?"
- Stating "I am fixin' to get a coke."
- Texting "R U ok?"
- E-mailing "7:00 at the library?"
- Skyping your baby cousin or nephew "Where is your nosey?"

In contrast to social language, academic language employs a more complex sentence structure and use of vocabulary. This is the type of language that occurs within the school day and, depending on a student's background, can be very different from his or her social language register. Sara at home is likely more similar to the within-school register since her parents likely speak to her with complex sentences and a variety of vocabulary as compared to Chris.

> An individual's own culture forms the template of reality; it operates a lens that allows some information to make sense and other information to remain unperceived. When two cultures come into contact, misunderstandings can result because members of these cultures have different perceptions, behaviors, customs, and ideas.
>
> *(Diaz-Rico & Weed, 2006, p. 20)*

The predominant school culture and out-of-school cultures that some students experience can sometimes be in conflict. This conflict may be viewed by the ineffective teacher as a deficiency rather than an area for growth.

Some examples of academic language include:

- Apples grow on trees, *but* carrots grow underground.
- Birds and bats are *similar because* they both fly, *but* they are *different* in that birds are *diurnal* and bats are *nocturnal*.
- When baking soda and vinegar are mixed, a chemical reaction occurs. *Consequently*, the volcano we created just erupted!

Most people have many registers that they switch between as the need arises. Picking a register for a certain time and purpose is similar to picking out an outfit. You wouldn't want to wear a bathing suit to an interview, just as it wouldn't make sense to solely use social language when leading a professional development workshop. Effective teachers support students in their acquisition of academic language, while still valuing the social language and cultural norms that all students bring to school. This less formal language can be used as a springboard for more complex vocabulary instruction.

The school's role is to socialize students into the language of school. This may be particularly important for English language learners or students who come from a lower-socioeconomic background. Acculturation of school language includes making explicit the purposes of language in the classroom, providing scaffolds to help students understand language norms and expectations, and affording students the opportunity to participate in classroom discussions. Depriving students of opportunities to engage in the language of school can lead to some unintended consequences. These may include:

- Defiant behavior, avoidance, or withdrawal
- Academic tracking based on invalid teacher judgments

- Watered-down curriculum focused on basic skills
- Rote instruction and lack of engagement

These unintended consequences will not shrink the language gap in schools; rather, they will serve as a catalyst to continue to widen the gap and decrease equity in the classroom.

Academic Language Defined

Remember that academic language is all about providing equity and access for those children who seem destined to fail even before they enter school. The definition of academic language can be divided into two distinct parts that are connected to one another, but are useful to look at separately before putting them back together when determining how to support these struggling students. These two parts are the purposes of language (functions) and the structures of language (forms: syntax or discourse) (Figure 7.2).

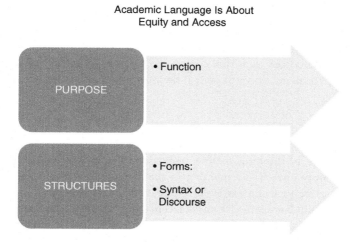

FIGURE 7.2 Relationship between the purpose and structures of academic language

Purpose of Language

Functions are the cognitive tasks that drive communication. They are the reason why we are communicating. The purposes, or the functions, of academic language are very different from the purposes of social language. The reason we communicate with friends may be to exchange a greeting or plan a special event. These types of exchanges rarely occur in the classroom. Instead, Chamot and O'Malley (1994) compiled a list of some of the most frequently used forms of language in the classroom. They consist of:

- **To Seek Information**—use who, what, when, where, how
- **To Inform**—recount information or retell
- **To Compare**—explain graphic organizer showing contrast
- **To Order**—describe timeline, continuum, or cycle
- **To Classify**—describe organizing principles
- **To Analyze**—describe features or main idea
- **To Infer**—generate hypotheses to suggest cause/outcomes
- **To Justify and Persuade**—give evidence why "A" is important
- **To Solve Problems**—describe problem-solving procedures
- **To Synthesize**—summarize information cohesively
- **To Evaluate**—identify criteria, explain priorities, etc.

It is not often that friends sit around at a restaurant classifying items on the menu, justifying why they placed certain items into certain categories, and trying to persuade others to agree that their system is the most useful. However, this type of conversation is expected regularly in classrooms.

Forms of Language

Once the purpose of communication is determined, then the ways in which the purpose is conveyed can be decided upon. This is the form of the language that can be considered the tools that convey the purpose (function) of talk. At the macro level, forms are discourse, and at the micro level, forms are syntax.

Discourse

Gee (1990) defines discourse as "a socially accepted association among ways of using language, of thinking, feeling, believing, valuing, and acting that can be used to identify oneself as a member of the socially accepted group" (p. 143). Therefore, to be part of a particular group, you must communicate in ways in which the group has deemed socially acceptable. Outside of the classroom during a book club meeting, you would ask clarifying questions about the shared text, you might ask philosophical wonderings about the roles and intentions of characters, and you might identify with situations or predicaments within the novel. Now if you were at the grocery store and you started analyzing the intentions of the clerk while going through the checkout line, you would probably receive odd stares accompanied by confusion of others. That is because the chosen form of discourse is not appropriate for the given time and location. Even within the classroom a variety of discourse modes are apparent. The ways in which questions are framed and activities are designed may be determined by the content area. Here are a few examples of how voice can change depending on the subject matter:

- Math and science: The purpose of the lesson may not be given, but rather, students are asked to explore and design their own equations to justify their thinking.
- Literacy: Figurative language and rich description are common.

When it comes to written communication, the structure of text also varies among content areas within school. In social studies, students might spend time analyzing a primary source (newspaper, correspondence, law), whereas in science class, the text they are working with might be instructions in a lab report. Within the literacy block, students might be required to read and write narrative, expository, and persuasive texts, which all are organized differently to suit their intended purpose.

Syntax

Syntax is the grammatical features and word usage of written or oral communication: the tools necessary for discourse, for reading and writing, for using complex language, and for engaging in cognitive processes (Dutro & Moran, 2003). Discourse can be considered the ways in which conversations or texts are organized, and syntax can be described as the ways in which sentences and phrases are organized. Considering syntax, what do you notice about the following three sentences?

A)   The girl stepped over the dog.
B)   The dog stepped over the girl.
C)   The stepped girl the over dog.

Likely it was evident that all three sentences contain the exact same words, but the words are placed in a different order. It is imperative to keep in mind that the organization of the sentence, not just the vocabulary it contains, provides the intent of the speaker. Syntax includes:

- Parts of speech
- Verb tenses
- Subject/verb agreement
- Use of pronouns
- Conjunctions

The organization of parts of speech in a sentence is predetermined based on rules within the English language. A substantial amount of time is usually spent in middle school having students diagram sentences to help them visualize the organization of written speech. For example, an adjective is placed before a noun (in Spanish, it is the other way around) and Yoda in *Star Wars* might say, "Much to learn, you still have," whereas we would say "You still have much to learn." Using the correct verb tense or having the subject and verb agree in a sentence is sometimes determined by what 'sounds right.' This idea of what 'sounds right' is based on the speaker's schema and prior experiences related to language. Sara may have heard her mother say multiple times, "You better have picked up your toys!" whereas Chris is more familiar with the syntax of "Has you picked up your toys yet?" Providing feedback to a student that includes the phrase "Does that sound right?" may preclude them from closing the language gap. More specific feedback, including examples of correct complex academic language, will be necessary to close this gap. The final section of this chapter will provide some sample activities that can be used to shrink the language gap.

Brick and Mortar Words

Within the category of syntax, Dutro and Moran (2003) identified two categories of words: brick and mortar. "'Brick' words are the vocabulary specific to the content and the concepts being taught" (Dutro & Moran, 2003, p. 237). They include examples of words like those in Figure 7.3.

Brick words are sometimes synonymous with vocabulary words. These are the words that are presented in bold face or italics in students' textbooks. Generally, when discussing academic vocabulary, this is what most educators think of first. Without mastery of these content-specific words that are typically not heard in general conversation outside of school, students will struggle to grasp the content being conveyed. Effective teachers know that intentional instruction of these vocabulary words is important, but with so many new words being introduced, how do effective teachers choose which vocabulary words to teach? Considering Beck, McKeown, and Kucan's (2002) three tiers of vocabulary is crucial when determining what vocabulary is most useful to teach:

- Tier 1: Common words that most students already know (baby, hat, grass, mommy)
- Tier 2: Words that are used frequently by mature language users (endurance, prospect, disinterested, gloomy)
- Tier 3: Words that are specific to discipline areas (histogram, axiom, enzyme, meiosis, municipality)

Consonant	Symmetry	Omnivore
Abbreviation	Obtuse	Equator
Idiom	Anemometer	Barter

FIGURE 7.3 Brick words

Little time should be spent instructing Tier 1 words, since most students should be familiar with these words. Deliberate instruction of Tier 1 words could be beneficial for English language learners in conjunction with visual representations such as photographs or graphic organizers to illustrate the relationships between words. Additionally, little time should be spent on Tier 3 words, since students will be exposed to these words infrequently when reading textbooks in school or during leisure reading time. When considering optimizing opportunities to close the language gap in school, the focus should be on teaching Tier 2 words. These are the words that students will engage with most frequently in texts and also serve to build a base of knowledge from which connections to other words can be made, therefore allowing students to internalize more words.

Most teachers are cognizant about teaching "brick" words to their students, but it is generally more challenging to generate instruction that focuses on the "mortar" words. "'Mortar' words and phrases are the basic and general utility vocabulary required for constructing sentences. They are words that determine relationships between and among words. They are words that hold our language together and are essential to comprehension" (Dutro & Moran, 2003, pp. 239–240). They include:

- **Connecting words**: because, then, but, sometimes, before, therefore, however, and whereas
- **Prepositions and prepositional phrases**: on, in, under, behind, next to, in front of, between, among, and in the background
- **Basic regular and irregular verbs**: leave, live, eat, use, saw, and went
- **Pronouns:** she, he, his, their, it, each other, and themselves
- **Academic vocabulary**: notice, think, analyze, plan, compare, proof, and characteristics

When introducing mortar words to students, it is best to integrate them into oral and written language rather than teaching them in solidarity since they are considered connecting words, and without the context surrounding those words, students will be less likely to actively process their meaning. Mortar words are overlooked in many classrooms and they are generally undervalued during instruction. Teachers may assume that students already know these words and their meanings since they are used so frequently in academic language. What is forgotten is that children who come from backgrounds like Chris most likely have not heard these connecting words regularly. If only simple, rather than compound or complex, sentence structures have been spoken in the home, then they will not be familiar with their usage. Deliberate instruction is needed to highlight the correct usage of these words in context; otherwise, struggling students will not be able to discern the subtle differences between many of these connecting words.

When thinking about instruction in academic language, it may be helpful to envision a table with an open puzzle box. The puzzle pieces are scattered all over the table and a few are still even in the box. Imagine that a few of the pieces are academic functions (the purposes of language during your lesson: to compare or to inform). A few more are discourse (text structure and organization of dialogue). Ten more are the Tier 2 words introduced or revisited in the lesson, five more are parts of speech, two are verb tenses, two are subject/verb agreement, seven are pronouns, and six are conjunctions. If only the ten vocabulary pieces are put together, it will be difficult to determine what the completed puzzle should look like. Without using all the puzzle pieces, the puzzle will never be completed and the picture will not match the picture on the front of the box. Without effectively teaching all the components of academic language, students will likely not understand the goal of the lesson. To them, the information presented will resemble an unfinished puzzle instead of the completed picture planned. The effective teacher must make sure that the lesson planned is the lesson taught with no missing puzzle pieces lost on the floor. Therefore, integrating strategies to teach the varied components of academic language are critical to student understanding of complex material.

Transform Your Instruction: Strategies to Support Academic Language Acquisition

Supporting your students' academic language development starts when you open your plan book. In addition to a learning objective for each lesson, the effective teacher plans a language objective for each day. This includes the language function(s) needed for all students to successfully participate in the lesson. These are generally tied to the learning objective of the lesson and are easy to determine. The language forms are a bit more difficult to plan for, but with some practice, they will become more evident and easier to include. When planning language forms, taking a backwards approach to planning is critical. An activity designed by Laura A. Hill-Bonnet (2013) at Stanford University instructs teachers to create a sample student response for the lesson assessments (formative or summative) that would illustrate understanding of the lesson objective (Figure 7.4). This sample response can then be deconstructed based on the academic vocabulary, syntax, and discourse necessary in order to be successful with the assigned task. Once effective teachers are aware of the language demands that are placed on the students, they can design activities that support specific needs, leading up to the required assessment of students' knowledge.

Common Core Standard	Grade One, Reading 2.7 Retell the central ideas of a simple expository or narrative passage.
Content Learning Goal for the Lesson	Given a read-aloud of "The Little Red Hen," students will be able to retell key events in the story.
Student Response	The little red hen (*found, planted, harvested, ground, baked*) a grain of wheat.
Language Learning Goal for the Lesson	Students will be able to *use regular and irregular past-tense verbs* to retell the story.

FIGURE 7.4 Deconstruction of student response to determine required academic language

To support academic vocabulary development, choosing the most appropriate words to focus instruction on is extremely important. Once these Tier 2 words have been identified, activities to build the required vocabulary to successfully enable students to demonstrate their knowledge can be designed. New vocabulary is acquired when it fits into a learner's existing schema, so tapping into a student's prior knowledge is a necessary first step when introducing novel vocabulary words. Johnson (2009) lays out a strategy to explicitly link vocabulary instruction to a learner's schema. In this exercise, which is similar to the Frayer model of vocabulary instruction (Frayer, Frederick, & Klausmeier, 1969), the student is responsible for writing the word in the center of a graphic organizer. Around the word, the student does the following: list synonyms, list examples, provide a working definition, draw a picture, list antonyms, and/or list nonexamples. This process can be modeled by the teacher at first, but then should systematically become the responsibility of the students.

Many primary classrooms have word walls organized in alphabetical order and composed of sight words students are expected to master in their reading and writing. These words are obviously not vocabulary words, but rather commonly used Tier 1 words. A spin on this idea would be to add subject-specific word walls organized around the content area, such as a math, science, and social studies word wall (see Figure 7.5). The words on these bulletin boards would be arranged by the relationships among each other rather than listed alphabetically. This would aid students' schematic understanding of multiple words simultaneously. Adding photographs or student-drawn pictures depicting the meaning of the words would also provide another layer of support.

Moving beyond academic vocabulary, effective teachers also consider how they will model and reinforce language demands such as syntax and discourse. Think-alouds and interactive writing with structured discussions are two powerful instructional frameworks that can be successful in closing the language gap within many classrooms. These frameworks offer the opportunity to model the unique organization of language found in the content areas.

Weather Word Wall		
Weather Events	*Weather Tools*	*Cloud Types*
Hurricane	Anemometer	Cirrus
Tornado	Barometer	Alto
Tsunami	Rain Gauge	Stratus

FIGURE 7.5 Subject word wall

> The key to an effective think-aloud is that the teacher is using the first person to describe how he or she makes decisions, implement skills, activates problem-solving protocols, and evaluates whether success has been achieved. Importantly, this is a chance for students to witness how an expert merges declarative, procedural, conditional, and reflective knowledge in a fluent fashion.
>
> *(Fisher & Frey, 2008, p. 31)*

Remember that many of your students have not heard complex academic language in their homes, let alone have had adults explain their own thinking out loud. Some students believe that adults just know how to make decisions about their daily activities and don't realize that we engage in internal conversations with ourselves on a regular basis to determine the best course of action. Think-alouds provide the opportunity to model the internal thought processes that otherwise would be invisible to learners (Wilhelm, 2001). As effective teachers plan think-alouds, they should consider the syntax and discourse necessary to effectively complete the task and explicitly point out the use of these language demands in their own speech. As teachers think aloud through the process, they discuss how they would employ a particular strategy or function of language (predicting, inferring) and describe their thinking (Johnson, 2009):

- I was confused by . . .
- I wonder why . . .
- I just thought of . . .
- This made me think of . . .

The think-aloud process should only focus on one or two functions of language at a time so as to not overwhelm or confuse students. As students begin to build a repertoire of functions, the effective teacher can build upon students' schemata and make connections to other novel functions during the think-aloud process.

Once students become familiar with the think-aloud process, the teacher can encourage students to think aloud as well through structured discussions. These structured conversations have also been described as accountable talk (Resnick & Hampton, 2009). After the teacher has explicitly taught the language skill or function and modeled its use through the think-aloud process, the effective teacher engages the students in academic conversations characterized by the following:

- The teacher elicits more extended contributions from students by inviting them to expand, by posing questions, and by restating.
- The teacher promotes students' use of text, pictures, and reasoning to support an argument or position.
- Much of the discussion centers on questions and answers for which there might be more than one correct answer.
- The teacher is responsive to students' statements and the opportunities those statements provide.
- The discussion is characterized by multiple, interactive, connected turns; succeeding utterances build on and extend previous ones.
- The teacher creates a "zone of proximal development," where a challenging atmosphere is balanced by a positive, affective climate (Johnson, 2009, p. 90).

The teacher offers sentence stems to help facilitate conversations both between the teacher and student and among students. These sentence stems can be general in nature and available for use during lessons in all content areas, such as: We concluded that . . . , I see it another way . . . , What do you think. . . . At other times, more specific sentence stems will be necessary based on the specialized discourse required in the content areas—for example, when comparing bats and birds in science class: _____ and _____ are similar because they both _____, but they are different because _____ _____ but, _____ _____. These sentence stems can be posted on the classroom wall or be available on a notecard or bookmark for quick reference for those students who need language support.

Teachers can also support students' understandings between function and forms with interactive writing and graphic organizers. "Interactive writing is a dynamic, collaborative literacy event in which children actively compose together, considering appropriate words, phrases, organization of the text, and layout" (McCarrier, Pinnell, & Fountas, 2000, p. xv). It can be thought of as a write-aloud, with similar characteristics to a think-aloud, but simply adding a written text element. The students and teacher work together to discuss a common writing piece in which students justify their ideas and extend their thinking. Composing a Venn diagram that compares birds and bats can serve as a visual entryway into the writing process for students who struggle with the language function of comparing and contrasting. By visually representing the information before requiring the information to be placed in syntactically complex sentences, those who struggle are offered an additional step of support. Once the graphic organizer is completed and agreed upon by the entire class, the teacher can model how to convert the information into complex academic language by employing sentence frames. The discourse surrounding the development of the text will be composed of accountable talk by both the students and the teacher, with the expectation that eventually the students will be able to compose complex texts in small groups and, finally, individually.

Final Thoughts on Academic Language

As with any robust instruction, the first step is knowing your students and their interests and background knowledge. Figuring out their individual levels of language proficiency will be fundamental to their success in school and, therefore, beyond school. Getting a grasp on a student's vocabulary knowledge can be accomplished through conversation and quick formative assessments. A student's level of syntactic knowledge may be more difficult to grasp. Effective teachers listen closely and do not dismiss the times when students like Chris skip transition words or cannot articulate what they mean. Some ineffective teachers seem to overlook their students' understanding of syntax, but it is important to be aware of this blind spot in order to overcome it and provide equitable education for all students.

DO YOU WANT TO KNOW MORE ABOUT ACADEMIC LANGUAGE? CHECK THESE OUT!

Hart. B & Risley, T. (1995). *Meaningful differences in the everyday lives of young American children*. Baltimore, MD: Paul H. Brookes.

Heath, S. B. (1983). *Ways with words: Language, life, and work in communities and classrooms*. Cambridge, England: Cambridge University Press.

Lareau, A. (1989). *Home advantage*. London, England: Falmer Press.

Connecting Pedagogy to Practice

1. What are the demographics of your classroom? How many of your students speak the 'language of school' proficiently?
2. Look at a text from your classroom and identify the Tier 1, Tier 2, and Tier 3 words. How will you teach the Tier 2 words?
3. Look at the same text and determine the mortar words. How will you teach them?

Putting Leadership into Action

Academic language can be a challenging topic for teachers, since they typically utilize it on a regular basis without even thinking. Now that you are aware of the critical nature of academic language, as a teacher leader, you have a responsibility to share your understanding with others. Think about how you would explain forms, functions, syntax, and discourse to one of your colleagues. Can you provide examples of each? Can you describe ways that you can support your students' academic language acquisition? What parts of academic language do you need to know more about? Make a list of questions and then begin searching for answers. Teacher leaders are always learning new things!

References

Beck, I.L., McKeown, M. G., & Kucan, L. (2002). *Bringing words to life: Robust vocabulary instruction.* New York, NY: Guilford Press.

Chamot, A.U., & O'Malley, J.M. (1994). *The CALLA handbook: Implementing the cognitive academic language learning approach.* White Plains, NY: Addison Wesley Longman.

Diaz-Rico, L.T., & Weed, K.Z. (2006). *Cross-cultural, language and academic development handbook: A complete K-12 reference guide* (3rd Ed.). Boston, MA: Pearson.

Dutro, S. & Moran, C. (2003). *Rethinking English language instruction: An architectural approach.* In G. Garcia (Ed.), *English language learners: Reaching the highest level of English literacy.* Newark, DE: International Reading Association.

Fisher, D., & Frey, N. (2008). *Better learning through structured teaching: A framework for the gradual release of responsibility.* Alexandria, VA: ASCD.

Frayer, D., Frederick, W.C., & Klausmeier, H.J. (1969). *A schema for testing the level of cognitive mastery.* Madison, WI: Wisconsin Center for Education Research.

Gee, J.P. (1990). *Social linguistics and literacies: Ideology in discourses.* London, England: Falmer Press.

Hart. B & Risley, T. (1995). *Meaningful differences in the everyday lives of young American children.* Baltimore, MD: Paul H. Brookes.

Heath, S.B. (1983). *Ways with words: Language, life, and work in communities and classrooms.* Cambridge, London: Cambridge University Press.

Hill-Bonnet, L.A. (November, 2013). *Demystifying "academic" language: Supporting candidates and colleagues in the everyday events of school.* Session presented at The National edTPA Implementation Conference, San Diego, CA.

Johnson, E.R. (2009). *Academic language! Academic literacy!* Thousand Oaks, CA: Sage.

Lareau, A. (1989). *Home advantage.* London, England: Falmer Press.

McCarrier, A., Pinnell, G. S., & Fountas, I. C. (2000). *Interactive writing: How language and literacy come together, K-2.* Portsmouth, NH: Heinemann.

Resnick, L. B., & Hampton, S. (2009). *Reading and writing with understanding.* Washington, DC: International Reading Association.

Stanovich, K.E. (1986). Matthew effects in reading: Some consequences of individual differences in the acquisition of literacy. *Reading Research Quarterly, 21*(4), 360–407.

Wilhelm, J. D. (2001). *Improving comprehension with think-aloud strategies.* New York, NY: Scholastic.

8

QUESTIONING AND FEEDBACK

Let's take a look at two different third-grade classrooms. In Mrs. Shuttleworth's classroom, the students are seated in groups and are discussing historical drawings from the Olympics in ancient Greece. As the students try to decipher what is going on in the drawings, the teacher moves around the room and checks in with each group's conclusions. She asks one group what they notice about the clothing worn and another group what they think is going on in the arena. The students in Mrs. Shuttleworth's classroom ask questions of each other and of the teacher. Instead of providing the answers, the teacher directs students to other resources in the room such as iPads, history textbooks, and other nonfiction texts to satisfy their curiosity.

In Mrs. Litton's classroom, the students are also learning about the Olympics in ancient Greece, but they are seated in rows. Students each have their own outline to fill in that goes along with the section of the social studies textbook that they are all taking turns reading out loud together. The same drawing that students are looking at in Mrs. Shuttleworth's class is on the second page of the outline. After a student reads a few paragraphs aloud, Mrs. Litton asks students to read the statements on the outline and for them to respond with the correct answer to fill in the blank. Then another student begins to read the next paragraph.

As you reflect on these two classrooms, what do you notice? Did there seem to be more engagement and learning in one classroom over the other? What factors do you think directly contributed to this? Most likely, it was the teacher's effective (or ineffective) use of questioning and feedback. These two concepts go hand in hand in supporting students' development of the types of critical thinking necessary for success both inside and out of school settings, and yet they tend to be an underutilized and overlooked means of supporting such student thinking.

Questioning

It is obvious that questioning takes place countless times throughout the school day. What might not be as obvious is the disparity between the rate and type of questioning occurring in the classroom and some teachers' perceived awareness of these questioning techniques. Susskind (1979) surveyed teachers and asked them how many questions they ask and how many questions their students ask in a thirty-minute period. Teachers predicted that they ask fifteen questions and their students ask ten. In reality, the teachers asked 50.6 and students asked 1.8. This study raised two interesting points. The first is that effective teachers must first notice their questioning techniques before they can truly understand if their questioning techniques are optimizing learning opportunities. It may be helpful to audiotape your own teaching and then chart how many questions are asked by the teacher and by the students. The other important aspect of these findings is the imbalance between the teacher and the students. If we are advocating for a constructivist classroom in which students can assimilate their own learning, the students should be more engaged in the questioning process. By moving away from merely asking questions to receive a right or wrong answer to thinking about questions as "vehicles for thought," effective teaching can occur (Walsh & Sattes, 2005, p. 9).

> We are shifting from viewing questions as devices by which one evaluates the specifics of learning to conceptualizing questions as a means of actively processing, thinking about, and using information productively. Many educators are weaning students from believing that questions are phrased to

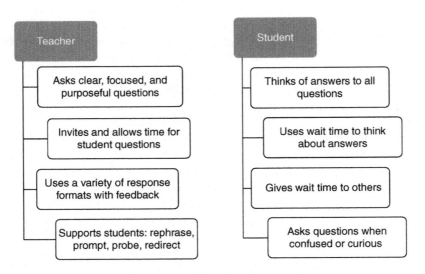

FIGURE 8.1 What a quality questioning classroom looks like (Walsh & Sattes, 2005, p. 8)

attain certain answers and are helping them to accept questions as key vehicles that elicit awareness of the diversity, complexity, and richness of knowledge. More educators are assisting students in comprehending that questions are linguistic goals that enable thinking and production of knowledge.

(Hunkins, 1995, p. 4)

Making this crucial shift will take time and effort, but will be well worth it in the end. These changes will challenge the traditional notion of roles in the classroom and may cause some disequilibrium at first as students relearn and transform their understandings of how conversation works at school (Figure 8.1).

Ways of Looking at Questions

There are two main purposes for asking questions in the classroom: to seek information and to process information. Effective teachers consciously spend more of their time focused on asking questions and helping students formulate their own questions in order to process information.

When thinking about the different types of questions, it is helpful to think about three categories: knowledge questions, skill questions, and big ideas (Knight, 2013; Wiggins & McTighe, 2005). If the goal is to assist students in processing information, teachers must emphasize big ideas in the classroom. Wiggins and McTighe (2005) define big ideas as "a concept, theme, or issue that gives meaning and connection to discrete facts and skills" (p. 5). These types of questions require students to demonstrate their understanding of the material and of how the information is connected to their learning. Effective teachers use a variety of question types to build up to big idea questions. Knowledge questions are usually closed ended and ask students to recall facts and ideas. Skill questions require students to apply the knowledge they have learned in a new context. Knowledge and skill questions should be used to lead up to the big idea questions of the lesson. For example:

- Knowledge: When did Columbus set out to explore India?
- Skill: Why did Columbus explore a new trade route?
- Big idea: Why do we explore?

One of the most widely used tools for distinguishing between question types is Bloom's taxonomy (Anderson & Krathwohl, 2001) (Figure 8.2). There are several other frameworks for questioning that are just as useful. What matters more than which framework a teacher uses is that the teacher and the students deliberately employ the framework and are consciously aware of its use and purpose.

1. Remember. These types of questions require the lowest level of cognitive processing, but are crucial in building a base of knowledge to get to the big idea questions. Students must be able to retrieve basic information to

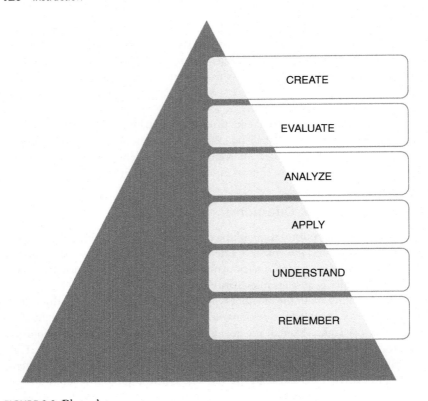

FIGURE 8.2 Bloom's taxonomy

use when constructing more complex understandings. Some verbs associated with remembering are memorize, recall, and repeat.
- Who was the eleventh president of the United States?
- What is condensation?

2. Understand. Understand moves beyond the cognitive level of remembering by allowing students to make connections between the new knowledge and their existing schemas. This requires students to use information that was not provided during the initial instruction, but rather, within their prior knowledge and conceptual understandings. Some verbs associated with understanding are classify, describe, identify, and predict.
- What is the main idea of the story?
- What do you predict will happen next in the story?

3. Apply. Application offers students the opportunity to apply a new procedure to a familiar or unfamiliar task. This entails a deeper understanding of the procedure than simply recalling the steps required. Some verbs associated with application are demonstrate, illustrate, and solve.

- Would you have reacted in the same way that the main character did?
- From the information provided, can you develop a set of instructions about how to build a greenhouse?

4. Analyze. Analysis requires students to take an idea and break it down into separate parts to then determine how all the parts are connected to one another. Some verbs associated with analyzing are compare/contrast, distinguish, and examine.
   - How are addition and multiplication similar?
   - What was the turning point in the American Revolutionary War?

5. Evaluate. Evaluation involves making a judgment based on a set of criteria. Generally, students are required to take a side or discuss the pros and cons of a particular issue. This necessitates the student grasping multiple sides to an issue and conceptualizing how the sides are similar and how they differ. Some verbs associated with evaluation are argue, defend, and support.
   - What would have been the implications if the South had won the Civil War?
   - Which is better: the traditional school year or year-round school?

6. Create. The final cognitive process is to create.

   The student must draw upon elements from many sources and put them together in a novel structure or pattern relative to his or her own prior knowledge. Create results in a new product that is something that can be observed and that is more than the students' beginning materials.

   (Anderson & Krathwohl, 2001, p. 65)

Some verbs associated with creation are construct, develop, and formulate.

- What are some possible solutions to cleaning up the environment?
- How would you test the theory of gravity?

Now that you are familiar with the categories of questions, go back and listen to the audiotape of your teaching. Categorize the types of questions both you and your students are asking. Are they of a high quality? Do you and your students address the big ideas or merely spend time asking knowledge and skill questions? Highly effective teachers spend time asking a larger proportion of questions on the top end of Bloom's taxonomy of cognitive levels. Let's examine how to integrate more demanding questions in the classroom.

How to Formulate Quality Questions

When considering how to choose which questions to ask of your students, it is important to remember the purpose of these questions. Effective teachers do not simply ask questions to quiz students' knowledge of memorized skills or facts. Rather, they ask questions to facilitate students' processing of new material. These types of questions help students:

- Focus their thinking on specified content knowledge
- Use cognitive processing strategies to develop deep understandings and long-term retention of content
- Ask academic questions to clarify or extend understandings
- Monitor progress toward learning targets through self-assessment (Walsh & Sattes, 2011 p. 3)

This creates a dynamic interchange between teacher and student (and even student and student) in which both are engaged in the learning process. Therefore, when effective teachers think about how they will formulate questions, they not only consider what they will ask, but also how students will engage with the material.

The role of the teacher in intentional questioning includes the process of formulating the question, determining required scaffolds based on cognitive demand, providing feedback, and creating a classroom atmosphere in which all students participate and understand the purposes of the questions being asked. Obviously, when formulating quality questions during planning, they should be directly connected to the lesson's expected learning outcomes. Effective teachers let the 'big ideas' of the lesson or unit drive instruction and questions. During a study of the water cycle, an effective teacher might ask the following:

- "Principal Darling told me that the water we drink out of the water fountain is the same water that the dinosaurs drank. I'm not sure I believe him. Is he correct?"
- "What can you do to decrease the impact humans have on polluting the Earth's water resources?"

These questions explore the concept that water continuously moves through the water cycle and also help students make a personal connection to the material. Both of these questions require a higher cognitive demand than asking "What step comes after evaporation during the water cycle?" Therefore, effective teachers must not only think about questions, but also follow-up prompts that can facilitate student understanding. These can come in the form of feedback, which will be discussed at length later in the chapter, but brainstorming possible student responses and thinking through how to redirect student thinking are vital to questioning that promotes learning.

Additionally, when formulating questions, the effective teacher must articulate who will be answering the questions. In an engaged classroom in which all students are learning, all students must be held accountable for their thinking. This dynamic version of a classroom will likely look and sound different from your own elementary classroom in which students may have quietly raised their hands to speak as the teacher called on one student at a time for an answer. Did any of the other students know the answer? Where any of the other students even actually listening? Student engagement can be achieved through allowing students to work in pairs or groups or requiring written responses that can be collected. During this practice time, the teacher can adapt the cognitive demand of the questions or provide individual scaffolds in the form of visual representations or prompting. By creating a dynamic learning environment, students who would regularly be inclined to 'opt out' of learning are not given that option. Instead, the effective teacher insists that all students be engaged with the material, which will likely prevent some of the disparity in academic success that occurs in some less effective teachers' classrooms. As students begin to realize that questioning has a purpose directly related to their learning and begin to see the effects on their understanding, their self-efficacy and motivation will increase, leading to even more engagement in the classroom!

Classroom renorming may be necessary to create a classroom environment in which students are willing to participate in quality questioning (Figure 8.3).

Student Behaviors	Student Outcomes
Pay attention to all questions and answers	Know facts
Think of answers to all questions	Develop understandings based on facts
Are on alert to answer all questions aloud	Use knowledge to solve problems and make decisions
Answer questions at the appropriate cognitive level	Develop new products and ideas
Use wait time to think about answers	Make inferences and draw conclusions
Give wait time to others when asking questions	Know and use effective questioning skills
Ask questions when confused	Thoughtfully answer teacher and peer questions
Ask questions when curious	Ask many high-quality questions
Make meaning out of facts	

FIGURE 8.3 Student behaviors and outcomes in a quality questioning classroom (adapted from Walsh & Sattes, 2005)

Creating time for students to think about and reformulate their thoughts is a vital part of the learning process. Traditionally, this time for reflection and thinking has been labeled wait time. Rowe (1986) found that three to five seconds is optimal for both the initial wait time when a question is asked and also for an additional wait time after a student ended his or her answer. The first wait time allows time for all students to formulate an answer. The second wait time allows students an opportunity to ask follow-up questions or expand on their peers' responses. At first, these wait times may feel awkward for students and the teacher will need to explicitly explain or model what is expected of them during these times. Also, it is vital that the teacher and students discuss the need to honor the wait time of others.

Building Student Learning Capacity

These quality questions should lead to building learning capacity. According to Walsh and Sattes (2011) the roles of the students include:

- Accountability
- Capacity to ask quality questions
- Collaboration

For all students to be accountable, teachers need to provide supports to allow them to enter into the conversation. This includes providing sentence stems ("What did you mean by . . . ?" or "Can you tell me more about . . . ?") to get the conversation started and grouping techniques to provide a comfortable environment in which students feel free to take chances and enter the conversation. Additionally, if we want students to ask quality questions, we need to provide opportunities for them to be interested enough to engage in the conversation. "Curiosity is one of the important skills in today's world; when teachers understand this, they value students who wonder, speculate, hypothesize, and imagine" (Walsh & Sattes, 2011, p. 113). For students to build learning capacity through questioning techniques, they must move from simply committing to the conversation to actually taking some ownership in the conversation. Students must feel as though their contributions to the conversation are worthwhile if they are to learn from the experience.

Finally, students must collaborate with their peers for questioning to build learner capacity. In many classrooms, teachers think that students are working collaboratively since they are placed in groups and are engaged in a shared task. Unfortunately, this is not collaborative learning. Collaborative learning must be explicitly modeled and practiced until students understand the expectations of this dynamic instructional strategy. To collaborate means that all students are expected to be involved and they are to build on one another's thoughts. Students need to begin by understanding the difference between listening to and judging other's ideas. Once students begin to listen, then they can be explicitly taught how to reformulate and expand a group member's ideas. When collaborative groups are not functioning smoothly, the teacher is usually aware because students begin arguing with each other. This usually stems from students making judgments about the worthiness of group members' contributions. When students are taught how to take ideas and adjust them to include all members' voices, true collaboration occurs and learning capacity is built.

Barriers to Implementing Questioning in the Classroom

If we know how powerful questioning can be, then why do we only see it in effective teachers' classrooms? The answer is that there are some barriers to implementing quality questioning. The first is time and content coverage. Teachers are always saying that they have too much content to cover and not enough time in the day to fit it all in. Asking higher-order, open-ended questions of students (and having them ask them of each other) takes up quite a bit of instructional time. Some teachers are worried that the students' answers will lead the lesson astray or move in a direction that is uncomfortable for the teacher. The idea of handing the conversation mainly over to the students also goes against some teachers' need to maintain 'control' of the classroom. The important point to remember is that just being in 'control' of the classroom is not ideal if the students are not learning. By readjusting the classroom dynamics and having students play a more influential role in their learning, the outcomes become more robust.

Another reason why some teachers do not ask challenging questions of their students is because they do not want to put students on the spot. It can be disheartening as a teacher to have a student who is unable to answer a question that has been posed in front of the entire class. One way to overcome this barrier is to plan questions that match the developmental levels of individual students or groups of students. Questions should be tailored to each student so that they are not too easy or too difficult. There is no need to determine specific questions for each student; rather, you should plan quality questions that can be modified to match the needs of your students. Another consideration would be to ask questions in small groups or individually so that students do not feel like they have been put on the spot in front of their peers. Finally, some less effective teachers simply find it easier to ask all the questions to which they already know the expected answer. Of course this is easier, but students quickly pick up on the idea that the questions aren't 'real' since the teacher already knows the answer, and therefore, their learning can be negatively affected. Students begin to realize that this type of conversation is not authentic and may disengage from these 'staged' conversations. Plus, effective teachers know that it is always better to do what is best for the child, not easier for the teacher.

Final Thoughts on Questioning

In summary, we know that questioning techniques by both the teacher and the students do make a difference in student learning outcomes. Thinking back to the chapters on assessment, quality questioning can be considered an effective form of formative assessment. When employed correctly, it will provide both the student and teacher with information that can be used to inform subsequent instruction. Providing feedback is a natural outgrowth of using quality questioning techniques and will be explored in the second half of this chapter.

Feedback

Research has shown that feedback is one of the most salient influences on student achievement (Hattie, 2009; Marzano et al., 2012; Norcini, 2010). Although we know that it is a powerful indicator of student growth, many teachers still struggle with integrating feedback into their instruction. Some teachers have conceptualized feedback in ways that don't always directly support students, but rather can be categorized as more evaluative techniques with little scaffolding and support provided to the students. According to Gipps et al. (2000), expressing approval or disapproval towards a student's actions or behaviors and, consequently, giving rewards and punishments merely serve as actions that evaluate a student based on the judgment of whether the teacher believes he or she is interacting in a positive or negative way. This type of feedback does not offer any advice on how the student can modify his or her actions (either academically or behaviorally) in a fashion that would support growth and optimize his or her learning trajectory. On the other hand, describing to a student why an answer is correct or incorrect, offering suggestions on ways students can improve, and encouraging students to suggest ways in which they can improve are all feedback strategies that are descriptive in nature and provide students with an opportunity to readjust their thinking, clarify their misunderstandings, and challenge them to grow intellectually.

What Is Feedback?

So you may be asking yourself, "What is feedback?" It is helpful to think about feedback in terms of the purposes and goals of giving feedback. "Effective feedback is concrete, specific, and useful; it provides actionable information" (Wiggins, 2005, p. 14). The goal of feedback "is to give students information about their performance relative to a particular learning objective so they can improve their performance and understand themselves better as learners" (Dean et al., 2012, p. 11). In describing feedback, these researchers make a designation between feedback and praise. Praise generally is not specific enough to be useful in supporting students' growth. Have you ever had a teacher who told you "Good job!" or

"You're smart!" or "Try harder next time!"? Did you truly understand whether you had mastered the goal of the learning segment or did you know what you needed to overcome to be successful in subsequent learning? Probably not. Praise is generally not effective (Norcini, 2010) and should not be used in place of feedback, although praising a student's effort can be motivating.

Earl (2013, pp. 101–102) states that feedback:

- Provides evidence that confirms or disconfirms an idea
- Gives students a chance to reflect on their learning and their learning needs
- Gives recognition and appropriate praise for achievement and for growth
- Is targeted to the specific learning needs of each student or group of students
- Gives clear directions for improvement
- Allows students to think about and respond to the suggestions
- Focuses on quality and on learning

Based on Earl's description of what feedback should accomplish, Figure 8.4 highlights specific examples and nonexamples of effective feedback.

Feedback should be connected to the goals of the lesson or unit. "Effective feedback requires that a person has a goal, takes action to achieve the goal, and receives goal-related information about his or her actions" (Wiggins, 2005, p. 13). Therefore, first and foremost, the effective teacher must understand what the goals of instruction are. Without planning clear goals, it will be difficult, if not impossible, to determine if students are approaching mastery of these goals and what feedback is necessary to continue guiding them towards mastery. Specific feedback tied to the lesson's goal might sound something like:

Examples of Effective Feedback	*Nonexamples of Effective Feedback*
You did an excellent job of incorporating adjectives in your writing to help the reader imagine the setting. Next time think about how you can also use adverbs to convey your thoughts.	Good job! You are so smart!
Those two questions are similar, so I can understand why you got confused. Let's review the definitions in your fraction book to determine the correct answers.	76% Try harder next time!
I noticed that when you got stuck on that word you tried to sound it out, but that didn't seem to work. Let's look at your strategy bookmark and see if another strategy might help in this situation.	You need more examples in your paper.
	I am so impressed with your project!

FIGURE 8.4 Examples and nonexamples of effective feedback

- "You did a great job explaining the events that led to the start of the Civil War. Do you think adding time words would help your reader follow the sequence?"
- "You tried to sound that word out, but that didn't help. Can you think of another strategy to use? Do you see any little words inside the word that you know or is it on the word wall?"

If we agree that feedback should be an integral part of instruction, then we should consider when feedback should be given. The answer is undeniably often. If our goal is the mastery of complex learning, the brain needs time to practice new material several times with slight modifications each time until assimilation of the new learning occurs. This requires setting aside time for students to reflect on the feedback, for them to consider how it fits with their prior learning, and for them to transform their understandings. Teachers claim they are giving vast amounts of feedback each day, but Hattie (2009) discovered that "at best, students receive 'moments' of feedback in a single day" (p. 174). To maximize student learning, teachers must consider intentionally altering components of their daily routines to allow time to incorporate feedback strategies at the beginning, middle, and end of daily lessons. Feedback should become part of your routine as an effective teacher in the classroom. Once this occurs, you can give timely feedback seamlessly, sometimes without students even realizing that feedback is being provided.

One way to provide ongoing feedback is through the use of rubrics. Rubrics should be directly tied to instruction and the desired outcomes of the lesson. For example, if you are expecting your second graders to write a story that includes a setting, the characters, the problem and solution, then handwriting, punctuation,

	Does Not Meet Expectations	*Partially Meets Expectations*	*Meets Expectations*	*Exceeds Expectations*
Grammar and Punctuation	Rarely uses correct punctuation and grammar	Sometimes uses correct punctuation and grammar	Generally uses correct punctuation and grammar	Consistently uses correct punctuation and grammar
Accuracy of Facts	Major inaccuracies	Inaccurate	Generally accurate; inaccuracies do not affect overall result	Completely accurate
Effectiveness of Persuasion	Ineffective	Somewhat effective	Generally effective	Highly effective
Clarity	Unclear; unable to follow	Lacks clarity; difficult to follow	Generally clear; able to follow	Exceptionally clear; easy to follow

FIGURE 8.5 Sample rubric

and spelling might not be included on the rubric. These are important facets of writing development, but depending on the goal of your lesson, these might not be included in the evaluation process or receive much attention related to feedback. Perhaps the next writing sample will focus on these conventions. In the beginning, these rubrics should be developed by the teacher, but as time goes on, the effective teacher can model expectations for student-made rubrics. One resource for developing teacher-made rubrics is available from McTighe and Wiggins (2004); their process was used to develop the rubric included in Figure 8.5.

Categories of Feedback

Feedback can generally be placed into one of three categories: self, peer, and teacher feedback. All of these categories are important components to student learning, and one should not be assumed more important than or subsume the others. Rather, these categories of feedback can be used in tandem and iteratively to promote students' understanding of complex material (Figure 8.6).

1. Self: evaluating or using metacognitive strategies, seeking information or correctives, creating a self-teaching or self-regulating situation
2. Peers: clarifying information or processing aloud for confirmation, peer teaching
3. Teacher: informal interactions in class, questions designed to seek reteaching, corrections to assignments, test and project evaluations (Pollock, 2012, p. 14)

Teacher

Teacher feedback is the most common type of feedback given in the classroom. This likely stems from the teacher's historical role as the giver of information in the classroom and the student's role of the receiver of information. As effective

Self-Feedback	Peer Feedback	Teacher Feedback
Goal setting	Think-pair-share	Questioning
Progress monitoring	Peer editing	Written feedback with suggestions
Self-evaluation on a rubric	Performance assessments with peer feedback	Journal writing
Recorded readings	Author's chair	
Writing portfolio	Gallery walk	
	Small group discussion	

FIGURE 8.6 Effective strategies that foster feedback

teachers become more proficient with offering feedback, the onus is then trans-ferred over to the students. The teacher remains engaged in the process, modeling effective feedback and offering suggested feedback when students get stuck, but students begin to offer each other authentic and useful feedback on a regular basis. It is important to remember that offering too much feedback can be as detrimen-tal to learning as not providing any feedback at all. The effective teacher provides feedback on only a few areas that are directly tied to the goals of instruction. These areas should be transferable to other areas of the curriculum and therefore offer the most 'bang for your buck.' For example, feedback on the correct usage of com-mon adverbs (carefully, loudly, quickly) during writer's workshop would transfer over to writing in all subject areas, but offering feedback on how to spell hippo-potamus to a kindergarten student will likely not inform her spelling of other similar words during writer's workshop.

Some examples of teacher feedback include:

- Questioning: Teacher verbally prompts students to think more deeply about the work they have produced. These prompts should be explicit enough to guide students to conclude their own next steps in learning without the teacher directly offering explicit guidance.
- Written feedback with suggestions: Teacher writes directly on student work and provides suggested tools and activities for improvement (Figure 8.7).
- Journal writing: Many teachers have students keep response journals in their desks, but without teacher feedback, these can be underutilized tools in the classroom.

Peers

Giving students the opportunity to give one another feedback can also be very powerful (Glaser & Brunstein, 2007). It gives students another opportunity to clarify what they understood or misunderstood. It is important to model your expectations for appropriate feedback and dialogue when peers are working together. Students will most likely start out simply giving each other praise and will need to be encour-aged to give more substantial feedback that is directly related to the learning goals. Additionally, peers should not be responsible for giving each other grades. Instead, they should serve as another place to 'practice' what they are learning on their jour-ney to mastery without any sort of high-stakes evaluative component.

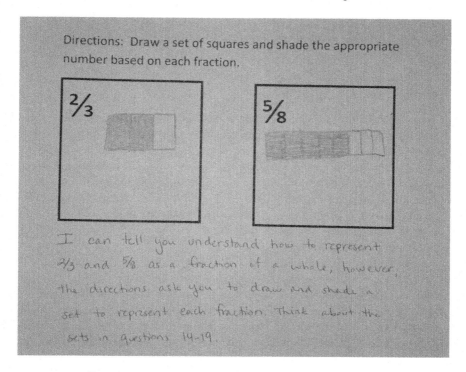

Directions: Draw a set of squares and shade the appropriate number based on each fraction.

2/3

5/8

I can tell you understand how to represent 2/3 and 5/8 as a fraction of a whole, however, the directions ask you to draw and shade a set to represent each fraction. Think about the sets in questions 14-19.

FIGURE 8.7 Effective teacher-written feedback

Some examples of peer feedback include:

- Think-pair-share: At predetermined points in the lesson, partners turn toward one another and share what they have learned or what they are thinking about the new material.
- Peer editing: Partners edit each other's written text based on a provided rubric or checklist.
- Author's chair: One student reads aloud his or her written work to the entire class and the audience provides accolades and suggestions to improve the text.
- Gallery walk: Student work is hung on the walls of the classroom and students move around the room as if they were walking around an art gallery. Classmates take notes and share suggestions for improvement at the end of the walk.

All of these types of peer feedback give students the opportunity to think out loud with a partner or small group of peers at predetermined points in the lesson. Through this process they will engage with the material and help support each other's learning. This process will also help individuals solidify their own learning since they will need to justify the feedback they are providing, which will support mastery of the objective.

Self

Giving feedback to one's self can be a daunting task for some students. This is not something that most students can perform intuitively and needs to be modeled before your students can be expected to successfully self-regulate. "Self-regulated learning helps students acquire the adaptive and autonomous learning characteristics required for an enhanced engagement with the learning process and subsequent successful performance" (Clark, 2012, p. 217). Open-ended questions, like those contained in Figure 8.8, are one way to build self-regulation in your students. By asking them to explain their thinking, you can help guide them to understand their mistakes.

As students continue to work with cognitively challenging material, they will begin to question themselves and force themselves to justify their conclusions before accepting the answer. This process becomes iterative and may begin to build self-esteem in some students who formerly believed in the fixed model of learning rather than the growth model of learning (Dweck, 1999). In the fixed model of learning, students believe that intelligence is predetermined and no amount of hard work will make a difference in how smart they are. Therefore, there is no use trying since the results are inevitable. On the other hand, students who hold the growth model of learning believe that academic success can be earned by everyone through dedication and hard work. More information on these models is included in Chapter 9. By creating a classroom culture in which asking for help is acceptable and working on challenging material is seen as a regular activity, students begin to self-regulate, offer internal feedback, and shift

---

I really had to think about . . .

I noticed that . . .

I was surprised about . . .

I discovered that . . .

I need more help learning about . . .

I would change this activity for next time by . . .

I am pleased with myself that I . . .

What helped me most was . . .

FIGURE 8.8 Sample open-ended self-evaluation questions

from the fixed model to the growth model of learning. Student self-regulation also offers a window into student learning that otherwise teachers might not have access to. By examining how students self-regulate (or neglect to self-regulate), the effective teacher can begin to pinpoint both strategies students have mastered and areas in which students need more explicit modeling and practice.

Some examples of self-feedback include:

- Goal setting and progress monitoring: This can occur within a lesson, a unit, or over a longer period. By setting goals, students have something concrete and tangible to work toward that is appropriate to their individual learning needs. As students work toward their goals, they can track their progress, which reinforces the growth model over the fixed model of growth (Figure 8.9).

- Self-evaluation on a rubric: By providing a rubric (or having students create their own), the effective teacher communicates the learning goals from the start and provides a roadmap of expectations. Students can compare their learning to the rubric and self-evaluate their progress.

- Recorded readings/writing portfolio: These activities provide a place for students to reflect on their literacy progress. By audio recording their reading over time, they can hear changes with their prosody and speed. Writing

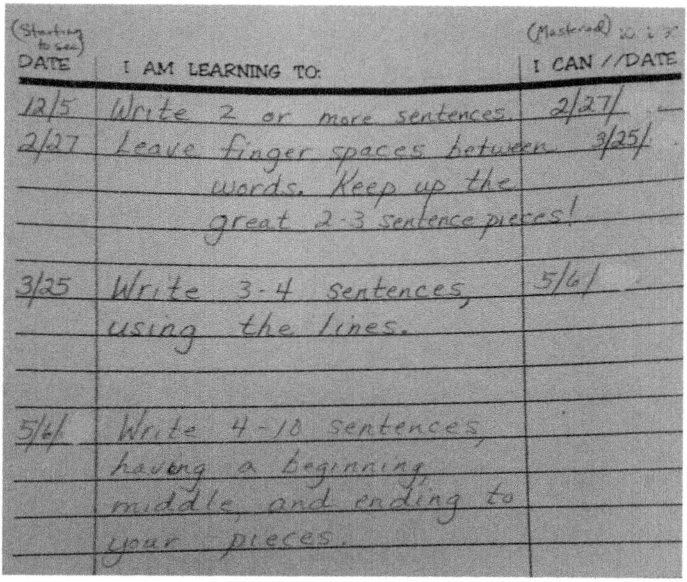

FIGURE 8.9 Goal setting as feedback to self

samples can be collected over time and placed in a portfolio to illustrate growth in phonics and writing semantics. These can also be used to determine areas for continued improvement.

Final Thoughts on Feedback

Quality and timely feedback is paramount for student success. Effective teachers realize they need feedback to improve also. This feedback obviously comes from outside of the classroom in the form of evaluative measures (principals, supervisors, state departments of education, parents), but perhaps the most powerful feedback is in the form of analyzing student learning within the classroom. By examining how your students are performing, most likely through formative assessments, you can begin to adjust and reformulate your ideas and plans to better suit the learning needs of your diverse students.

DO YOU WANT TO KNOW MORE ABOUT QUESTIONING AND FEEDBACK? CHECK THESE OUT!

Questioning

Anderson, L. W., & Krathwohl, D. R. (Eds.). (2001). *A taxonomy for learning, teaching, and assessing: A revision of Bloom's taxonomy of educational objectives.* New York, NY: Addison Wesley Longman.

Walsh, J. A., & Sattes, B. D. (2011). *Thinking through quality questioning: Deepening student engagement.* Thousand Oaks, CA: Sage.

Feedback

Pollock, J. E. (2012). *Feedback: The hinge that joins teaching and learning.* Thousand Oaks, CA: Sage.

Connecting Pedagogy to Practice

1. Audiotape a segment of your instruction. What types of questions do you hear you and your students asking? Are they of a high quality?
2. What have been your experiences with feedback as a student? Was the feedback you received helpful? Why or why not?
3. Who do you think should be giving feedback in the classroom? How often?
4. Next time you are in a classroom, focus on feedback. Is it present? Who is offering the feedback? Is it effective?

Putting Leadership into Action

Earlier in the chapter, we suggested audiotaping a segment of your teaching in order to notice the kinds of questions you're asking. That's just the kind of thing that teacher leaders do: critically examine their own teaching. Not only do we suggest audiotaping a segment of your teaching, but we also suggest audiotaping segments of your teaching across the school day and over time. What kinds of questions do you tend to ask? Do your questioning techniques change according to subject area? Why might that be? Track your progress over time. Do you have evidence that your questioning practices are changing in the way that you intended them to? Do the audiotapes suggest that student learning is being positively affected?

References

Anderson, L.W., & Krathwohl, D.R. (Eds.). (2001). *A taxonomy for learning, teaching, and assessing: A revision of Bloom's taxonomy of educational objectives.* New York, NY: Addison Wesley Longman.

Clark, I. (2012). Formative assessment: Assessment is for self-regulated learning. *Educational Psychology Review, 24*, 205–249.

Dean, C. B., Hubbell, E. R., Pitler, H., & Stone, B. (2012). *Classroom instruction that works* (2nd Ed.). Alexandria: VA: Association for Supervision and Curriculum Development.

Dweck, C. S. (1999). *Self-theories: Their role in motivation, personality, and development.* Philadelphia, PA: The Psychology Press.

Earl, L. M. (2013). *Assessment as learning: Using classroom assessment to maximize student learning* (2nd Ed.). Thousand Oaks, CA: Sage.

Gipps, C., McCallum, B., & Hargreaves, E. (2000). *What makes a good primary school teacher? Expert classroom strategies.* London, England: Routledge.

Glaser, C., & Brunstein, J. C. (2007). Improving fourth-grade students' comprehension skills: Effects of strategy instruction and self-regulation procedures. *Journal of Educational Psychology, 99*, 297–310.

Hattie, J. (2009). *Visible learning: A synthesis of over 800 meta-analyses relating to achievement.* London, England: Routledge.

Hunkins, F.P. (1995). *Teaching thinking through effective questioning* (2nd Ed.). Boston, MA: Christopher-Gordon Publishers.

Knight, J. (2013). *High-impact instruction: A framework for great teaching.* Thousand Oaks, CA: Sage.

Marzano, R. J., Pickering, D. J., & Pollock, J. E. (2012). *Classroom instruction that works: Research-based strategies for increasing student achievement* (2nd Ed.). Alexandria: VA: Association for Supervision and Curriculum Development.

McTighe, J., & Wiggins, G. (2004). *Understanding by design: Professional development workbook.* Alexandria: VA: Association for Supervision and Curriculum Development.

Norcini, J. (2010). The power of feedback. *Medical Education, 44*(1), 16–17.

Pollock, J. E. (2012). *Feedback: The hinge that joins teaching and learning.* Thousand Oaks, CA: Sage.

Rowe, M. B. (1986). Wait time: Slowing down may be a way of speeding up! *Journal of Teacher Education, 37*, 43–52.

Susskind, E. (1979, Summer). Encouraging teachers to encourage children's curiosity: A pivotal competence. *Journal of Clinical Child Psychology, 8*, 101–106.

Walsh, J.A., & Sattes, B.D. (2005). *Quality questioning: Research-based practice to engage every learner.* Thousand Oaks, CA: Sage.

Walsh, J.A., & Sattes, B.D. (2011). *Thinking through quality questioning: Deepening student engagement.* Thousand Oaks, CA: Sage.

Wiggins, G., & McTighe, J. (2005). *Understanding by design.* Alexandria, VA: Association for Supervision and Curriculum Development.

9

ENGAGEMENT THROUGH MOTIVATION

"Time on task." Was this the first phrase that came to mind when you spotted the word engagement beside Chapter 9? How about "paying attention"? Engagement is often linked to these two concepts, although it is usually discussed in the context of classroom management or behavior epitomized by the traditional vision of a classroom full of students sitting quietly in rows, writing. We argue that looks can sometimes be deceiving and that not all students who are seemingly doing what they are supposed to are actually actively engaged in the lesson. Although we agree that engaged students are generally well behaved, paying attention, and on task, we believe there is more to engagement than that.

"Anyone who has spent time in classrooms knows that a teacher cannot make headway without engaging students in the learning process, and this is not as straightforward as it might appear" (Darling-Hammond & Bransford, 2007, p. 88). Perhaps it is not straightforward because learning occurs at all times, not just the moment teachers present the punch line for the lesson. Learning can occur before and after lessons, as well as inside and outside of the classroom, because learning is personal. Teachers can't 'make' students learn, although we can try to establish the prime learning conditions through engagement.

Another reason engaging students does not seem straightforward is because paying attention is an internal mechanism—one we can't really observe from the outside—that involves orienting and maintaining neural networks by excluding and suppressing internal and external distractors (Jensen, 2005). Despite our proclivity to believe we can multitask, brain research generally suggests that we don't do it well at all. (If you have never watched the videos associated with the research that preceded the book *The Invisible Gorilla: And Other Ways Our Intuitions Deceive Us* by Chabris and Simons [2010], you might take a look!) We humans, of any age, need time to process information—to think—in order to get it into our brains, and no one but we can make that happen. No matter what teachers or administrators or anyone else would like to believe, the act of teaching can only go so far; in order for learning to occur, students have to actually do the work. Thus, if student learning is our goal, we have to convince our students that learning is worth the effort, which makes engaging them in the process—hooking them, so to speak—a critical component of effective instruction.

The word engagement has been a rising star in the English language since the 1980s. Word use for engagement has increased by over 40 percent from 1978–2008 ("Engagement," 2014). Much in the same way that the word leadership is defined and employed in many different ways, the overuse of this word in the educational arena has broadened and/or blurred its meaning in the classroom, and thus needs a bit of clarification. Engagement is a result of motivation, just as integrity is the result of telling the truth. Engagement can be thought of as the outward, observable result of inward motivation. Therefore, the goal for engagement must be targeted at motivation. So far in this book, we have talked at length about assessing student needs and planning for instruction based on those needs. It is likely not surprising then that again student needs come into play here. In order to engage students, you have to tap into what motivates them, and despite what some would like to have us believe, not everyone is motivated in the same way. Not only do we have to catch students' attention, but we have to sustain it; needless to say, this can be challenging when the twenty-five nine- and ten-year-olds in your fourth-grade class are used to being bombarded with information as they watch television while playing video games and listening to music on their electronic device of choice. Simply demanding that they sit up and pay attention is not likely going to work in the same ways that it seemed to in the iconic classrooms of the 1950s and 1960s.

Basic Needs of Motivation

Engaging students in the learning process is clearly not straightforward, but it can be modeled and taught (Darling-Hammond & Bransford, 2007). In order for that to happen, the basic needs of motivation should be met.

Understanding the Basics of Motivation

Understanding that students own their learning as individuals and that teachers serve as mediators of this process is crucial to establishing a mindset that will support motivation. Psychologist Carol Dweck (2006) offers two distinct mindsets for teachers to consider as they observe their students: growth or fixed. A growth mindset views intelligence as something that can be developed, whereas a fixed mindset views intelligence as something that is static. The mindsets have profoundly differing traits in three areas: appearance to others, responding to setbacks, and talent versus effort. When it comes to appearance, students with growth mindsets tend to aim to learn, whereas those with fixed mindsets more often strive to appear clever. Their response to setbacks takes a similar turn, in that those with growth mindsets are willing to confront mistakes and deficiencies, whereas those with fixed mindsets tend to attempt to mask mistakes and deficiencies. Finally, those who have growth mindsets believe that hard work and effort garner success, whereas those with fixed mindsets often attribute that success to natural ability (or inability). In practice, it is important for teachers to embrace a growth mindset in order to most effectively model and teach it to students.

Environmental Distractors

In order to successfully engage students, teachers must understand, modify, and accommodate for the environmental distractors in students' lives that can inhibit motivation. In Chapter 6, we discussed Maslow's hierarchy and the associated need for security within the classroom environment. We will explore more potential classroom distractors here, but believe that it is important to recognize that distractors can also spill over into school as a result of students' home lives. In addition to our discussion of classroom distractors, we consider how home life affects students. We recognize that many of these issues fall well within teachers' circles of concern; however, since they generally remain outside of teachers' circle of influence, we don't advocate spending too much time dwelling on them.

Home Life

Although teachers are limited in ways they can reduce distractors that occur outside of the school building, they do have an obligation to students while they are at school. In order for school and classroom time to be spent diligently, teachers should work hand in hand with school administrators and counselors to help students facing distractors such as lack of food, lack of sleep, or issues associated with parental irresponsibility. If students come to school late and without breakfast, that is already two strikes against them being able to pay attention. They've missed out on instruction and they are likely distracted by their hunger. Not assigning blame ("Nice to see you finally got here!") and having healthy snacks available in the classroom for situations like these can serve to mediate the disengaging effects of the before-school stressors. Everyone realizes that teenagers are notoriously groggy in the early morning hours, but sleepy students are also a challenge in elementary schools. Although we would certainly hope that every student arrived at our door having received the proper amount of sleep for their age, generally at least ten hours for school-aged children (National Institute of Health, 2014), we know that doesn't always happen. Generally speaking, we are all sleepy from time to time, and taking short breaks to do some kind of physical activity can get the blood and brain moving in a way that saves time in the long run. However, there are times where the best course of action in relation to the needs of a sleep-deprived child is simply to let him or her sleep. Of course, if this is an ongoing issue with a particular child, school support staff should certainly be notified and involved. Finally, we have to recognize that elementary-aged students have few options for affecting the choices their parents make on a daily basis. No matter what teachers personally think about home-life considerations, we have a professional responsibility to set those judgments aside when dealing with the students in our classrooms. For example, we once had a second-grade student who arrived at school around 9 AM every day, thus missing the first forty minutes of school and a significant portion of the reading block. After weeks of being frustrated by the fact that this little girl would interrupt guided reading and small-group work almost every day, we finally thought to ask her why she couldn't get to school on time. She calmly explained that she just couldn't get everything done in enough time to get to school, and then went on to explain that it was her job to get herself up and ready, before waking up her two-year-old brother to get him dressed and feed him breakfast. Only then could she wake her mom up so she could be driven to school. And, she added, "Sometimes mom isn't that easy to wake up." Although there was really not much we could do to modify the expectations set for this child at home, we could certainly stop making her feel guilty about her late arrival at school and simply do our best to work within the parameters we had. She was doing more before school than most seven-year-olds did all day, and acknowledging those responsibilities went a long way to making her feel like a valued member of the class.

Classroom Life

What goes on inside your classroom is a lot easier to control than what goes on outside of it. The physical arrangement of space, lighting, and noise levels can all inhibit engagement if they are distracting. Students should be able to both hear and see the teacher well, not just because common sense tells us that eye contact helps draw students into the learning, but because visual and auditory systems connect during cognitive focus (Jensen, 2005). Although it may make our teaching lives easier, isolating that one student who tends to distract others by moving the desk to the back of the room or turning it around to face the wall will not generally do much to improve the student's engagement . . . or learning.

Noise levels are also important to take into consideration. We each have our own personal tolerance levels for noise. If you grew up with three younger brothers (like one of us), your tolerance for noise might be pretty high. If, on the other hand, you grew up in a calm household where you were used to quiet study time, your noise tolerance might be a little lower. The point is that it doesn't really matter what your preference is as a teacher; it is the students who matter most. As such, we suggest that teachers manage noise levels in many ways, including keeping the classroom door closed or nearly closed to lower hallway noises, having distinct group work and quiet areas not right next to each other in the classroom, and even, in some cases, allowing students who need a quiet environment in order to focus to wear noise-cancelling headphones as they work independently.

Based on the industrial fluorescent lighting present in most schools, you might think that those were the best kinds of lights for facilitating learning. This is not the case, despite the fact that good lighting has been shown to have a direct relationship with students' performance (Phillips, 1997). We suggest adding lamps as a way to soften the harshness (and incessant humming) of the fluorescent lights during times where bright lighting isn't necessary for working. If you are lucky enough to have windows, natural light can also serve as a good alternative.

Finally, the physical classroom layout and décor can also be distracting. We acknowledge that space is typically at a premium in most classrooms, and that makes it even more critical to consider how to most thoughtfully use it. Clutter around the room and on the walls can be extremely distracting for students—especially those who have been diagnosed with attention-impeding disorders. Regularly scheduled clean-up times (for teachers and students!) and open wall space can help reduce the sensory stimulation that may negatively affect the environment. This doesn't mean that we expect to see bare walls, but rather that we expect to see purposeful use of space in general and wall space in particular. For example, as mentioned earlier, word walls are commonly found in elementary classrooms. However, if they are never referred to by the teacher and go largely unused by the students, you might consider the cost/benefit ratio of leaving them hanging on the walls.

The Double Standard of Motivation

Once all of the housekeeping items are checked off the list and the room is primed and ready for optimal student engagement, then what? Most teachers move on to establishing what seems to be the obligatory behavior chart, valuing extrinsic motivators for behavior over the more elusive intrinsic motivators. It is common for people to believe that a dichotomy exists between the two approaches of motivation, but much in the same way as the two instructional framework models, the dichotomy may exist due to the history of psychology and learning theories. In the past, extrinsic motivation (behavior driven by external rewards) has been associated with behaviorism, and intrinsic motivation (behavior driven by internal rewards) has been associated with constructivist theorists (Dimitriadis & Kamberelis, 2006). In the classroom, extrinsic and intrinsic forms of motivation do not always have to be mutually exclusive; both can occur simultaneously.

We believe that extrinsic and intrinsic motivation can both have a place in the classroom just as both a microwave and an oven have a place in your kitchen. Extrinsic motivation can be likened to a microwave; objects can be cooked or recooked with heat that enters and exits quickly; it is a quick fix, but doesn't always result in the tastiest treats. Intrinsic motivation can be likened to the oven; objects can be cooked or recooked with heat that enters and exits steadily; it takes longer, but it's worth the wait. Sometimes we need to react in a way that addresses issues quickly, but we cannot only use the quick-fix approach and expect it to result in meaningful and lasting change.

Extrinsic Motivation

Extrinsic motivation has some advantages and many disadvantages. On a positive note, external rewards, when used with the intention of being reduced and eliminated, can be effective in developing self-efficacy (Cameron, 2001). However, such rewards may lead students to connect the causes of their behavior to things outside of their control (Pintrich & Schunk, 1996). Students who take this approach often struggle to sustain the effort toward and quality of their work over time (Deci & Ryan, 2000; Pintrich & Schunk, 1996; Brewer, Dunn, & Olszewski, 1988; Lepper, Keavney, & Drake, 1996).

External motivation, often associated with carrots and sticks, is then best used for improving students' facility with classroom procedures, and works best when external rewards and consequences are reduced and eliminated as the desired behavior is changed. The disadvantages of extrinsic motivation revolve around the notion that behaviors become associated with external causes through the use of rewards and punishments. The loss of task quality often leads to loss of interest, working against rather than for engagement. For example, research suggests that when reading is tied to external rewards, even those students who started out enjoying reading become less enamored with it once the rewards are removed (Krashen, 2003).

We acknowledge that there may be a place in the classroom for extrinsic motivation. In fact, schools often implement school-wide extrinsic motivation programs in which you will be required to participate. Because these programs are typically explicit and easy to follow, the majority of our discussion will focus instead on intrinsic motivation, which tends to be more challenging to understand and facilitate.

Intrinsic Motivation

An array of research supports an emphasis on intrinsic motivation in the classroom. Humans typically want self-direction and control over their own lives (Darling-Hammond & Bransford, 2007), and internal rewards may result in increased expectations, support, and confidence (Bandura, 1997; Eccles, Wigfield, & Schiefele, 1998; Pintrich & De Goot, 1990; Schunk, 1991; Stipek, 1996). We believe that both teachers and students, in the long run, reap the most benefits from shifting from a focus on extrinsic to a focus on intrinsic motivation (Stipek, 2002).

Extrinsic practices are easy to visualize, whereas intrinsic practices are more abstract. Many teachers can quickly explain token economies in classrooms, as well as sequences of negative consequences as a result of not following rules and procedures. However, asking teachers how they intrinsically motivate students often results in responses that revolve around the use of praise related to effort and accomplishment. Praise may be a small part of engagement through motivation, but it is not all that should occur for lifelong learning to be promoted. The social scientist Dan Pink (2009) helps clear the abstraction of intrinsic motivation with his book *Drive: The Surprising Truth about What Motivates Us*. The three broad concepts (autonomy, mastery, and purpose) presented in his book align with the educational research about engagement.

Autonomy

Autonomy is people's desire to direct their own learning. "Our 'default setting' is to be autonomous and self-directed" (Pink, 2009, p. 222). Deci and Ryan's (2000) seminal work with self-determination theory laid the groundwork for this statement to be true. Self-direction of learning involves choice, both in terms of having choices and having the ability to self-select. Who has the power of choice in the classroom: teachers or students? We believe they both hold potential power, but in many classrooms it is the teacher who consistently demonstrates authority over students rather than offering them opportunities to demonstrate autonomy. Teachers who want to engage their students have a responsibility to not only select interesting tasks based on what they know about their students' needs and interests (Blumenfeld, Puro, & Mergendoller, 1992), but should also consider integrating options for student choice, which research suggests will result in positive engagement outcomes. Students' choices for what, where, how, and with whom work is done along with variety within the routines and structure of the school day can also be motivating. Furthermore, students tend to find teachers who shift their focus away from grades/rewards, as discussed in Chapter 3, motivating (Brophy, 1987; Lepper, 1988).

Teachers who invest in assessment and planning around four 'T' areas of task, time, team, and technique are likely to find that students are more engaged in their instruction as a result of promoting students' autonomy. As mentioned in Chapter 5, students can be given choices within the tasks they work on. In a reading lesson, the focus is typically on the level of book the child should be reading, but students can easily be given choices regarding the subject matter or topics of the book. There may even be room for students to demonstrate their understanding of their assigned reading though different assignments. Whereas one may choose to design a poster highlighting the key characters and depicting their personalities through visual representation, another may choose to create a digital book trailer, and yet another may actually enjoy writing a more traditional book report. Students can also have choices with time. Should teachers be focused on progress by the end of a class period or the ringing of a bell? We believe that progress should be the focus. The industrial-style blocks of time with bell systems that many schools operate with should not sway teachers to snatch papers off desks because 'time's up.' Although this is undoubtedly more challenging in departmentalized classroom settings, short periods of flexible time in which students can choose what to work on can be incorporated throughout the day and may actually build responsibility and independence that benefit students' future study skills. Team refers to both a class of students and the variety of ways in which they can be grouped for instruction. It is not only teachers who can assign groups; once teachers establish expectations for group work (and students demonstrate that they understand them), it isn't too hard to invite students' input as the teams are determined. Finally, students can have an impact on the learning techniques employed by teachers. As discussed in Chapter 6, instructional approaches can be blended based on the topic, goals of instruction, and students' needs. There are even times where student input can be solicited as teachers make these kinds of instructional decisions.

Mastery

Pink (2009) defines mastery as people's urge to make progress to get better and better. Making progress toward a task may be among the most motivating aspects of work. With his influential work, Csikzentmihaly (1991) introduced the term flow, the positive aspect of total involvement with an experience. Many of us have had the experience of being so totally involved in something that the rest of the world simply fades away. Some may find that flow in running, whereas others find it in online gaming or between the pages of a good beach book. We want our students to find similar kinds of flow in school during work in academic subject areas. Total involvement with an experience is more likely to occur if the experience is appropriately rigorous. If tasks are challenging (Brophy, 1987; Lepper, 1988), but appropriate support for progress is in place (Blumenfeld et al., 1992), experiencing flow—and thus engagement—is possible. Teachers' confidence in students' abilities also helps promote positive feelings of getting better and better at a task (Bandura, 1997; Eccles et al., 1998; Pintrich & De Goot, 1990; Schunk, 1991; Stipek, 1996).

Teachers can take action with assessment and planning to ensure that students have opportunities for total involvement by planning academic experiences that have just the right level of difficulty. We suggest, however, that teachers too often fail to take into account the varying needs of students when establishing appropriately rigorous tasks. Struggling readers who are consistently given grade-level reading materials are unlikely to ever get to the point where they can experience flow; facing consistently challenging tasks with little success does not facilitate engagement among students. Planning for the right level of difficulty should be based on the kinds of formative and diagnostic assessments discussed in Chapter 2. As discussed in Chapter 7, academic language selection can also make challenging content and skills more accessible for students, and questioning and feedback, as discussed in Chapter 8, can help teachers drive instruction and students self-assess, engaging both more fully in the learning process.

It is important to note that in presenting students with engaging and challenging learning opportunities, there will likely be setbacks. Not all students will welcome the challenge, nor will all students find consistent success. Plans must be in place to address both concerns. Students' mastery, as defined by Pink, can be promoted with the right mindset and opportunities for total involvement.

Purpose

Purpose represents people's yearning to learn in the service of something larger than themselves. We have already established that humans desire self-direction through choice, but Pink suggests that they often seek to use these choices to make contributions and be part of something bigger and more lasting than self. Holocaust survivor Victor Frankl's (1985) famous work *Man's Search for Meaning* introduced the idea of logotherapy, the notion that finding meaning is the primary force for human existence. Yearning to have purpose and meaning for experiences is certainly a factor echoed by many researchers for motivation and engagement in the classroom (Brophy, 1987; Lepper, 1988).

Teachers who teach with purpose utilize relevance and goal setting within the classroom walls. Relevant teaching can be assessed and planned for by knowing students: knowing their goals, their dreams, and what makes them tick. Students are passionate in ways that are so personal and individual. Finding out these passions is key to helping students unlock their many purposes. Allowing students to utilize their passions can take many forms cross-curriculum. For example, a student concerned about the environment may be assisted in writing a school-wide petition to improve recycling options in the cafeteria. Other students might be encouraged to write letters to local government officials regarding additional environmental concerns. Effective teachers could provide these purpose-driven opportunities within a unit of study in science or writing . . . or both! Goal setting can help students see their progress over time. Teachers and students who work together to set and monitor academic and social goals (remember the example in Figure 8.9?) can positively affect classroom opportunities to capitalize on students' sense of purpose.

Reflecting on Engagement

We believe that engagement through intrinsic motivation can be enhanced by reflection. Reflection best enhances teaching and learning when it is ubiquitous

---

QUESTIONS FOR ENGAGEMENT

Teacher Questions

1. Do I have their attention?
2. Are they engaged?

Student Questions

1. How do I feel?
2. Am I interested?
3. Is this important?
4. Can I do this?

FIGURE 9.1 Questions for engagement (adapted from Marzano et al., 2011)

and continuous throughout the day. In this last section, we examine how Marzano et al.'s (2011) engagement questions, listed in Figure 9.1, can facilitate reflection through the three aspects of intrinsic motivation: autonomy, mastery, and purpose.

Teachers can constantly evaluate their employment of engagement through motivation by utilizing teacher questions numbers one and two throughout the day. If the answer to these questions is "No" at any point, then teachers can envision themselves in the place of the students to answer student questions one through four. Teachers who know their students well enough to put themselves in their students' shoes have more opportunities to discover multiple ways to increase motivation. Explanations of the questions follow.

Teacher Question #1

Teachers who ask themselves the question "Do I have their attention?" at the beginning of each lesson tend to be more in tune with students' levels of engagement. Being able to consistently answer this question with "Yes" is imperative. Teachers have many choices while planning specific lesson leads and attention grabbers: using videos, songs, skits, and humor are great ways to engage students in the lesson. We think this initial planning is a fun and exciting part of the job, although the introductions have to be in alignment with the rest of the lesson! We are not advocating showing Weird Al Yankovic's song "Word Crimes" as a way of getting students' attention for a lesson on plane figures in geometry, though it might be the perfect option for a grammar lesson. The bottom line is that securing students' attention at the beginning of a lesson can set the stage for effective use of instructional time.

Teacher Question #2

Teachers who ask themselves the question "Are they engaged?" during each lesson are more in tune with sustaining engagement, and thus positively affecting students' learning. This question should be on repeat in teachers' heads throughout lessons and throughout the day, and if at any time the question yields doubts about students' engagement, teachers must take responsibility for reflecting on how to re-engage individual students. This could include changing the proximity of teacher and/or student within the room or changing the tempo of the lesson. Pink's lenses of autonomy, mastery, and purpose serve to help teachers focus on engagement in general, but considering students' feelings, interests, passions, and abilities before and throughout the lesson can help with the fine-tuning.

Student Question #1

Checking in with students at the beginning of the day can give teachers a sense of how students feel. Though the goal is to eventually have students self-monitor their own levels of engagement and adjust accordingly, teachers who take the time to actually ask students how they are feeling can gain insights into how much time and energy may be necessary to secure and sustain students' attention. These interactions must be authentic; we are not advocating the kinds of actions we have sometimes observed in which the teacher intentionally asks students who are clearly off task how they are doing in front of the whole group as a means of getting them back on track. Humiliation is never a good route to real engagement. Recess, bathroom breaks, and hallway walks can also be utilized to secure time for these well-being check-ins, and, depending on the situation, teachers may want to document the students' response using a checklist or other means of formative assessment. We have even seen teachers who have focus students for each day of the week, meaning that they pre-identify the four to six students they will be sure to check in with as a means of holding themselves accountable for this kind of personal interaction. Though we believe that the most effective teachers find ways to connect with every student on a daily basis, this kind of structure may serve as a useful and less overwhelming starting point.

Although out-of-school factors that influence a student's well-being are outside of a teacher's circle of influence, the effective teacher can employ certain teaching strategies that will help keep students' energy levels in check and their minds focused. When planning a lesson, administrative duties, transitions, and instructional delivery should all be considered. Tasks such as taking role should not be done while students sit idle. Instead, independent work or some other meaningful activity should be provided or a meaningful routine established so that students know what to do when they walk through the door. Some primary-grade classrooms even have students sign in as they enter the classroom, allowing students to practice writing their name and allowing the teacher to quickly determine who is absent. It also serves to increase the students' responsibility in regard to attendance and frees the teacher to mingle with students as they enter the classroom.

Transitions can also be a challenge to engagement and need to be varied and seamless. Establishing the student role in these kinds of transitions requires modeling and practice at the beginning of the school year. Establishing procedures for things like distributing materials, returning papers, and demonstrating readiness for listening can help facilitate smooth transitions.

When it comes to delivering instructional content, effective teachers vary their pacing based on the difficulty of the material and the verbal and nonverbal cues received from students. If students begin to misbehave or zone out, it is likely that the lesson pacing is either too slow or too fast for the majority of the students, and in many cases, simply adjusting the rate of exposure to new information should get students back on track. This means that despite a teacher's best efforts, sometimes a forty-five-minute lesson can either turn into a twenty-five-minute lesson or a two-day lesson, depending on the students' response. The most effective teachers are ready and willing to adapt to either scenario, though most of the time, their thoughtful planning leads to relatively accurate lesson time estimates.

Student Question #2

We are not really suggesting that teachers should regularly ask their students, "Are you interested?" Asking that could lead to the awkward but honest answer of "No!" effectively shutting down chances of engagement. Although we hope that students will self-monitor their own interest levels and compensate in some ways when their levels start to drop off, teachers who keep students' interests at the forefront tend to offer more opportunities for student choices. Remember the four 'Ts' from earlier in this chapter? Choice leads to autonomy, responsibility, and hopefully engagement. According to Marzano et al. (2011), choice can come in many forms and should be woven into your instructional frameworks. By planning your lessons around game-like activities or opposing sides of a debate, students tend to be automatically interested since the learning format is more closely aligned with their out-of-school activities. Allowing students to choose which side of the debate to take or how the game's winner will be determined provides additional opportunities for ownership in the process and leads to increased autonomy.

Student Question #3

"Is this important?" is a question teachers may rehearse in order to consider students' purpose, and preceding that question with the word "How" can be especially important for making learning relevant to students' lives. Just because curricular materials include certain topics for certain grade levels doesn't mean that students will automatically find the topics relevant. This is when understanding your students' prior knowledge and interests becomes paramount. Let's imagine you are teaching a lesson on the Earth's surface and analyzing the differences between various types of soil, sand, and rocks. You know a particular student would likely not find this topic very important until you reminded him how this new information is connected to his goal in life: becoming a heavy machinery operator. By explaining that without a deep understanding of how different solids are composed, and therefore act, a track hoe driver will have a difficult time building a retention wall on the jobsite, once you make this connection for the student, he will be hooked! When learning and lessons appear unimportant to students, lack of relevance may be at the heart of the matter. Considering students' passions and goals in addition to application to real-life situations can help make lessons more engaging.

Student Question #4

Teachers typically plan activities that they anticipate students being able to do—at least with support. However, sometimes during instruction, teachers forget to continue considering the question of whether or not the students can actually do what they are being asked to do. We want students to be able to answer the question, "Can I do this?" with a resounding "Yes," though we must be willing to recognize that not all students will. Engagement hinges on teachers' abilities to convince students that they have potential. Believing in oneself is pivotal for active participation in the practice needed to advance learning. Thinking about the just-right levels of difficulty and providing opportunities accordingly can help students become fully involved in the learning activities and processes. Teachers can help improve students' attitudes and perceptions about learning by encouraging and modeling a growth mindset. One way to encourage a growth mindset in your students is to engage them in setting goals and tracking their progress over time (Marzano et al., 2011). As students begin to see their progress over time toward their individual goals, they will begin to realize that growth is possible, which in turn will lead to intrinsic motivation to keep persevering even with appropriately challenging material.

Final Thoughts on Engagement

Time on task and paying attention are often associated with student engagement in the classroom. Unfortunately, in our opinion, these two concepts are often managed exclusively through the lens of extrinsically motivated behavior programs and charts. We argue that real engagement involves so much more. Engagement is a result of motivation, and intrinsic motivation is the gold standard for lifelong learning. The nuances of intrinsic motivation can be more easily understood through the overlapping components of autonomy, mastery, and purpose. Goal-driven teaching, student choices, and challenging but achievable tasks hold great power for facilitating active engagement in the classroom, and it is the responsibility of the teacher to carry out instruction in this vein.

DO YOU WANT TO KNOW MORE ABOUT ENGAGEMENT THROUGH MOTIVATION? CHECK THESE OUT!

Jensen, E. (2005). *Teaching with the brain in mind*. Alexandria, VA: Association for Supervision and Curriculum Development.

Marzano, R. J., Pickering, D., & Heflebower, T. (2011). *The highly engaged classroom*. Bloomington, IN: Marzano Research Laboratory.

Pink, D. H. (2009). *Drive: The surprising truth about what motivates us*. New York, NY: Penguin.

Connecting Pedagogy to Practice

Autonomy:

1. Make lists of students' choices in the 4 'T' areas: task, time, team, and technique.

Mastery:

2. Have students list their preferred times of focus to help inform your scheduling.

Purpose:

3. Have students write a "Dear Ann" letter to a caregiver to ask for advice in discovering passions and purposes.

Putting Leadership into Action

Teacher leaders know that they set the tone for the classroom. Take some time to reflect on your own views of learning.

*   Do you have a growth mindset or a fixed mindset? Does it depend on the subject?
*   Do you find some subjects more important than others? Why?

- Have you had teachers that you find more engaging than others? What characteristics made them so engaging?

  How about in terms of your students? Have you ever found yourself saying, "Well, she's just not capable of thinking in that way"? It may sound cliché, but believing that all of your students can learn is a must if learning is going to really occur. Teacher leaders take this approach—and the responsibility—for engaging students in learning.

References

Bandura, A. (1997). *Self-efficacy: The exercise of control*. New York, NY: Freeman.

Blumenfeld, P. C., Puro, P. & Mergendoller, J. R. (1992). Translating motivation into thoughtfulness. In H. H. Marshall (Ed.), *Redefining student learning: Roots of educational change* (pp. 207–239). Norwood, NJ: Ablex.

Brewer, E.W., Dunn, J.O., & Olszewski, P. (1988). Extrinsic reward and intrinsic motivation: The vital link between classroom management and student performance. *Journal of Education for Teaching, 14*(2), 151–170.

Brophy, J. (1987). Synthesis of research on strategies for motivating students to learn. *Educational Leadership, 45*(2), 40–48.

Cameron, J. (2001). Negative effects of reward on intrinsic motivation—A limited phenomenon: Comment on Deci, Koestner, and Ryan (2001). *Review of Educational Research, 71*(1), 29–42.

Chabris, C. F. & Simons, D. J. (2010). *The invisible gorilla: And other ways our intuitions deceive us*. New York, NY: Crown.

Csikzentmihaly, M. (1991). *Flow: The psychology of optimal experience* (Vol. 41). New York, NY: HarperPerennial.

Darling-Hammond, L., & Bransford, J. (Eds.). (2007). *Preparing teachers for a changing world: What teachers should learn and be able to do*. San Francisco, CA: John Wiley & Sons.

Dimitriadis, G., & Kamberelis, G. (2006). *Theory for education*. New York, NY: Routledge.

Dweck, C. (2006). *Mindset: The new psychology of success*. New York, NY: Random House.

Eccles, J. S., Wigfield, A., & Schiefele, U., (1998). *Handbook of child psychology* (5th ed.) (Vol. 3) (pp. 1017–1095). New York, NY: Wiley.

"Engagement." 2001. *The Oxford American College Dictionary*. Retrieved through Google. com.

Frankl, V.E. (1985). *Man's search for meaning*. New York, NY: Simon and Schuster.

Jensen, E. (2005). *Teaching with the brain in mind*. Alexandria, VA: Association for Supervision and Curriculum Development.

Krashen, S. (2003). The (lack of) experimental evidence supporting the use of Accelerated Reader. *Journal of Children's Literature, 29*(2): 9–30.

Lepper, M.R. (1988). Motivational considerations in the study of instruction. *Cognition and Instruction, 5*(4), 289–309.

Lepper, M.R., Keavney, M., & Drake, M. (1996). Intrinsic motivation and extrinsic rewards: A commentary on Cameron and Pierce's meta-analysis. *Review of Educational Research, 66*(1), 5–32.

Marzano, R.J., Pickering, D., & Heflebower, T. (2011). *The highly engaged classroom*. Bloomington, IN: Marzano Research Laboratory.

National Institute of Health (2014). *How much sleep is enough?* Retrieved June 1, 2014, from http://www.nhlbi.nih.gov/health/health-topics/topics/sdd/howmuch.html.

Phillips, R.W. (1997). *Educational facility age and the academic achievement of upper elementary school students* (unpublished doctoral dissertation). University of Georgia, Athens, GA.

Pink, D.H. (2009). *Drive: The surprising truth about what motivates us*. New York, NY: Riverhead Books.

Pintrich, P.R., & De Groot, E.V. (1990). Motivational and self-regulated learning components of classroom academic performance. *Journal of Educational Psychology, 82*(1), 33.

Pintrich, P.R., & Schunk, D.H. (1996). *Motivation in education: Theory, research, and applications*. Englewood Cliffs, NJ: Merrill.

Ryan, R.M., & Deci, E.L. (2000). Self-determination theory and the facilitation of intrinsic motivation, social development, and well-being. *American Psychologist, 55*(1), 68.

Schunk, D.H. (1991). Self-efficacy and academic motivation. *Educational Psychologist, 26*(3–4), 207–231.

Stipek, D. (1996). Motivation and instruction. In D. Berliner & R. Calfee (Eds.), *Handbook of educational psychology* (pp. 85–113). New York, NY: MacMillan.

Stipek, D.J. (2002). *Motivation to learn: Integrating theory and practice*. Boston, MA: Allyn & Bacon.

SECTION IV

Teacher Leadership

Introduction: Teacher Leadership

Teachers—especially beginning teachers—often find themselves caught up in management, particularly in relation to time and behavior. Although there is good reason for this focus (the common recommendation, "Don't let the kids see you smile until Christmas!" given to beginning teachers comes to mind), novices also have a tendency to overlook their role in the academic successes and failures of their students. We are not suggesting that management isn't important; it is! We all know that if we have to be out of school for a day, we cross our fingers that we will be graced with a substitute teacher who has strong classroom management skills, meaning behavior issues and noise levels will be kept to a minimum and, hopefully, some learning will take place. However, an exclusively managerial focus can lead classroom teachers to potentially faulty assumptions, such as quiet students are engaged students, or well-behaved students understand the material being taught. Managers focus on doing things right, whereas leaders do the right things (Bennis & Nanus, 1985). Teachers who get caught up in the management side of doing things the 'right' way have a tendency to abdicate their own authority as they look to others (supervisors, administrators, etc.) for approval. In doing this, they miss the bigger picture of classroom leadership, failing to see that moving away from the script and making evidence-based decisions not only supports the students' growth, but also energizes and empowers the teacher.

We believe that leadership is a choice, meaning that you are never too old or too young to lead; you can step up at any time. A mind-set for leadership is not necessarily determined by an official role or title, but rather by how you choose to live your professional life. In their book *Finding Your True North*, George, McLean, and Craig (2008) suggest that authentic leaders have a passion for their purpose, practice their values, hold themselves accountable, acknowledge their mistakes, develop connected relationships, and, possibly most importantly, are prepared to go their own way. Again and again, the literature suggests that the most effective teachers are unorthodox (Liesveld & Miller, 2005), have to go against the organizational grain (Allington, 2002), and pose a threat to the status quo (Redfield, 2014). Taking this type of approach is rarely an easy choice for teachers, who have "been socialized to receive knowledge generated by others rather than trust their own capacities to assign meaning through action and reflection" (Pine, 2009, p. 92). Since it is our goal that teachers step into leadership roles when they step into the classroom, we have framed this final section on teacher leadership around these two general concepts: thinking and action.

References

Allington, R.L. (2002). What I've learned about effective reading instruction from a decade of studying exemplary elementary classroom teachers. *Phi Delta Kappan, 83*, 740–747.

Bennis, W. & Nanus, B. (1985). *Leaders: The strategies for taking charge*. New York, NY: Harper & Row.

George, B., McLean, A., & Craig, N. (2008). *Finding your true north: A personal guide*. San Francisco, CA: Jossey-Bass.

Liesveld, R. & Miller, J. (2005). *Teach with your strengths: How great teachers inspire their students*. New York, NY: Gallup Press.

Pine, G.J. (2009). *Teacher action research: Building knowledge democracies*. Thousand Oaks, CA: Sage.

Redfield, C.A. (30, April 2014). A 'divergent' path: Tips on becoming a teacher leader. *Education Week*. Retrieved August 6, 2014, from http://www.edweek.org/tm/articles/2014/04/30/ctq-redfield-teacher-leader.html?tkn=PVWDgZCLKIy03zLKbDDC9wMGH80iDqEh1ht3&intc=es.

10
THINKING

This chapter is dedicated to describing the kinds of informal, quiet leadership that can take place in the confines of your own classroom. We know that this can be important to novice teachers especially because of their overwhelming desire to be accepted by and "fit in" with their colleagues and the school community in general. Despite the best intentions, there is almost always tension between the idealistic, new teachers fresh out of the university and filled with academic knowledge of research and best practices and the experienced classroom teachers who have seen educational trends come and go . . . and maybe come back again. Acknowledging that this tension exists should not insinuate blame on either group; in truth, the strongest teachers have both knowledge and experience, as well as an honest assessment of their strengths and shortcomings, the ability to critically reflect on their own beliefs and practices, and the willingness to explore new ideas and research. The good news is that these things are not dependent solely on years of teaching; new teachers can develop more expert practices even in their first years (Hammerness et al., 2005).

Assessing Your Leadership Skills

We have already discussed the importance of acknowledging your biases and assumptions before entering the classroom. It should be clear at this point that in order to be an effective teacher, you must be able to think about and understand teaching in a different way than you have experienced it as a student. Teacher leaders must be willing to go even further, looking at themselves through the lens of leadership. Leadership characteristics are not typically discussed in teacher preparation programs, as they are more often associated with coursework leading toward advancement into an administrative role. Unfortunately, few beginning teachers—and not even many experienced classroom teachers—actively consider what leadership characteristics they possess. In fact, many teachers shrug off the notion that they might be seen as a leader, suggesting instead that they are just focusing on their students and their students' learning. We disagree. In fact, we would argue that in order to best meet the needs of your students and their learning, you have a responsibility to see yourself as a classroom leader. When discussing authentic leadership, George, McLean, and Craig (2008) suggest that "to become great in any endeavor . . . you must use the unique strengths you were born with and develop them to the fullest while acknowledging and learning from your shortcomings" (p. xiii). Take a few minutes to consider the list of characteristics associated with teacher leaders in Figure 10.1. Notice that it builds on all of the characteristics of effective teachers highlighted in Chapter 1. What would you say are your strengths here? What are your shortcomings? Be honest! Acknowledging your imperfections is a critical step in assessing your teacher leader self.

The characteristics in the figure are not meant to be an exhaustive list of important leadership characteristics, nor do we intend to suggest that one must possess all of these characteristics in order to be a good leader. Good leaders—in the classroom or outside of it—lead differently; some want to be in charge and others want to collaborate. The expression of leadership is individualized, though we believe that all leaders sometimes have to be willing and prepared to go their own way.

We know that novice teachers "regularly fall back on existing curriculum, textbook suggestions, and an emphasis on classroom control" (Berson & Breault, 2000, p. 33). In fact, people in general tend to stick to what they know because "the difficulties loom much larger than the joys when spheres of activity feel alien" (St. John & Deane, 2012, p. 325). Making use of professional autonomy becomes even more challenging as teachers step into systems where they are asked to set aside their own understanding to follow scripts written by 'experts.' Following someone else's script does little to develop the responsiveness necessary for effective teaching. Thus, one of the most critical characteristics of teacher leaders is a willingness to accept responsibility for what goes on (or doesn't go on) in your classroom.

Principled	Supportive	Accepting	Open-minded
Honest	Altruistic	Vulnerable	Resilient
Focused	Accessible	Confident	Organized
Resourceful	Decisive	Committed	Perceptive
Fair	Intelligent	Collegial	Empathetic
Enthusiastic	Innovative	Flexible	Understanding
Hopeful	Caring	Ethical	Trustworthy

FIGURE 10.1 Characteristics of effective leaders

Emily: So, do you feel like you're changing things?

Neal: I always say, "No," to what the other kindergarten teachers offer me. I don't do it in a mean way, not like, "That's trash," just, "No thank you."

Emily: I always say, "Yes," and then throw it away when I get back to my classroom.

Neal: I don't let it get that far. But I also offer ideas.

Emily: I'm just insecure, I guess. I just close my door and do my thing.

FIGURE 10.2 Listening in: A conversation between two teachers nearing the end of their first year in the classroom

We have, unfortunately, heard teachers at all experience levels take solace in the idea that because they are doing what they have been told to do, they can't be blamed if the students don't learn. We sincerely hope that you find this shocking, because it still shocks us despite our over forty years of combined teaching experience. Teacher leaders do not take this approach. Instead, they accept ownership for student learning, take meaningful risks in an attempt to affect that learning, and recognize that failure is a necessary part of any learning. When something isn't working—even if it is the script, or the textbook, or the research-based practice that is supposed to work—they realize that it is their professional responsibility to attempt to solve the issues that arise in their classrooms. Teacher leaders know that "[p]rograms don't teach children, teachers teach children" (Cooter & Perkins, 2011, p. 563), and that sometimes that means they must swim against the tide, always aiming toward aspirational rather than what may be perceived as 'normal' classroom teacher behavior in their schools. We aren't saying it is easy, and we aren't suggesting that there is a 'right' way to go against the grain. We are, however, saying it is possible, as evidenced by the excerpt from a real conversation between first-year teachers contained in Figure 10.2.

Building Your Knowledge

Teacher leaders are not only committed to student learning, they are also committed to personal learning. Zemelman and Ross (2009) say that building your own knowledge and capacity is the first step toward teacher empowerment. Generally, we think of two types of knowledge: experiential and academic (sometimes called propositional). These are certainly not the only two types of knowledge, but for our purposes, they will suffice. Experiential knowledge is, of course, that which you gain through your daily encounters with people. When it comes to teaching, it encompasses all of your experiences with students, parents, colleagues, bus drivers, lunchroom supervisors, custodians, administrators, and so on. Traditionally, those in power (administrators, politicians, and, even to an extent, teacher educators) tend to diminish the importance of experiential knowledge, whereas those practicing in the field tend to rely heavily on it as a means of informing their daily practice. On the other hand, academic knowledge is related to knowing about a topic, like fractions, the water cycle, guided reading, or vocabulary instruction. The importance of this type of knowledge is generally privileged by those in positions of power. Sadly, the words written by Chittendon, Charney, and Kanevsky (1978) over thirty-five years ago still ring true today:

> Historically teachers have been told that the source of knowledge about learning resides somewhere outside their classrooms, perhaps in curriculum or research labs. Given such conditions, it's not surprising to find some teachers so lacking confidence in their own views that they doubt the legitimacy of their experience with children when confronted with 'expert' evidence that goes against it.
>
> *(Chittendon, Charney, & Kanevsky, 1978, p. 58)*

We believe that both types of knowledge are important, as having one without the other not only negatively affects efficacy in the classroom, but also reduces the potential of talking knowledgeably with people who are important in your professional life, thus reducing the power you have to make informed choices about teaching and learning in your classroom.

Building your professional knowledge doesn't have to be a public activity; reading blogs, professional books, and journals; taking a class; or joining a professional education organization can provide access to a network of knowledgeable people and information. Paying close attention to how your students see school—or even asking them questions about their perceptions—can expand your experiential knowledge and allow you to understand them more deeply. The authors of *Tensions and Triumphs in the Early Years of Teaching* (2006) indicate that knowledge was the key resource in enabling them to teach in their own ways because they could use that knowledge to warrant the use of alternative approaches to the widely used programs in their schools. In just about every situation, knowledge is power, and schools are no different. Seeking out knowledge can generate new ideas, help you refine old ones, or provide you with justification for not following common practice . . . and it can be done in the confines of your own classroom. Unless you are at the point where you are comfortable sharing your knowledge with others, you don't have to say a word about it to anyone—the important thing, the empowering thing, is that *you* know that you know.

Researching and Exploring New Ideas

Many teachers focus on practices that seem to 'work' in their classrooms. And these practices typically do work if the focus of the evaluation is purely managerial: kids are busy doing things and there is evidence of 'work,' typically in the form of worksheets and other such papers. Unfortunately, this kind of 'work' does not usually result in much actual student learning, and teachers may become overwhelmed with the stacks of papers and amount of grading they have to comb through on a daily basis. It is likely that many of these teachers, because they are not actively thinking about the purposes of their assignments and the impact of their instruction, remain unconcerned with this cycle of busywork. Teacher leaders, on the other hand, take active responsibility for making learning deeper and more powerful for their students. As such, they often engage, at least to some extent, in teacher research in their classrooms.

All teachers are exposed to new teaching ideas on a regular basis, whether informally through social media and conversations with other teachers, or from more formal sources like a professional book or a district-level in-service. It's not uncommon for teachers to take an idea back to their classrooms and give it a go after these kinds of experiences. What is more uncommon is for teachers to take an idea back to their classrooms, think about how they might evaluate its impact on students, determine an appropriate time frame for trying it out, and then give it a go. This kind of intentionality in implementing new ideas raises the bar and allows teachers to engage in research of their own. A potential plan for conducting teacher research is included in Figure 10.3. Although this kind of research is certainly informal and does not follow the protocols typically associated with research, it is no less valuable to the teacher conducting it. In fact, Zemelman and Ross (2009) suggest that becoming more intentional and organized about your inquiry processes can not only help differentiate instruction and prevent you from falling into teaching ruts, but it also promotes professional growth, provides a means of justifying your teaching methods, and can be an energizing source of empowerment.

1. Decide what it is you want to know and write your research question(s).
2. Conduct a review of the literature; see what research says about your question.
3. Make a plan!
    a. Decide who you are going to study. (The whole class? A specific group of students? More than one group of students? An individual?)
    b. Decide what you are going to do, how often, and for how long you are going to do it.
    c. Decide what exactly you are going to measure (Achievement? Motivation?) and how you will measure any changes.
4. Implement your plan and collect your data.
5. Analyze your data.
6. Make changes in your instruction based on what you find out.

FIGURE 10.3 Sample plan for teacher research

Teacher research can be inspired by a reaction to a stimulus—a new idea or program—but often teachers who see themselves as active participants in the learning process are much more proactive about their inquiry. They question their practices, generate their own questions, are open to research, and entertain the idea that there may be better strategies for teaching what they are trying to teach. They become quite intentional about finding answers to their questions, documenting their attempts to improve their practice, and collecting and analyzing their classroom data. Teachers who engage in these research practices see it as a means of improving their practice and professional growth. This approach to exploring new ideas gives them the power to find meaning in what they are doing and generate solutions to the complex problems that appear in their classrooms.

Reflecting, Reflecting, Reflecting

If you read only one section of this chapter, we hope it is this one. This is the one that all teachers have the power to put into practice, regardless of the situation in which they find themselves. It is at the heart of what this chapter is all about: thinking. Far too often, those in charge of schools are concerned with having teachers follow the 'correct' procedures rather than encouraging them to draw on their professional knowledge to make decisions about what works. Many teachers are by nature peacemakers, who in an attempt to avoid conflict, give in to the pressure and, without reflection, end up accepting as reality that things are done in a certain way rather than realizing that it is simply one of many possible ways. It is not surprising that this repeated acquiescence can result in teachers who withdraw or feel victimized and ultimately grow less optimistic over time (Markow & Martin, 2005). Reflection is a way of combating this victimization, as it "emancipates us from merely impulsive and routine activity . . . enables us to know what we are about when we act" (Dewey, 1933, p. 17).

What do we mean by reflection exactly? It's a fair question, since reflective thinking is generally not well defined and is often criticized for being both overused and vague. It is important to first note that not all thinking is reflective, and not even all thinking about teaching is reflective. Our attempts to define reflection rely primarily on descriptions provided by Dewey (1933) and Schon (1983), although their work explores the concept at much deeper levels than we will here. We define reflective thinking as that which involves intentional questioning and critiquing of beliefs, practices, or knowledge with the intent to become more mindful of and responsive to the associated implications and assumptions. That means that when you finish teaching a lesson and think, "Wow! That went well!" you are not thinking reflectively. However, if you finish teaching a lesson (or are in the middle of teaching a lesson) and think, "Wow! This really seemed to make sense to everyone but Hannah and Andrew. They were really hard to keep on task after the first five minutes. I need to take a close look at their work while they're in the computer lab so that I can check in with them before we wrap up the day," you are probably in the reflective thinking ballpark.

Reflection is typically triggered when you find something confusing or experience what Piaget (1985) called disequilibrium. Of course, this insinuates that you will recognize when you are receiving conflicting or confusing information. In the field of teaching, those experiences do not just happen in response to a particular teaching event or assessment; moments of disequilibrium can be triggered by teaching materials and programs; mandates and directives handed down from above; education policy; or anything that happens within the context of the classroom, school community, or education at large. Dewey's (1933) work suggests that those who think reflectively share three characteristics—characteristics that have shown up in a number of other discussions within this book:

- Open mindedness (the desire to see more than one side and recognize the possible error of our ways)
- Responsibility (the willingness to move beyond whether something works and take into consideration the consequences)
- Wholeheartedness (the belief that new learning is always possible, accompanied by a commitment to finding possible solutions)

Reflection is holistic; involves intuition, emotion, and passion; is influenced by context and situation; and can't be easily packaged (Zeichner & Liston, 1996). In today's efficiency-oriented society, those characteristics can be challenging. Still, we place a high value on long-term development over immediate proficiency and recognize that efficiency can, in fact, be a direct threat to reflection.

Aligning Beliefs with Practices

Reflective thinking should lead to reflective practice, and one of the most important things you can do to bring this kind of thinking and practice together is to determine your beliefs about teaching. We are not talking about an academic answer to "What is your philosophy of education" kind of belief statement (though it has benefits, too). We are talking about deciding what it is that you believe based on your knowledge of kids, learning, and teaching. Debbie Miller (2008) cautions that if you don't define your own beliefs, you can bet that someone else will try to do it for you, adding that "success in the classroom depends less on which beliefs we hold and more on simply having a set of beliefs that guides us in our day-to-day work with children" (p. 4). You may find it hard to believe, but not all teachers have spent time thinking about things like this, and some don't even realize what they are giving up by not having a set of beliefs to guide them. They are left to rely on others to tell them what they need to do and how they need to do it. They are not bad teachers; in fact, one that comes to mind was very well regarded in her school and community. She had been teaching for over twenty years and had mentored many new teachers in her career. In a casual conversation, we asked her what it was she was focusing her professional development on that year and were astounded when she responded that she didn't really know, but that she would check with her evaluator to see where her focus should be. She was willingly handing over control of her own development to someone else because she had either never taken the time to cultivate her own awareness of who she was as a teacher or she had given in to the ever-present pressures of teaching. We don't want you to end up in the same situation. Having a set of beliefs will not only allow you to make conscious decisions about what you're doing in the classroom, it will also provide you with a vision for what you need to be doing and where you should be focusing your efforts. Miller (2008, p. 19) suggests a few questions to get you started:

- How do you go about teaching kids something new?
- What principles guide you?
- How do you know if kids are getting it?
- What do you do when they don't?

Once you take the time—and it may take a long time!—to establish your beliefs about teaching and learning, you are, of course, not done. The next step is to carefully examine your practices. Is there evidence that what you are doing matches your beliefs? If you are doing the kind of reflective thinking we have been promoting throughout this book, you will likely find that there are places where they do not match. The good news is that this will give you more opportunity for practicing your reflective thinking. In fact, you ultimately have to decide whether it is your belief that needs to be changed or your practice. And that takes research and—you guessed it—more reflection. It requires you to be aware and present in every moment and it requires you to question all that you do. Eventually, if you take this process seriously, you will arrive at a place where your beliefs and practices are in alignment, providing you with a clear guide for filtering what matters and what doesn't and allowing you to be authentic and do what you have to do to meet the needs of your students. It is recognized, even in the broad realm of leadership, that practicing your values in a consistent way brings meaning and congruency to life (George, McLean, & Craig, 2008).

Final Thoughts on Thinking

For far too long, teachers have been considered consumers of knowledge, lacking the skills and acumen to either create or critique it. Unfortunately, many teachers continue to fall into that trap, blindly following the directions given to them by their principal, their colleagues, or textbooks. We advise you instead to put your efforts into developing habits of mind—valuing and regularly taking time to think—that will allow you to continually assess your assumptions and practices in light of your students and their learning. We are not suggesting that you walk into your classroom ready to prove that you know everything. In fact, we would argue that the most effective teachers, in addition to regularly engaging in honest self-assessment, actually search out and welcome critical feedback from others. However, we believe that receiving the feedback should actually start the thinking process. Feedback has to be filtered through what you know about your students, what you know about teaching, and what you know about learning. It has to be filtered through your belief system. And if it still has merit after you've taken the time to run it through all of those filters, you have to decide what to do with it. Schon (1983) says that professionals work in environments where "problems are interconnected, environments are turbulent, and the future is indeterminate" (p. 16). If teachers are to really be considered professionals, they need to embrace the messiness that comes with a classroom full of students who are expected to learn and take responsibility for deciding what to do for students in their classrooms.

In a nutshell, teacher leaders do more than follow 'the book'; they think. They reflect on their own beliefs and practices, they reflect on their students' performance, and they reflect on the relationship between their students' performance and their own practice. They use their knowledge of research to inform their classroom practice, they conduct their own research as they implement new practices with a keen eye, and they analyze how those practices influence student learning. Teacher leaders do not simply do what they are told without thinking about the consequences and, when necessary, they quietly resist.

At this point, you may be talking to yourself saying, "Enough! I get it! We have to think about our teaching." If this is the case, rest assured you are not alone. Our students often complain about how much we ask them to reflect, how we answer their questions with more of our own, and how we always ask for opinions while trying to avoid giving our own. But we do this with one primary purpose: to prepare our students to withstand the pressures of efficiency, mandates, other teachers, parents, principals, and policies. We know they make fun of us when they think we're not looking. But, sometimes, if we're lucky, after they've been out in the classroom on their own for a while, they come back and talk to us. And if we are really lucky, they tell us that they have come to appreciate our focus on reflective thinking. And if we're really, really lucky, we have moments like this one, when one of our former students, at the end of his first year in his own classroom, exhaustedly reported, "There are times I want to stop reflecting but I can't. Maybe that's the key. Keep thinking." Yes. That's the key. Keep thinking.

References

Berson, M.J., & Breault, R.A. (2000). The novice teacher. In B.E. Steffy, M.P. Wolfe, S.H. Pasch, & B.J. Enz (Eds.), *Life cycle of the career teacher* (pp. 26–43). Thousand Oaks, CA: Corwin Press.

Chittendon, E., Charney, G., & Kanevsky. R. (1978) Collaborative research: Implications for in-service development. In R. Edelfelt & E. Smith (Eds.), *Breakaway to multidimensional approaches* (pp. 49–59). Washington, DC: Association of Teacher Educators.

Cooter, R.B., & Perkins, J.H. (2011). Much done, much yet to do. *Reading Teacher, 64,* 563–566. doi:10.1598/RT.64.8.1.

Dewey, J. (1933). *How we think.* Chicago, IL: Henry Regnery.

George, B., McLean, A., & Craig, N. (2008). *Finding your true north: A personal guide.* San Francisco, CA: Jossey-Bass.

Hammerness, K., Darling-Hammond, L., Bransford, J., Berliner, D., Cochran-Smith, M., McDonald, M., & Zeichner, K. (2005). How teachers learn and develop. In L. Darling-Hammond & Bransford, J. (Eds.), *Preparing teachers for a changing world: What teachers should learn and be able to do* (pp. 358–389). San Francisco, CA: John Wiley & Sons, Inc.

Long, S., Abramson, A., Boone, A., Borchelt, C., Kalish, R., Miller, E., Parks, J., & Tisdale, C. (2006). *Tensions and triumphs in the early years of teaching: Real-world findings and advice for supporting new teachers.* Urbana, IL: National Council of Teachers of English.

Markow, D., & Martin, S. (2005). *The MetLife survey of the American teacher, 2004–2005: Transitions and the role of supportive relationships.* Retrieved August 4, 2014, from http://files.eric.ed.gov/fulltext/ED488837.pdf.

Miller, D. (2008). *Teaching with intention: Defining beliefs, aligning practice, taking action.* Portland, ME: Stenhouse.

Piaget, J. (1985). *The equilibration of cognitive structures: The central problem of intellectual development.* Chicago, IL: University of Chicago Press.

Schon, D. (1983). *The reflective practitioner.* New York, NY: Basic Books.

St. John, B., & Deane, D. (2012). *How great women lead: A mother-daughter adventure into the lives of women shaping the world.* New York, NY: Center Street.

Zeichner, K.M., & Liston, D.P. (1996). *Reflective teaching: An introduction.* Mahwah, NJ: Lawrence Erlbaum Associates.

Zemelman, S., & Ross, H. (2009). *13 steps to teacher empowerment: Taking a more active role in your school community.* Portsmouth, NH: Heinemann.

11
ACTION

Chapter 10 focused on how you could be a leader within your classroom: continuing to gain knowledge, aligning your beliefs and practices, conducting research on your own practice, and consistently engaging in reflective thinking. This chapter is about building on this kind of thinking, finding your voice, and translating your thinking into actions that are visible outside the comfort of your own four walls. We remain steadfast in our belief that novice teachers are capable of the kinds of actions we will describe here, though we recognize not all will be ready or willing to take this step. With that in mind, we explore both subtle and overt ways to take action as you continue to build your leadership skills.

Before we jump into ways that you can go public with your thinking, we believe that it is important for all teachers to understand the politics of teaching. Few teachers enter education because they want to be involved in politics. Yes, they know that over the past nearly thirty years education has been in the political spotlight. They know that their lives will be shaped by education policies set at all levels from the federal government all the way down to their own school boards. And they know that the general public doesn't really understand teaching, but thinks they do. (Remember the 'apprenticeship of observation' from Chapter 1?) In spite of this knowledge, most teachers plan to simply ignore the politics and teach the kids who show up in their classrooms. We don't really want to burst the ideological bubble that suggests you can step foot in a school—let alone teach in one—without encountering some kind of politics, but guess what? You can't really teach in a school without encountering some kind of politics. So you have to make some decisions about how you will handle the tough issues.

You can try to ignore it: keep your head down, don't say anything, and just go about your daily routine. However, if you choose that route, you will likely begin to feel disenfranchised and powerless, and you may become one of the casualties of the first few years of teaching, never making it past your fifth year. Another option is to follow the guidance of Chapter 10: keep your eyes and ears open, read and build your own knowledge, critically examine your teaching, keep quiet, and think. Reflective thinking and classroom leadership can make you feel empowered and might just be enough to sustain you through the struggles associated with the first years of teaching. But teaching in that way can be lonely. Novice teachers in general report feeling isolated and alone as they try to prove themselves capable colleagues alongside their more experienced peers. Those who are intentionally making decisions that go against the grain, even if they are doing it very quietly, can burn out quickly if they don't have some outlet for their fears, frustrations, joys, and . . . you guessed it, reflection.

This is where taking action comes into play. We frame taking action around two general purposes: advocating for yourself and advocating for others. They aren't mutually exclusive; you can do one or the other or both, depending on your needs and your comfort zone. We do believe, though, that you need to recognize two things before moving down this path of action. First, you must understand there is a long tradition of dismissing or silencing teachers' voices. If you dig into the research, you will find lots of hypotheses as to why, but for our purposes, the why doesn't matter so much. What matters is that you embrace the fact that even as a beginning teacher, you are in possession of valuable knowledge, you have a voice, and you have something to say. Second, you must understand that using your voice is a political act. It's not writing letters to the editor or chatting with legislators political; we like the way Julie Parks, one of the teacher authors of *Tensions and Triumphs in the Early Years of Teaching: Real-World Findings and Advice for Supporting New Teachers* (2006), defines being political as "engaging in acts, no matter how large or small, that honor one's core beliefs and philosophies" (p. 160). These teacher authors go on to say:

> While we still find great frustration with the federal and local politics of educa-
> tion, we know there are many windows of opportunities for new teachers to
> be heard. We also know that taking such action happens in both gentle and
> boisterous ways and that no action is more or less courageous than another.
>
> *(p. 160)*

We hope that the following pages will help you to determine how you find your voice and use it gently or boisterously as you take an increasingly active role in your teaching career.

Speaking Up: Being Your Own Advocate

Arguably, the line we have drawn between thinking and action is a fine and some-what arbitrary one. It would be easy to argue that simply teaching according to your knowledge and values is a way of taking action—especially if it means modi-fying or stepping away from mandated programs. Seeking knowledge, whether about new instructional strategies or federal and local education issues, could also be considered an action, though we have categorized both under the heading of thinking, primarily because you don't have to go public with them. That said, there are some good reasons for speaking up. Most novice teachers wisely shy away from taking bold actions early in their career. Our suggestion is to start by selectively speaking up about a subject you know intimately for reasons that have an immediate purpose. We suggest becoming your own advocate by searching out mentors, joining a professional organization, and selectively sharing your knowledge. This approach (hopefully) allows you to slowly gain the respect of your colleagues and the relational power that comes with that respect.

Finding a Mentor (or Two)

There is a body of research that suggests that teachers who are mentored are more likely to have long-term success in teaching (Ingersoll, 2012). It is not a surprise then that almost all new teachers seem to be assigned an official mentor who is tasked with guiding them through their first year of teaching. That's great, mostly. But not all who are assigned to that role know how to support a novice teacher, and often, a visit from them can tend to feel a little more like an evaluation and less like a conversation. If this is the situation in which you find yourself, we suggest you treat meetings with your mentor in that vein; keep them professional. Ask your assigned mentor for feedback on specific issues (questioning, academic language, etc.), and try to be open to the feedback you get.

There are many things to be learned from developing relationships with assigned mentors, but really, that is not the kind of mentoring we are talking about. We are talking about finding people—often multiple people—who have characteristics that you admire, who are willing to make time for you, who are willing to share their stories and expertise with you, and, most importantly, whom you can trust. We are talking about taking the task of finding a mentor into your own hands. Rami (2014, selected from pp. 7–8) suggests a number of questions that can help guide you in your pursuit of mentors based on your own needs:

- What am I already doing well that I would like to get even better at?
- What do I know off the bat that I would like to improve about my teaching practice?
- What have others (administrators, parents, even students) told me that I need to improve? Which of the suggestions seem to have merit?
- Which of the goals that I had when I became a teacher am I still working on achieving?
- What would help me feel more energetic about my work?

Although your needs are important, there are other aspects of mentors that are worth considering. Should you search for a mentor at your school or outside of it? Is it important that you and your mentor work at the same grade level? Are you comfortable sharing your concerns about your teaching with the person? Do your personalities mesh? There is not a formula or set of correct answers to this or any list of mentor-related questions; the process of finding a strong mentor match is as unique to each individual as his or her beliefs, values, and personalities are. We've included one teacher's story about how she found what she considered her first mentor in Figure 11.1.

Once you have identified (and secured) a mentor, the trick is to maintain communication. In a world where there is never enough time to write plans, grade papers, and complete all of the required paperwork that somehow seems to magically multiply in your school mailbox, making time for meaningful conversations with a mentor can be more challenging than you might think. But it's exactly that communication—the shared thinking—that is the reason for having a mentor at all. You have to be willing to put yourself on the line, questioning curriculum, asking the 'silly' questions, figuring out why things worked—or not, brainstorming

---

FINDING A MENTOR: ONE TEACHER'S STORY

My first real mentor who taught in the way I wanted to teach wasn't assigned to me, and I definitely didn't officially ask her if she would mentor me. I found her during my fourth year of teaching. It was my first year of teaching sixth grade, and it was about her thirty-somethingth year of teaching eighth grade. If you just saw her, you might assume she was 'old school.' But I watched her and listened, and I could just tell we clicked. She believed in setting high standards and expected the kids to rise to them, but she also believed in the kids and taught them that reading was something bigger than school. I really just started going to her with both my successes and questions. We bonded over a movement to combine reading and language arts, or whatever you want to call it, all into one class; not many other teachers seemed to understand that they went together hand in hand. Even though she was near retirement she was still open to trying new things and always searching for better ways of teaching her kids. We both toyed with readers' response notebooks and writers' notebooks. She was more successful with readers, while I was more successful with writers. While she guided me, she also respected my thoughts about teaching practice even though I was a newer teacher. We talked like colleagues, and the conversations we had about our failures and successes were priceless. I was lucky to have taught with her for three years before she retired. She was a true mentor to me.

FIGURE 11.1 Finding a mentor

possible solutions to instructional hurdles, and, in many ways, baring your professional self to another expert in the field. Wiggins and McTighe (2005) state that we find personal meaning in our work when we reflect and question ourselves in a supportive environment, and that is why it is worth the risk.

Joining a Professional Organization

We'll be honest. We debated whether to categorize this as thinking or action. Technically, you can join a professional organization without having to announce it to the world—or anyone, really. But, we settled on action for two, or maybe three, reasons. One, it really does involve intentionally taking action; you should really take time to figure out which professional organization best fits your needs (check out our list for you in Figure 11.2). And two, it costs money; having to spend money almost always moves something out of 'thinking' and into the 'action.' Professional membership in national organizations can cost anywhere from $40 to $100 and up, depending on the benefits (newsletters, journals, etc.) offered. The invaluable part of joining an organization, though, is the networking and professional development opportunities that it offers. Reduced prices for convention attendance is another benefit; there are few things more invigorating for a teacher than spending a few days in a big city surrounded by like-minded colleagues learning about their area of teaching from some of the biggest experts in the field. This is where our third reason for including this in action comes into play. If you are lucky enough to attend one of these national conferences with the support of your school—even if it just means they gave you professional leave rather than making you take personal days—it is likely that you will be asked to share at least a portion of what you learned with the rest of the faculty upon your return. We believe this is a great way of beginning to share your ideas aloud, because you are simply reporting what you saw and heard without having to own the ideas. It serves as a good stepping stone to sharing your own knowledge in a public forum.

Sometimes sharing your knowledge in a public forum of people you don't know can be much less intimidating than sharing with your fellow teachers. Active membership in a professional organization can also provide you with opportunities for sharing both your practice and knowledge. There are often state and local levels of larger national organizations like the International Literacy Association or the National Council of Teachers of Mathematics. Although these local and state organizations may not consistently attract the attendance of celebrities (both from outside and within education) and those with the most recognizable names in the field, they provide opportunities to interact with others who are as interested in and dedicated to professional development as you are. It can provide you with local support, potentially both within and outside of your school. Often, they do have meetings or conferences where teachers present on aspects of their own classroom practices. These can be invited presentations (often at the local level), or

---

CONSIDER JOINING ONE OF THESE NATIONAL PROFESSIONAL ORGANIZATIONS AND THEIR STATE AND LOCAL AFFILIATES EARLY IN YOUR CAREER! MOST OFFER SIGNIFICANT DISCOUNTS FOR STUDENT MEMBERS.

Association for Childhood Education International (ACEI): An organization dedicated to promoting the optimal education and development of children in a changing world through various programs and projects; www.acei.org

ASCD (formerly the Association for Supervision, Curriculum & Development): A global community dedicated to excellence in learning, teaching, and leading; www.ascd.org

International Literacy Association (ILA): A global network of individuals and institutions committed to worldwide literacy; www.reading.org

National Association for the Education of Young Children (NAEYC): The nation's leading voice for high-quality early childhood education for children from birth through age 8; www.naeyc.org

National Council for the Social Studies (NCSS): An association whose mission is to provide leadership, service, and support for all social studies educators; www.socialstudies.org

National Council of Teachers of Mathematics (NCTM): The public voice of mathematics education, supporting teachers to ensure equitable mathematics learning of the highest quality for all students through vision, leadership, professional development, and research; www.nctm.org

National Science Teachers Association (NSTA): The largest organization in the world committed to promoting excellence and innovation in science teaching and learning for all; www.nsta.org

---

FIGURE 11.2 Select possibilities for professional membership

the organization may accept proposals, which then go through some kind of vetting process (typically at the state and national levels). Sharing your knowledge and expertise beyond your local community can be an especially empowering experience.

It is also important to note that many of these organizations are consistently on the lookout for people willing to step into leadership roles, whether at the organizational level or of various committees within the organization. This can be a perfect means of 'trying on' leadership and developing leadership skills without direct implications to your teaching position. Taking on these kinds of leadership roles in a professional organization often feels safer than doing so in your own school.

Sharing Research and Practice at "Home"

Novice teachers often find themselves in the unique position of walking into their first teaching position with some of the most current knowledge about research in effective teaching and learning coupled with little independent experience in actually transferring that knowledge into practice. In many school settings, respect and power are earned through experience, meaning the knowledge beginning teachers bring to the table may be summarily dismissed by those teachers with more experience. This has two very significant implications for novices who are ready to speak up: they must find a way in which to present the information that doesn't come across as arrogant, and they must be thoughtful about when and with whom they share the information.

Do not kid yourself; the manner in which knowledge about research and practice is shared matters. There are internal networks and hierarchies in every organization, and schools are no different. Novices can often unintentionally alienate themselves from their colleagues if their enthusiasm for changing the world is interpreted as a means of establishing superiority over the common practices of the school. Hammerness and colleagues (2005) discuss how prospective teachers need to first understand the reasons for constraints within a system before considering how to work within it. We suggest aiming for the middle ground between willful and compliant—humble but bright. Few colleagues respond well to a new teacher who already seems to have all the answers.

As for when and with whom to share your ideas, we have four specific recommendations. First, spend at least a few weeks watching your colleagues, especially the other teachers on your team. (In elementary schools, most teams are arranged by grade level, and in middle and secondary schools typically by content area, although other team structures are possible at both levels.) Pay attention to nonverbal communication. Watch behavior during professional development sessions. Who is engaged and who is grading papers? Note who speaks up (and who doesn't) at staff meetings. Are they adversarial, or do they make valid and rational points? Paying close attention to the subtleties of human behavior should give you a good indication of who might be receptive to actually listening to what you have to share. Second, run your plan by your mentor—the one you trust, not necessarily the one assigned to you by the school. Practice what you plan to say out loud and ask your mentor to critique you, pointing out any potential trouble spots. There is a big difference between starting your sharing with "I think we should . . . " as opposed to "I was wondering about . . .". Intentionality in word choice can make a big difference when you're building relationships with colleagues. Third, rather than speaking up in a faculty meeting, start small. Share your knowledge and thinking with individuals or small groups of people with whom you are familiar. There is always less room for misinterpretation of your intentions in more intimate settings. Plus, it is easier to gauge the nonverbal reactions of colleagues in a small group setting.

Our final recommendation regarding sharing ideas related to research and practice involves interacting with your principal. The same observational rules apply; watch their nonverbal reactions to other teachers' comments and listen closely to what they say (and don't say) in staff meetings and professional development settings. Perceptions gained from these observations should give you additional insight into how willing your principal is to entertain your ideas. However, principals can often be a better first audience than your colleagues because they have a vested interest in your success. They hired you, so if you honestly conveyed your beliefs, values, knowledge, and practice in your interview, your principal may not be at all surprised by the information you are ready to discuss! This does not mean we are suggesting you simply invite yourself into the principal's office and proceed to lay out all the reasons you're not going to do what everyone else is doing. We advocate a much more strategic approach. You should go in with a specific plan for what you hope to do, an implementation timeline, an identified means of evaluating whether it worked or not, and solid research-based documentation to support your plans. (If this sounds somewhat familiar, take a look back at Chapter 10 and the way we suggest you research and explore new ideas.) Our experiences suggest that most administrators will allow even novice teachers to experiment with new practices if they come forward with a clearly organized plan and a willingness to discuss it.

Each of the actions described in this section is a way in which you can begin to test the water, so to speak, in regard to the willingness of your colleagues and administration to listen. These actions also serve as a means of building human capital—relationships on which you can build. Building and maintaining a successful team of like-minded individuals can allow you opportunities to practice your leadership skills on a small scale. Actions taken in a public forum—even in a one-on-one meeting—affect others and set a tone for future interactions. Starting small allows you to build influence and power in a way that will allow you to have a larger impact on issues beyond your own classroom.

Speaking Out: Advocating for Others

If we surveyed teachers about what keeps them from speaking out and taking more visible leadership roles, we would get a wide range of seemingly valid reasons. Our guess is that the lack of time would top them all. Anthony Coulucci (2013), a National Board Certified Teacher, identified five additional beliefs that he thinks hold teachers back from leading:

- Belief that politics isn't part of teaching
- Lack of confidence in public speaking (or writing, or networking, or other) abilities
- Fear of offending administrators
- Fear of drawing more ire from the public
- Belief that time spent out of the classroom will harm students' learning

We have already spent time addressing a couple of these: Politics is always part of teaching, and administrators generally want successful teachers—it makes them look good! Coulucci counters each of the others with compelling arguments and concludes with a challenge encouraging teachers to reject the fallacies and stop excusing themselves from involvement in leadership activities that challenge the top-down decision making that is so prevalent in public education today.

Zemelman and Ross (2009) suggest that "[l]eadership . . . means taking a more active and constructive role in the professional community and developing an authentic kind of power that legitimizes and strengthens this role" (p. 5). We believe that despite the fact that there are many excellent teachers across the United States, few view themselves as potential leaders. Although they willingly wield power and influence in their classrooms, they are reluctant to step into more publically recognized leadership roles that employ these two key components. We hope that by helping you understand the relationship between power and influence and their roles in facilitating change, you will be willing to speak out and advocate not only for yourself, but for others. One of the best explanations of the difference between power and influence came out of a leadership development session led by, of all people, an engineer. She made an analogy to a car, noting that power was like the horsepower—it's potential energy, just sitting there waiting to be used. The key, she said, was influence; in a car, the horsepower goes untapped until acted upon by the gas pedal. In leadership, influence is like the gas pedal. You can have all the power, but without influence, it's going to be really hard to get things moving. We are not suggesting that you should aim to garner power and influence for the sake of having it; rather that by gaining power and influence, you have the potential to positively affect the culture of your school, empower other teachers, and challenge the policies that negatively influence the daily work of students and teachers.

Even armed with power and influence, teacher leaders would be remiss to simply start a single-handed vocal campaign. Teachers at all stages of their careers can be susceptible to the effects of public opinion, but beginning teachers who have yet to secure tenure—which does not ensure job security, but rather the right to due process—often fear the ramifications of speaking out. As such, it is even more important to make sure that if you do make the choice to speak out, your voice is not left quietly hanging in the air. Figure 11.3 includes one teacher's story of speaking out. What this humble rebel didn't say was how her courage and voice became a rallying point for many teachers in her district after the video of her impassioned speech was posted online. At the next school board meeting, seats were filled with teachers wearing red in solidarity. By speaking out, she gave voice to others and became a recognized teacher leader in her district.

If you want to be taken seriously, speaking out should not be done on the spur of the moment. It is much easier to simply dismiss an understandable but generalized emotional outburst like "It is crazy to spend so much time assessing instead of

Lauren's story: During the first year of Tennessee's new evaluation system, as part of the Race to the Top initiative, I spoke to the local Board of Education about many of the concerns I had with the way it was being implemented and its effect on teachers and students. I had genuinely thought that a teacher making the effort to show up at a meeting to voice very specific concerns would garner their attention and action. I was mistaken. Instead of pursuing the issue further, I just went back to my classroom, tried for the next two years to keep my head above water, and bonded in misery with my coworkers. As overstressed as we were, as many days as we left meetings in tears, we still held on to a belief that all the unrealistic demands were just going to flush out the "bad teachers," and the rest of us would be ok as we waited for the pendulum of micromanagement and flawed mandates to swing the other way. We were wrong.

My anger and frustration at how my coworkers and I were being treated grew as our pleas to administrators for help seemed to fall on deaf ears . . . or ears that heard but were powerless to do anything about our situation. As the arbitrary nature of the evaluation system became more obvious, I started to see the walls closing in on the "good teachers." The process wasn't flushing out "bad teachers," but experienced teachers whom I admired were starting to leave and stress was taking its toll on all of us.

One afternoon, as I was planning for my class after school, I went to borrow something from a coworker and found her sitting behind her desk in tears as the school counselor tried to console her. At first she didn't want to share the source of her distress, but finally relinquished the letter she had received from the school system that said she was an ineffective teacher and her job was in jeopardy solely because of one year of test scores. In that instant, it dawned on me, that in such a flawed system, no one was immune to losing their job, not even an excellent teacher like my friend . . . and not me.

The decision to go public again was made in an instant, really, in a fit of rage. I remember loudly proclaiming that the madness had to stop and then instantly trying to quell my anger so as to protect my friend, who was too humiliated for anyone else to know. For a solid week, I woke up in the middle of the night rehearsing what I was going to say at the next board meeting, dreaming about berating them for allowing this to happen with their inaction and, eventually, waking up to the realization that I needed to be more constructive. Judging from the reaction, or lack of, that I had gotten two years before, my only goal was really just to make sure none of the board members could say they hadn't been told about the suffocating climate in our school system. They would not hear silence from me.

FIGURE 11.3 One teacher's story of speaking out

After much internal debate, I chose to go with my personal story. Not accusations or generalities, but the narrative of what I witnessed every day in my building. I wasn't afraid of getting facts or details confused, because it was my story, my truth. I spoke my truth to a largely empty boardroom, and incidentally the school board video camera. What I learned afterward is that sometimes your truth can be many other people's truth as well. Sometimes that truth is the only thing that will give that pendulum the energy it needs to start swinging the other way.

FIGURE 11.3 Continued

teaching!" than it is to engage the speaker in meaningful conversation. Although we recognize that passion and frustration (and sometimes outrage) are harbingers of speaking out, as they were in Lauren's story, we warn that they cannot be the leading emotions associated with sustained action. Lauren, too, realized that her emotional "gut" reactions would not likely be taken seriously, and so she thought and planned what it was she wanted to say. Without knowing it, she walked herself through many of the thoughtful guidelines for helping ensure that speaking out actually leads to some sort of productive action offered by Zemelman and Ross (2009) in their book *13 Steps to Teacher Empowerment: Taking a More Active Role in Your School Community*.

- **Consider the risks**—Is this the battle you're willing to fight for? A good gauge is to consider whether the issue at hand is negatively affecting your ability to work productively within your value system to meet the learning needs of students. Keep in mind, though, the story "The Boy Who Cried Wolf." Wise leaders are taken seriously because they are able to speak out without being viewed as whiners, complainers, and annoyances.
- **Have a clear goal in mind**—Know the difference between throwing out an idea and discussing a plan of action. If you are going to take the risk of speaking out, it is always best to know what you want to accomplish—and to have research and data handy to back you up.
- **Talk with your administrator(s)**—We are not really suggesting that you should ask for permission to make your voice heard, but few administrators react well to being taken by surprise. If for no other reason, letting your administrator know that you are planning to speak out demonstrates a level of respect and professionalism that likely sets you apart from others who simply complain in the comfort of their own classrooms. You might find out that your principal supports you and is glad for an ally, or you may gain insight into the hurdles you will need to overcome. In either case, you can decide how best to strategically proceed.

- **Get others on board**—This is the step where your power and influence really come into play. Hopefully, you have built positive relationships with other teachers in the building (or district). Talking with these others can provide you with alternative perspectives and concerns, but most importantly, it can build grassroots support for your idea and leave you feeling less alone.
- **Know your audience**—Consider who you need to make aware of the situation in order to move your cause forward. Do you need to move beyond the walls of the school in order to have an impact, or would your intentions be better suited for one-on-one meetings with select people? Should you involve parents? Community members? School board members? Remember that whether you are speaking out informally or formally, your choices regarding who you involve have implications.
- **Overplan**—Leave as little as you can to chance. Know who supports your ideas and who doesn't. Know how you will answer the hard questions. Write out what you want to say, making intentional word choices that point out the problems while keeping the tone positive and clearly articulating what needs to change.
- **Stay focused**—No matter what setting you choose to speak out in, it is likely that you will have detractors who will try to derail you. Keep your plan in view and don't be distracted by their attempts to sidetrack your ideas or launch personal attacks.

Whether you are speaking out in support of one of your students, in opposition to a program or policy, or for teachers' rights; whether your audience consists of a legislator, those in attendance at a school board meeting, or even just your grade-level colleagues, keeping these guidelines in mind will help you translate your thinking into action. The authors of *Tensions and Triumphs* say

> . . . [r]ecognizing retrospectively that we *did* effect change for ourselves and others helps us understand that new teachers have a responsibility to use their voices to improve their own situations . . . *You are not powerless* . . . We don't recommend storming the gates, but we do know that, through quiet example that becomes respectfully louder and louder, new teachers can effect change from their very first days in the classroom.
>
> *(p. 186)*

We wholeheartedly agree.

Final Thoughts on Action and Leadership

Teachers are often reluctant to take on formal leadership roles that have the potential to vault them into the public spotlight. This may be a result of the kinds of personalities that are called to teach—many, but certainly not all, of the teachers we know are compassionate individuals who prefer any spotlights to shine on their students while they remain firmly behind the curtain. It may also be a result of the culture of education, where teachers are seen as the consumers rather than producers of knowledge and make daily decisions that are often questioned by non-educators. Regardless of the reasons, proportionately few teachers have found ways to make their voices heard beyond the four walls of their classrooms. What we've noticed, though, is that when they do, they make an impact.

Historically speaking, unless proposed educational changes are embraced by teachers, any kind of success is fleeting. St. John and Deane (2012) say that people don't respond well to command-and-control approaches to leadership anymore and suggest that the complexities of our global society demand leadership that is more collaborative. Unfortunately, both federal education policy and corporate reformers in education appear to continue to rely on the tactics of fear and intimidation associated with the command-and-control approach.

We include leadership as a key component of this book because we believe that real and lasting change can only come from those on what are often called the front lines of education. We believe teachers must begin to see themselves not as compliant cogs in the wheels of assembly line education, but as knowledgeable leaders, capable of influencing the practices and policies that affect them—and their students—on a daily basis. We believe that teachers are the only ones able to truly step into the role of what Meyerson (2001) calls tempered radicals, those

> . . . who want to succeed in their organizations yet want to live by their values or identities, even if they are somehow at odds with the dominant culture of their organizations. Tempered radicals want to fit in and they want to retain what makes them different. They want to rock the boat and they want to stay in it.
>
> *(p. xi)*

She suggests these people find a way to navigate a middle ground between resignation to and defiance of the organizational status quo. Her model of the actions of tempered radicals, pictured in Figure 11.4, falls in line with our approach to teacher leadership; it can be so quiet that it is nearly invisible to outsiders and feels quite safe, or it can be very public and thus risky.

In general, teacher educators and administrators don't do a very good job of preparing teachers for leadership roles. As a group, we unintentionally send the message that leadership is for principals and superintendents, and that if you don't want to pursue these kinds of administrative roles, you really don't need to worry about leadership skills. We personally disagree and believe that taking on a leadership role for the first time can be an uncomfortable position for anyone. Generally, people in all jobs start off as novices, but quickly gain experience and knowledge that move them into the role of experts. It is these experts who are often asked to step into leadership roles, where their status returns to novice—not because they

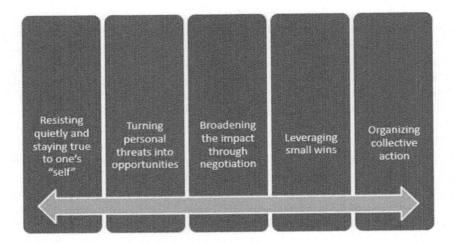

FIGURE 11.4 How tempered radicals make a difference (adapted from Meyerson, 2001)

have limited knowledge and experience, but because they have limited knowledge and experience in regard to leading others. It is no different in education: novice teachers become expert teachers, who are then asked to take on leadership responsibilities and find themselves in what is often an awkward-feeling role of novice educational leader. We hope to break this cycle by helping all teachers—even novices—understand the kinds of thinking and action that serve to develop leaders, because we firmly believe leadership is a choice and that you are never too young or too old to make the choice to become a leader.

FOR MORE INFORMATION ON LEADERSHIP, CHECK OUT THESE RESOURCES:

George, B, & Sims, P. (2007). *True north: Discover your authentic leadership*. San Francisco, CA: Jossey-Bass.

Meyerson, D. E. (2001). *Tempered radicals: How people use difference to inspire change at work*. Boston, MA: Harvard Business School Press.

Activities to Connect Pedagogy to Practice

1. In what areas of your life do you have mentors? How did they become your mentors? Who do you admire in the field of education? Write to that person and ask them for teaching insights.

2. Explore websites and blogs written for and by outspoken teachers (e.g., Jersey Jazzman, @the chalk face, Badass Teachers Association, Mercedes Schneider, etc.). What do you notice? Do you consider the authors of these sites/blogs leaders? Why or why not?

3. Practice speaking up! Choose a topic that you are passionate about and scour the literature in order to become more knowledgeable. Examine the research. Read the popular media. Investigate respected bloggers. Get to know the issues and the arguments pro and con. Then compose a letter stating your opinions and back them up with the research you have done. Finally, send your letter off to its intended recipient. (Consider writing to school board members, a local newspaper, your congressional representative, professional organizations, etc.)

References

Coulucci, A. (10 September, 2013). Five beliefs that hold teachers back from leading. *Education Week Teacher*. Retrieved August 8, 2014, from http://www.edweek.org/tm/articles/2013/09/10/ctq_colucci_leaders.html.

Hammerness, K., Darling-Hammond, L., Bransford, J., Berliner, D., Cochran-Smith, M., McDonald, M., & Zeichner, K. (2005). How teachers learn and develop. In L. Darling-Hammond & Bransford, J. (Eds.), *Preparing teachers for a changing world: What teachers should learn and be able to do* (pp. 358–389). San Francisco, CA: John Wiley & Sons, Inc.

Ingersoll, R.M. (2012). Beginning teacher induction: What the data tell us. *Kappan, 93*(8), 47–51.

Long, S., Abramson, A., Boone, A., Borchelt, C., Kalish, R., Miller, E., Parks, J., & Tisdale, C. (2006). *Tensions and triumphs in the early years of teaching: Real-world findings and advice for supporting new teachers*. Urbana, IL: National Council of Teachers of English.

Meyerson, D. E. (2001). *Tempered radicals: How people use difference to inspire change at work*. Boston, MA: Harvard Business School Press.

Rami, M. (2014). *Thrive: 5 ways to (re)invigorate your teaching*. Portsmouth, NH: Heinemann.

St. John, B., & Deane, D. (2012). *How great women lead: A mother-daughter adventure into the lives of women shaping the world*. New York, NY: Center Street.

Wiggins, G., & McTighe, J. (2005). *Understanding by design*. Upper Saddle River, NJ: Pearson.

Zemelman, S. & Ross, H. (2009). *13 steps to teacher empowerment: Taking a more active role in your school community*. Portsmouth, NH: Heinemann.

12

PULLING IT ALL TOGETHER
Being a Professional

We believe most teachers begin their careers with good intentions. They tend to be a bit idealistic, striving to help kids love school and learning (often in the same way they loved school and learning), and hoping to make the world a better place. They often cite warmth, patience, and love of children as characteristics that will make them good teachers, and they believe that their own memories of school, textbooks, and common sense will give them what they need to be successful (Berson & Breault, 2000). They want to be good teachers who do their jobs well. What they too often find is a classroom reality that doesn't match their own classroom memories. Not all kids love books, not all parents are active participants in their children's education, not all teachers use assessment to inform instruction, and not all administrators recognize quality instruction when they see it. We know that good intentions will only go so far in sustaining a teaching career—about five years, according to research.

Although we certainly don't try to dissuade our students from becoming teachers, we make every effort to help them understand the complexity of the job and the contexts in which they will be spending (hopefully) the next thirty or so years of their lives. We share the statistics that say only half of them will make it to the five-year mark. We talk about the public perception of teachers, the arguments for and against teacher tenure, who benefits (and who doesn't) from a heavy reliance on student test scores for teacher evaluation, and the fact that education is always political (Freire, 1973), whether they want it to be or not. As our students work through the more challenging aspects of a year-long, unpaid teaching internship in which they are full-time co-teachers and full-time graduate students enrolled in classes, we discuss the implications associated with increased alternative licensing programs like Teach for America, whose "teachers" get hired and paid after a six-week summer training period. By the time they leave us, our students know that they will likely be told to forget what they learned in their teacher preparation program and to just pay attention to how things are done in the schools where they are hired. And we try desperately to help them understand that despite all these challenges, they are entering one of the most intrinsically rewarding and arguably one of the most important careers available.

But we don't stop there. We push them more, continuously reinforcing the idea that we expect our students to be more than teachers; we expect them to be teaching professionals. Although it does not seem that teaching is yet accepted by society as a true profession in the same sense that the practices of law, medicine, or engineering are, we believe that we educators are currently in the midst of a long-standing attempt to gain professional legitimacy. Part of formalizing a profession involves respecting the choices of those within the group in terms of setting standards for how membership within the profession is granted, what qualifies as good work, and what happens when a member does not uphold the expected standards (Cheney, Lair, Ritz, & Kendall, 2010). Although there have long been accrediting bodies associated with both pre-K–12 schools and teacher education programs, as well as specific requirements for both initial and ongoing teacher licensure, their rigor has often been called into question. Traditionally, educators as a group have responded sporadically to such calls. Notably, The National Board for Professional Teaching Standards established a challenging process for earning an advanced teaching credential in the late 1980s, and, more recently, the use of edTPA, a performance assessment tied to initial licensure, has been slowly taking hold across the United States as a means of earning acceptance into the profession. Yet there remains much debate about the meaning of "good work," both from within and outside the profession; Karseth (2011) states that "the nature of professionalism and the meaning of professional responsibility are contested not only at the level of the profession and practice, but also at the level of policy" (p. 159). Clearly, we have a long way to go before educators in the United States are viewed, on the whole, as true professionals.

What do we mean, then, when we tell our students that they need to be teaching professionals? For us, it comes down to doing the right thing—consistently aiming for what Aristotle would call the "golden mean," that sweet spot between two extremes. We know they won't always (ever?) hit that mark, but if they are consistently focusing on doing what's right as they use what they know about their learners, teaching, and the particular situation in their decision-making processes, we believe they will at least be in the ballpark. Although we don't typically bring up formal discussions of normative ethics in our coursework, we do discuss the application of such approaches—paying particular attention to how we believe virtue ethics plays out in the reality of classrooms and schools. Our bottom line is that it is not enough to talk the talk, not enough to follow the rules, and not enough to rely on the ends justifying the means. We want our students, when faced with one of the thousands of decisions they will make on a daily basis, to ask themselves, "What would a good teacher do?" We want them to make intelligent choices mediated by practical wisdom and prudence. We want them to be intentional about their decisions and be able to articulate why they have made them. We want them to shift from a focus on accountability, in which the primary relationship is between the school and the state, to a focus on responsibility, in which the primary relationship is between the teacher and student (Biesta, 2004).

Stengel (2013) echoes our emphasis on this professional responsibility, stating, "Teaching is a moral endeavor, a relational practice of response and responsiveness that both requires and gives rise to responsibility" (p. 45). We expect that our students, when they reach the classroom, will be the teachers who are taking stock of their own students' needs; using their knowledge of subject matter, development, and pedagogy; and intentionally making the best possible choice for the particular situation because it is the right thing to do. We want them to realize that, to paraphrase Peter Parker's Uncle Ben, with a license to teach comes great responsibility, and as such, there are significant, lasting consequences associated with failing to meet that responsibility—not only for them, but for the students they serve.

We strive to develop teachers who both believe in themselves and hold themselves accountable for making the right choices. We believe that Dumbledore had it right when he told Harry Potter, "It is our choices . . . that show us what we truly are, far more than our abilities." At the same time, we hold on to Margaret Mead's sentiment, "Never doubt the ability of a small group of people to change the world. Indeed, it is the only thing that ever has," and hope that those who pass through our classrooms, and now those who read this book, will also take seriously the responsibility associated with teaching. We hope they will challenge themselves to make the right choices for their students on a daily basis. Indeed, the future will be sitting in their classrooms.

If You Want to Know More about Ethics and Their Application to Teaching:

Aristotle's *Nicomachean Ethics*.

    Devettere, R. J. (2002). *Introduction to virtue ethics: Insights of the Ancient Greeks*. Washington, DC: Georgetown University Press

    Gunzenhauser, M. G. (2012). *The active/ethical professional: A framework for responsible educators*. New York, NY: Continuum.

    Sanger, M. N. & Osguthorpe, R. D. (2013). *The moral work of teaching and teacher education: Preparing and supporting practitioners*. New York, NY: Teachers College Press.

If You Want to Know More about Sustaining Your Energy for Teaching:

Graves, D.H. (2001). *The energy to teach*. Portsmouth, NH: Heinemann.

Long, S., Abramson, A., Boone, A., Borchelt, C., Kalish, R., Miller, E., Parks, J., & Tisdale, C. (2006). *Tensions and triumphs in the early years of teaching: Real-world findings and advice for supporting new teachers*. Urbana, IL: National Council of Teachers of English.

References

Berson, M.J., & Breault, R.A. (2000). The novice teacher. In B.E. Steffy, M.P. Wolfe, S.H. Pasch, & B.J. Enz (Eds.), *Life cycle of the career teacher* (pp. 26–43). Thousand Oaks, CA: Corwin Press.

Biesta, G. (2004). Education, accountability, and the ethical demand: Can the democratic potential of accountability be regained? *Educational Theory, 54*, 233–250.

Cheney, G., Lair, D.J., Ritz, D., & Kendall, B.E. (2010). *Just a job? Communication, ethics & professional life*. Oxford, England: Oxford University Press.

Freire, P. (1973). *Education for critical consciousness*. New York, NY: Seabury Press.

Karseth, B. (2011). Teacher education for professional responsibility: What should it look like? In C. Sugrue & T.D. Solbrekke (Eds.), *Professional responsibility: New horizons of praxis* (pp. 159–174). Abingdon, England: Routledge.

Stengel, B.S. (2013). Teaching moral responsibility: Practical reasoning in a pedagogical "wonderland." In M.N. Sanger & R.D. Osguthorpe (Eds.), *The moral work of teaching and teacher education: Preparing and supporting practitioners* (pp. 44–59). New York, NY: Teachers College Press.

INDEX